THE FBI
They Eat Their Young

Written By

William Alan Larsh

Published in the United States of America by CreateSpace
Independent Publishing Platform, North Charleston, South
Carolina
www.createspace.com
Library of Congress Control Number: 2017914572
ISBN-13: 978-1544029269

All photographs were taken by and/or are the sole property of
William Alan Larsh.
Cover art by Cynthia Lynn Larsh
10 9 8 7 6 5 4 3 2 1
First Edition

This book is dedicated to all the hardworking, conscientious FBI agents who had to put up with unfair, petty, illogical, stupid, irrational, vindictive, or otherwise insufferable supervisors.

CONTENTS

INTRODUCTION

During my years of employment with the FBI, there was an old joke among FBI employees: "What's the difference between sharks and FBI executive management? Sharks don't eat their young." Unfortunately, this was no joke, but a fairly accurate depiction of FBI management. The FBI might be considered the premier law enforcement agency and the most feared by criminals, spies, and terrorists the world over, but it was also the most feared by its own employees. Time and time again, FBI managers referred to their employees as the "FBI family." As my career progressed, this notion of family became more and more absurd to me. FBI managers normally made critical decisions for the right reasons, but countless others were implemented with selfish, petty, and vindictive motives by power-hungry, egotistical, and small-minded individuals.

I believed this mentality was derived from a deep-seated tradition in the FBI, a throwback to the J. Edgar Hoover era. Agents under Hoover were supposedly transferred to Butte, Montana, for the slightest of infractions. If Hoover wanted to make an example of an agent, he exiled them to Butte. During my more than twenty-seven and a half years in the organization, I witnessed similar spiteful behavior demonstrated by the powers-that-be. Sadly, FBI management exerted vengeful power at their whim and discretion. Any injustice or retaliation against FBI personnel was easily justified under the umbrella of "the needs of the Bureau." This convenient and often used term could justify virtually any frivolous action made by FBI management.

Countless managers in the FBI accepted the bad decisions of their superiors without expressing any opinion, mainly out of fear of jeopardizing their chance for career advancement. In my experience, FBI executive management typically operated with a team of sycophants. Most of these pathetic "yes men" were seemingly highly educated, intelligent individuals. However, they were merely followers, too afraid to rock the boat. Their behavior reminded me of those surrounding Donald Trump on his popular television program years ago, *The Apprentice.* In the boardroom, Trump decided which contestant to fire at the conclusion of each show, repeating his famous line, "You're fired." His subordinates seated on either side of him invariably agreed with him, usually stating, "You made the right decision" or "You had no other choice." No one ever disagreed with him or told him he was in error.

This scenario from *The Apprentice* took place frequently in the FBI. I rarely ever witnessed anyone disagreeing with management. No one dared to go against the FBI family. Marlon Brando, who starred in the movie, *The Godfather,* famously said the often-imitated line, "Never go against the family." In the mafia, this meant certain death if you crossed them. In the FBI, going against the FBI family obviously did not mean death, but it was a career killer. Even worse, it meant retaliation by management for the offender.

An outsider might think this critique of the FBI was coming from a bitter, disgruntled former employee. This premise could not be further from the truth. I loved my work and was proud of my accomplishments. Throughout my career, I never gave anything less than my best on every investigation, mission, or task. I was a diligent, efficient, conscientious, and dedicated agent. I took my oath to uphold the Constitution of the United States and enforce federal laws very seriously. I was very happy with my career, my life, and my family (not to be confused with the FBI family). I will admit that I believed in the FBI family early in my career, but management slowly ruined it for me. By the second half of my career, I no longer bought into the idea of the FBI family, especially after witnessing and personally experiencing the wrath of so many petty and power-hungry managers. I saw a hilarious bumper sticker recently which summed up my experience nicely. It read, "I used to be a people person, but then people ruined that for me."

Despite management's objectionable behavior, I had an entirely satisfying career. I believed firmly from the beginning of my career to the end that I was making a difference. I generally enjoyed most of the people with whom I worked, making many life-long friends. My family, friends, and co-workers always seemed entertained by my countless stories regarding the FBI.

THE FBI – THEY EAT THEIR YOUNG

Many told me I should write a book. The public would never believe it, some said. If nothing else, this book will provide the reader with more information about the FBI than they previously thought they knew, warts and all.

This book was based on my personal FBI experiences, a completely honest narrative, sometimes at the expense of my own embarrassment. Every person in this book was real and every detail was a true depiction of events based on the best of my knowledge and my memory. I omitted names or changed individual names for the most part, except my own, my family's, public officials', and those found in court records and newspapers. The opinions expressed in this book are solely those of the author and not those of the FBI. My story began with me as an eager, ambitious young man, starting his first job out of college in what I perceived as the greatest organization imaginable, the FBI.

CHAPTER 1

FBI HEADQUARTERS

When I was hired on September 10, 1984 as a GS-3 file clerk with an annual salary of $11,080 at FBI Headquarters in the J. Edgar Hoover Building in Washington, D.C., I was very excited and thrilled to be earning money that required no sweat on my part. I had spent the previous summer cutting grass. I was twenty-two years old and had recently obtained my Bachelor of Science degree majoring in political science, graduating with magna cum laude honors from Towson State University in Towson, Maryland. I had many part-time and summer jobs during college, including working as a waiter at a restaurant; a security guard at a trucking warehouse; a cashier at a bowling alley; a telephone cable installer at the telephone company; and a laborer at a country club.

I was never sure what I wanted to do in life. My passion was playing golf, but unfortunately my skills were lacking to play the game for a living. I had considered being a greenskeeper and planned to major in agronomy at the University of Maryland. However, that all changed after working at the Towson Golf and Country Club during the summer after high school. I didn't like the job. One of my co-workers reminded me of Bill Murray's character in the movie, *Caddyshack;* however, this guy was not even remotely humorous. The assistant greenskeeper lived in a broken down hovel on the course. He was up at the crack of dawn every morning with the rest of the crew to cut grass, change the cups, rake the traps, and perform all of the other manual labor necessary for the upkeep of the course. The entire summer was a depressing experience.

In early August of that summer after work, I was on a boat with a friend on Back River near the Chesapeake Bay. I dove off the rear of the boat catching my foot on a metal vent. I lifted my foot out of the dirty Back River water to inspect my injury to find a giant wad of sludge embedded in the deep cut on the bottom of my big toe. My friend later took me to the hospital where I required nine stitches. The only saving grace to this accident was that it precipitated the end to my job at the golf course two weeks earlier than scheduled. I subsequently did not attend the University of Maryland. My father, an alumni of Loyola College in Baltimore, was able to get me enrolled at Loyola at the last minute. I still had no idea what I should do. I attended for only two weeks and quit. I played golf that fall and then worked at a department store during the Christmas season. I realized I needed to go to college. I enrolled in the winter mini-semester at Essex Community College the following January. I remained very uncertain about my future, but finally committed myself to school.

While playing a round of golf two and a half years later at Mount Pleasant Golf Course in Baltimore City between my junior and senior years of college, I was paired with a middle-aged man who asked me what I was going to do after college. I told him I honestly didn't know. He proceeded to tell me his son's future plans. His son had recently graduated from college and went to work at the FBI as a support employee with plans to apply as an agent after three years. In order to become an agent, an applicant with a college degree, who was at least twenty-three years old, needed three years of work experience before becoming an agent. The work experience prerequisite could be waived if an applicant possessed a degree in law, accounting, science, or a foreign language. From that day on, I had a plan for my future.

I applied to the FBI in April 1984 as a file clerk and received a letter that summer to report to FBI Headquarters in Washington, D.C. On my first day, I reported to a large hall on the first floor in the J. Edgar Hoover building for orientation with about fifty or a hundred other new FBI support employees. We were warmly welcomed and then instructed to fill out innumerable forms, a trend that continued for more than twenty-seven and a half years.

I had no idea where my assignment might be. The suspense ended when I was escorted to the front office of the Organized Crime Section in the Criminal Investigative Division (CID) on the third floor. I was introduced to the two secretaries, and then the Section Chief, a tall, amiable man in his fifties. I met the two Assistant Section Chiefs, one of whom was a short Italian man in his forties. I immediately thought how appropriate it was for him to be working in the Organized Crime Section. The other Assistant Section Chief was my immediate boss. He was also in his forties, but not as fit or distinguished looking as the other two executives. He treated me well and was always very nice to me. His favorite person in the section was my predecessor, who had recently been promoted to the position of a GS-7 Narcotics Analyst. My boss was also in charge of the Narcotics Policy Group, consisting of three Supervisory Special Agents (SSA). I worked for these three agents as well.

The FBI's responsibility investigating drugs derived from President Ronald Reagan's Executive Order in November 1982 giving the FBI concurrent federal jurisdiction with the Drug Enforcement Administration (DEA). By all accounts, the DEA resented the FBI infringing on their once exclusive jurisdiction, particularly since the FBI was already responsible for investigating over three hundred other federal statutes besides drugs. By the time I began working, the FBI still had no entity at its headquarters other than the Narcotics Policy Group to handle this enormous new responsibility. This group played an essential role in formulating policies, guidelines, and plans to handle the FBI's new jurisdiction in drugs. Working for these agents proved helpful to my fledgling career.

My predecessor left shortly after my arrival to attend the Defense Language Institute (DLI) in Monterey, California, to study Italian. In his nine-month absence, I assumed all of his Narcotics Analyst duties. The benefit to me was that I could prove myself as more than just a file clerk. The downside was that I was not compensated. My position as file clerk allowed me an automatic promotion to a GS-5 after six months. Under the federal pay scale promotion rules, however, I had to wait another year before being promoted to a GS-7. My predecessor returned from the DLI nine months later. Fortunately for me, he did not return to his position as Narcotics Analyst, but received a promotion to a GS-9 Organized Crime Information System (OCIS) Analyst. I worked as a Narcotics Analyst for about a year and a half before officially being promoted.

The position allowed me to learn how the FBI investigated drugs. My job was largely maintaining statistics regarding the FBI's drug investigations in the then fifty-nine field divisions (currently there are only fifty-six field divisions). I kept track of the number of court authorized Title III wire interceptions, undercover operations, arrests, indictments, and convictions in drug cases, as well as seizures and forfeitures made in connection with drug cases. I compiled these statistics monthly, which the Section Chief of the Organized Crime Section ultimately received and reviewed. These statistics proved to be very important because the Section Chief used them periodically in his testimony to Congress. His testimony, bolstered by these drug statistics, helped to provide justification to increase the budget for the FBI in the enforcement of drug trafficking.

Although I was assigned meaningful work, I was often utilized as an errand boy. Between the Organized Crime front office and the SSAs in the Narcotics Policy Group, someone was always sending me somewhere in or outside the building to deliver or retrieve something. I really didn't care, though, and would do anything I was asked. I made trips to the Director's Office, Assistant Directors' offices, the Department of Justice, and other federal agencies, routinely. On some occasions, I was the chauffeur for my bosses. Sometimes, I would search the basement of the FBI building to locate a more comfortable chair or some other piece of furniture for one of the agents. One SSA from the Narcotics Policy Group called me "Radar," referring to the character, Corporal Radar O'Reilly from the television program *M*A*S*H*, since I always seemed to find what they wanted.

Federal Bureau of Investigation
Performance Award
Presented to
WILLIAM A LARSH
in recognition and appreciation of exceptional performance of official duties throughout the past year.

SEPTEMBER 30, 1985

Date

Director
Federal Bureau of Investigation

I became acquainted with many support personnel in the J. Edgar Hoover building. A clerk assigned to CID to the Executive Assistant Director's office showed me a computer printout a foot high listing every agent in the FBI in alphabetical order. I found it fascinating that it contained each agent's vital statistics, office of assignment, entry on duty (EOD), date of birth, Social Security Number, etc. The most interesting aspect of this list was a column on the far right designating if the agent was overweight. There were not many agents listed as overweight, but I always wondered if they knew they had been tagged as fat or were told to lose weight.

On one occasion, I met Joe Pistone, the famous undercover agent, also known as Donnie Brasco, who successfully infiltrated the mafia in New York. Pistone was visiting with the Italian Assistant Section Chief in the Organized Crime Section. I had no idea who he was. My predecessor told me all about his undercover work and said, "Joe Pistone is a legend in the FBI."

By late 1985, plans were under way for the Narcotics Policy Group to break away from the Organized Crime Section and become a unit in a newly formed Drug Section. One of the agents from the Narcotics Policy Group advised me to apply for new analyst positions being created in the units of the Drug Section. My current position as Narcotics Analyst did not go beyond a GS-7. The new analyst positions in the Drug Section, called Intelligence Research Specialists (IRS), offered a grade series progression for promotion to a GS-11.

The new Drug Section Chief was a very affable fellow and made passing comments to me on two different occasions in the hallway, referring to me as the smart guy with two college degrees. I only had one college degree, but I never corrected him. I assumed he misread my personnel file that contained my transcripts from three colleges, all with different majors. I attended Essex Community College in Baltimore, Maryland, as a physical education major; then I spent a year as a pre-physical therapy major at the University of Georgia. I spent my last two years at Towson State University, majoring in political science.

After I was officially promoted to the GS-7 Narcotics Analyst position, I read the FBI memorandum regarding the promotion, which revealed that the ranking criteria was based on experience, possessing a college degree, and scores on the Missouri College English Test (MCET). I was rightfully credited with vast experience, since I had been performing the job for almost a year and a half. To my surprise, despite the Drug Section Chief's previous comments to me, they actually wrote in the memorandum that I possessed two college degrees. When I was hired, support employees were encouraged to take the MCET for possible future promotions. I had not become aware that the MCET scores were being used as part of the criteria for the Narcotics Analyst position until I saw the final rankings.

When I had the opportunity to take the MCET shortly after entering on duty in the FBI, I went home and told my wife about it. She was a high school history teacher at Linganore High School in Frederick County, Maryland. Her school had the MCET practice test on file (not the actual test), and offered to get me one. When I later took the test at the FBI, I realized I was going to get every answer right, so I purposely missed some questions. I doubted that anybody in the FBI scored higher, unless they had a practice test, too, or were English majors.

Employe[ ] have less than[ ] year's experience in the Bureau and therefore were no[ ] eligible for the promotion. In addition, less than a year of experience in the Bureau is deemed inadequate to satisfy the knowledge requirements for this position.

The remaining candidates are ranked as follows:

1. William A Larsh, EOD 9/10/84, GS-5, Comprehensive Employment Test (CET) score 143; Missouri College Series (MCS) score 157. Mr. Larsh has experience not only in the Organized Crime Section but also in the position for which he is being recommended. The employee previously assigned to that position went on temporary duty seven months ago, and Mr. Larsh has assumed a portion of those responsibilities since then. In addition, he has experience with the Organized Crime Information System (OCIS) and NADDIS. His educational background was greater than that of the other candidates in that he holds two Bachelor degrees, one in Pre-Physical Therapy and a second in Political Science. His performance rating for 1985 was Exceptional. His test results on the CET and MCS ranked first amongst all candidates.

b6, b7c
3RD PARTY
INFO

FBI Memorandum (p. 2), dated 3/3/1986, promoting me to the Narcotics Analyst position.

When it came time for my interview for the IRS position, it was obvious to me that management wanted me for the job. One of the SSAs interviewing me for the IRS position was an SSA from the Narcotics Policy Group. He was clearly willing to help me along during the interview. I cannot remember exactly what some of the questions were, but I recall responding to a question stating that I had no experience in a particular area. The SSA immediately corrected me and said I did have that experience. He then prompted me to answer the question fully by reminding me of some task I had performed for him as a Narcotics Analyst. Needless to say, I had a successful interview.

THE FBI – THEY EAT THEIR YOUNG

After I was promoted to the IRS position, a list was disseminated of the rankings and scores for all of the candidates. The Drug Section selected the first ten candidates from the list to fill two IRS positions for each of the five new units. I was ranked number one and promoted in September 1986. I was assigned to the Colombian/South American Drug Trafficking Unit. The other IRS in my unit was an intelligent thirty-five-year-old white female with a great sense of humor and a biting wit. Her good friend was hired as an IRS in the La Cosa Nostra Drug Trafficking Unit. Shortly after we began working together, they told me I looked like the actor, James Dean. From then on, they referred to me as "Jimmy Dean." They were great for my ego. I only worked with them for a little more than a year, but our paths would cross in the FBI for the next twenty-plus years and they never once called me by my given name.

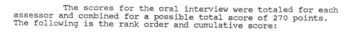

The scores for the oral interview were totaled for each assessor and combined for a possible total score of 270 points. The following is the rank order and cumulative score:

Ranking	Name	Score
1	Larsh, William E.	258
2		
3		
4		
5		
5		
7		
8		
9		
10		
11		

b6, b7C

3RD PARTY INFO

Mr. William E. Larsh, EOD 9/10/84, was ranked first after oral interview based on his knowledge, skills and abilities. Mr. Larsh is experienced in organized crime matters having served as a GS-7 program analyst in the Organized Crime Section. As such, he has familiarity with the organized crime program, objectives, and has enhanced his analytical ability through the utilization of computerized research tools, i.e., OCIS and NADDIS DEA system. He was rated exceptional in his last performance appraisal which included, ability to collect, analyze, and report results either orally or in the written format. His interview score and pertinent experiences exceeds that of the other ranked candidates. Mr. Larsh, therefore, is recommended for the Intelligence Research Specialist GS-7 position.

FBI Memorandum (p. 3), dated 9/4/1986, regarding my promotion to the IRS position.

The problem working in this new position was that it was initially unfulfilling, insofar as management did not seem to know what to do with all of the new IRSs. The SSAs in the new units utilized the new analysts largely by having them assist with menial tasks, rather than having them conduct any type of analysis.   Finally, the Drug Section Chief decided that a worthwhile project would be to determine what connection existed between Colombian and Mexican drug trafficking cartels. I was given the assignment and was thankful for the opportunity to finally research, analyze, and write something of value for the FBI.

My FBI credentials as an Intelligence Research Specialist (IRS), 1986.

I spent the next nine months working on and completing this project. I queried all fifty-nine FBI field divisions for cases where intelligence or evidence existed indicating ties between Colombian and Mexican drug cartels. I analyzed the information and began organizing it into a report.   An SSA in the unit reviewed it for accuracy and was quite impressed with it. My Unit Chief signed off on the report and it was sent to the Special Projects Section for professional binding. I was very proud when the bound copies were returned.   More importantly, however, I believed that the information contained in the report might be of assistance to agents in the field conducting drug investigations. The last step was to attach airtels to each booklet for all fifty-nine field divisions.   An airtel was the FBI's form for written communications between the field offices. They were later changed to Electronic Communications, or ECs. All that was needed for dissemination was a signature by the Drug Section Chief. However, the Section Chief who initially gave me this assignment transferred to the field by the time I completed this project. My old Unit Chief from the Narcotics Policy Group became the Acting Section Chief.

I was told by my colleagues that he was apparently unhappy with me for leaving the Narcotics Policy Group, although he had never said anything directly to me. At any rate, the Acting Section Chief balked at disseminating the reports to the field because he said they needed to be classified "Sensitive." I followed his instructions and sent them all back to the Special Projects Section to be bound again with the appropriate classified markings. After the booklets were returned with the appropriate markings, however, the Acting Section Chief still would not sign off to disseminate them to the field. I was later hired as an agent and was attending New Agent Training Class at the FBI Academy six months later. My IRS co-worker from my unit told me while I was at Quantico that the Acting Section Chief never disseminated my report. She said she believed it was out of spite because I left his unit the previous year. The only saving grace was that the Assistant Director of CID utilized the information from my report as part of his testimony before Congress as justification to increase the FBI's budget in the area of drug investigations.

During the time I had been promoted and was working diligently on the drug cartel report, I was also focusing on my ultimate goal of becoming an FBI agent. With my college degree, the FBI required me to have three years full-time work experience before becoming an agent. The FBI application rules would not allow me to take the written examination until after two and a half years working there. My OCIS analyst friends had already taken the written test and failed. The first section of the agent test involved reading comprehension. The second part was a psychological test. My one OCIS Analyst friend told me he failed the psychological part of the test. Although in retrospect, he would not have known which, if not both portions of the test, he had failed.

My friend gave me a great tip regarding the psychological portion of the test, telling me that I needed to answer the questions honestly and instinctively. He explained not to answer how I might think the FBI would want me to answer because the same question was asked repeatedly throughout the test in different ways. He said that the way in which to pass the psychological part of the test was with consistency in my answers. This advice would turn out to be of great help to me. However, when my two OCIS friends failed the test, it shook my confidence in my own plans in becoming an agent. They were allowed to take the test again six months later, but they both failed again. They were then precluded from ever taking the test again.

The one OCIS Analyst became a DEA agent, and the other became a federal agent with the Naval Intelligence Service. Both jobs were 1811 series, meaning they were authorized to carry guns and had arrest powers, similar to FBI agents. However, neither agency had the prestige of the FBI, nor were they the jobs they both dreamed of having. I figured that if these two presumably bright guys could not pass the test, then my chances might not be good. Although I had not given up on my goal of becoming an agent, which for me started three years earlier with the suggestion from the stranger at the golf course, I thought now for the first time that it might not materialize.

With my friends' failures, I began thinking I needed a backup plan. I applied to the DEA at the end of 1986 and took the Department of the Treasury agent test in the beginning of 1987. At that time, the Department of the Treasury consisted of the Internal Revenue Service, the Bureau of Alcohol, Tobacco, and Firearms (BATF), Customs, Border Patrol, and Secret Service, all of which had 1811 series federal agents. I also applied to the Howard County Sheriff's Office in Maryland, where I lived. I was scheduled to take the FBI agent written examination in April 1987 when the DEA called me for an interview. I remember an SSA from my unit asking why I would want to work for the DEA, detecting a hint of disdain for the agency. I explained that I wasn't sure I would pass the FBI agent's test.

The DEA interview was a disaster. I believed the interview had been going fine at the beginning. I was responding to the panel's questions adequately, I thought, most of which related to situational scenarios. They asked a series of "What would you do?" types of questions. For instance, they asked, "What would you do as a DEA agent if you saw someone smoking marijuana socially at a private party you were attending?" Another was, "What would you do if your partner was shot, administer first aid, or leave your partner to catch the shooter?" Then a black female

DEA agent on the panel asked me why I was not considering becoming an FBI agent since I was already an analyst in the FBI. When I proceeded to tell her that I was scheduled to take the FBI agent's test in April, she became indignant, agitated, and downright hostile toward me. She started yelling at me that I needed to prove to her why I wanted to be a DEA agent. It was quite obvious that becoming a DEA agent was my backup plan. Needless to say, I never heard back from the DEA.

Luckily, my FBI agent written test was scheduled a few weeks later. I could do nothing to prepare for the psychological part, except to heed the advice I had been given by my friend. As for the reading comprehension portion of the test, I had been practicing from an SAT preparation book. I wished I had purchased this book in high school. I had done very poorly on the SAT tests in high school, staying out until 2 a.m. when the exams were scheduled at 7:30 a.m. the same morning.

I would not make that mistake again. I was determined to have a career that was more than just a job to go to every day. I wanted some self-satisfaction in my work and to do something I believed would make a difference in the world. My current job working as an IRS in the Drug Section did not come close to fitting that bill. The SAT practice tests paid off. One part of the agent test was a timed three-minute read of a one-page description of a bank robbery. I then had two minutes to answer thirty questions about the bank robbery without looking back at the narrative. I aced it. Maybe the stars were in alignment for me that day, but the practice tests definitely helped. I was memorizing everything I read on each and every narrative on the test. I had never been able to focus that way before on a reading comprehension test. The psychological test went just as well. The same questions were occurring a second and third time throughout the test in different forms. I had never felt so confident on a test in my life and it could not have happened at a better time. I knew doing well would give me the exciting career I coveted.

After passing this test with flying colors, I was scheduled for a panel interview in June at the Washington Metropolitan Field Office (WMFO). An SSA from the Narcotics Policy Group, one of the nicest agents I ever met, offered suggestions for the interview. First, he said, "Just be yourself and you'll do fine." Then, he offered advice regarding my attire. Rattling off a list, he said matter of factly, "Bill, first thing, agents don't wear tassels on their shoes, get a pair of wingtip shoes. Also, buy a new suit and tie. And wear a white shirt." I tended to wear a lot of plaid shirts. I followed his advice to the letter. I thought this SSA was a great guy. I bought the wingtip shoes, an Evan-Picone suit, and a new silk tie. I felt very good about my appearance. I also firmly believed in the old adage, "Clothes make the man!"

The day of my FBI agent interview, 6/18/1987.

An SSA from the Colombian/South American Drug Trafficking Unit also provided me with some valuable advice for the interview. He told me to make sure I knew current events and to be able to describe my accomplishments in great detail. This SSA had previously worked at WMFO with one of the three agents on my panel interview. I assumed he must have told him I was a good candidate.

His advice was hugely helpful for the interview. At the outset, my knowledge of current events impressed the panel. I had studied the newspapers for months, especially the Iran-Contra scandal, which was prominent in the news at the time.

The interview panel finally had to cut me off after I went on and on providing them with every excruciating detail of the scandal: the illegal sale of arms to Iran for hostages held in Lebanon; the diversion of funds from the arms sales to anti-Communist Contra rebels in Nicaragua; the violation of the Boland Amendment which prohibited assistance to the Contras; the history of the Sandinista government; Colonel Oliver North accepting responsibility; and the rest of the Reagan administration's involvement; until they realized I knew everything there was to know about it.

The interview seemed to get better for me at every turn. My confidence was high. I was knowledgeable, articulate, personable, and charming. I spoke of my accomplishments in golf, which included my second place finish in the Baltimore County High School Championships; my first place finish in the A-flight of the 1979 Baltimore City Public Links Championship; and my win in the 1979 Baltimore City Two-Man Team Championship at Clifton Park, where I shot my career low round of 68. They seemed impressed, even though it was all a bit of braggadocio on my part. I felt a little self-conscious about the golf, partly because these events took place seven or eight years previously. My golf game had deteriorated significantly since high school, which I disclosed, too.

When describing my accomplishments at work, I described my nine months of work producing a report on the Colombian/Mexican drug cartel connections. I brought them a copy to review. When I told them that the Assistant Director of CID used the information in the report in his testimony to Congress to help justify an increase in the FBI's drug budget, they seemed suitably impressed. I then explained to them the details regarding how FBI Headquarters and the Acting Section Chief had not yet disseminated it to the field. They shook their heads in disgust, conveying their apparent understanding of the matter. Throughout my entire career, FBI Headquarters was never highly regarded by the field. Field agents often referred to it as the "Puzzle Palace" or some other disparaging term. The general impression was that FBI Headquarters often made the field agents' jobs more difficult and was usually a hindrance to their investigations. The agents on the panel were not at all surprised at FBI Headquarters' failure to disseminate my report. They recognized how ridiculous their lack of action was and seemed more amused by it, if anything.

My FBI report, dated 1987, never disseminated.

The interview had clearly gone well. I felt extremely comfortable and confident. They liked me and I believed I answered their questions more than satisfactorily. The final boost to my confidence came at the very end of the interview when an agent on the panel began describing to me how cool it was to be an agent and the extra-added benefits agents received. He told me how he was once in Detroit at Tiger Stadium attending an Orioles game and badged his way into the press box where Brooks Robinson was broadcasting the game to the Baltimore television audience. He not only got to meet his hero, but Brooks introduced him to the television viewers. I was quite fascinated with the agent's story, due to the fact that I had gotten an autograph from Brooks Robinson when I was fifteen years old. I proceeded to tell him how Brooks was at the opening of a Pizza Hut in 1977 in Perry Hall, Maryland. I rode my bicycle two miles and stood in line for about an hour to get his autograph. Brooks was one of my childhood heroes, as he was to nearly every Baltimore kid of that era. I felt encouraged about my chances of becoming an agent following this interview.

THE FBI – THEY EAT THEIR YOUNG

Brooks Robinson, the greatest third baseman of all time.

I was later notified by letter of my combined score for the written test and the interview, making me eligible to become an agent. I needed only to pass a background investigation, a medical examination, a trigger-pull test, and a physical fitness test. The requirements for the fitness test were doing a minimum number of sit-ups, push-ups, pull-ups, and completing a two-mile run. I was well on my way to becoming an agent. I had already passed a background investigation three years earlier when I was hired as a file clerk, so this was not going to be a problem. I was twenty-five years old and in great physical condition. Fitness requirements were not any real difficulty. The trigger-pull test was not a problem either, as it required the applicant to be physically strong enough to pull a trigger on a Smith and Wesson .38 caliber revolver a minimum number of times in sixty seconds. This test was clearly designed to weed out extreme weaklings. The only other hurdle was passing a medical examination.

My appointment for my physical took place during the summer of 1987 at the Walter Reed Army Hospital in Washington, D.C. The elderly doctor who examined me was at least in his seventies. He had autographed pictures on his wall of every President from Ronald Reagan back to Dwight D. Eisenhower. I thought everything went fine until I received a letter a month later stating that I had scoliosis, or curvature of the spine, which could preclude me from becoming an agent. The letter further instructed me to be examined by an orthopedic specialist. This was a shock to me, inasmuch as I never had any back pain other than some occasional stiffness when I was on the high school football team. My fears were quickly erased when the orthopedic specialist examined my back and told me, "You have a slight curvature of the spine of about five degrees, but your back should be good for another sixty years."

The last hurdle was the spousal interview, which took place at the FBI Baltimore Division. The FBI wanted to make sure that the spouse of the applicant was willing to transfer anywhere. My wife, Cindy, was giving up a lot in her teaching career by following me. She had received several awards in only her third year of teaching. She was even interviewed by the *U.S. News & World Report* magazine regarding her innovative and enthusiastic teaching methods. Cindy, of course, told the Baltimore FBI agent in the spousal interview that she was one hundred percent behind me and had no problem moving anywhere.

In September 1987, the FBI sent me a letter stating that I had received my appointment as an FBI Special Agent. I was instructed to report to the FBI Academy in Quantico, Virginia, on November 1, 1987 for New Agent training. At the end of October, the Drug Section planned a big party for me at Blackie's Restaurant on Northwest M Street in Washington, D.C. It was all very exciting and everybody at work seemed extremely happy for me, except for one person.

My OCIS Analyst friend came back to visit the OCIS Unit following his DEA graduation in October. I ran into him in the hallway with one of the female OCIS analysts. He looked different physically, as he obviously had gotten into shape during his training. Sadly, however, he was no longer his gregarious, jovial self. He was as serious as I had ever seen him. I congratulated him on becoming a DEA agent and how fit he looked. He told me he was being assigned to New York. I told him that it was great for him and his wife. His wife was an OCIS analyst in the FBI New York office. My wife and I attended their wedding in Queens. The reception was held at the Downtown Athletic Club in Manhattan where the Heisman Trophy was presented annually. When the female OCIS analyst told him I had passed the agent's test and was on my way to New Agent Training class in

November, a queer look crossed his face. He was obviously not pleased. He did not even congratulate me. I thought we had been friends. It was very disappointing and I never saw him again.

My going away party was the biggest luncheon I would ever have in my career. My wife took off from school to attend. The strange part of this affair was a comment made to Cindy from the SSA from my unit, the same SSA who had previously given me such good advice for my agent interview. Shortly before lunch, he cornered Cindy and said, "After Bill becomes an agent, if you ever see him on the street with a pretty girl, just ignore it because he could be working undercover. You might compromise an investigation." She was not buying his bull and developed an immediate dislike for him. This had been the first time they had ever met and he completely insulted her intelligence. She was also struck by his obvious sense of entitlement.

I received a pewter mug with my name and the dates I worked in the Organized/Drug Section engraved on it, and a garment suitcase bag as a gift, which I would use throughout my FBI travels over the next twenty-four and a half years. It was a great send-off, in spite of the SSA annoying Cindy. He definitely riled her up. Another SSA from my unit was at the luncheon who Cindy told me looked just like Christopher Reeve from the *Superman* movies. In my speech, I told the crowd, "My wife met Pat and was surprised that Superman was attending my luncheon." It got a good laugh and Cindy was quite pleased with my remark, especially considering what the other SSA said to her earlier.

TO   : Mr. David Rarity,   August 4, 1987   **b7C**

FROM   : Mr. Storey

SUBJECT: WILLIAM ALAN LARSH
          CRIMINAL INVESTIGATION DIVISION
          BUAP-SA

      Enclosed herewith are memoranda prepared by supervisors and support staff that are assigned to the Drug Section who are acquainted with captioned employee. The following additional information is being submitted by Section Chief Storey:

      Intelligence Research Specialist Larsh has been under the overall supervision of Section Chief Storey for the past two years. He is a dedicated, conscientious, and extremely bright employee who has contributed significantly to the work being performed in the section. He has a pleasing, outgoing personality, can work under pressure, and has never had any difficulty following instructions or getting along with his fellow employees.

      On many occasions, Larsh demonstrated the ability to initiate projects on his own that directly related to his responsibilities. This was particularly true relating to the analysis work he has done in connection with the Colombian/South American drug trafficking problem. He has prepared written communications and reports concerning his assignment in a clear, concise, and articulate manner. He also has delivered oral reports and briefings concerning the analysis work he has performed in a similar manner.

      Section Chief Storey has been an Agent for 22 years, the last 12 years of which have been spent in a supervisory and management capacity. Based on his experience, Section Chief Storey would not hesitate to recommend Larsh for the position of Special Agent and considers him to be one of the most outstanding candidates that he, Section Chief Storey, has observed in recent years.

87-   -28

1 OCT 16 1

 b7C

FBI Memorandum (p. 1), dated 8/4/1987, regarding the Organized Crime Section Chief recommendation for me as a Special Agent.

Memorandum

To   :   Mr. Shafer   Date   10/8/87

From :   D. Rarity, Jr.

Subject :   WILLIAM ALAN LARSH
EOD 09/10/84; FBIHQ, (CRIMINAL INVESTIGATIVE DIVISION)
INTELLIGENCE RESEARCH SPECIALIST, GS 9, $22,458
AGE 25; MARRIED (NO CHILDREN)
BUAP – SPECIAL AGENT (DIVERSIFIED)

PURPOSE: To set forth the results of employee's background
investigation in connection with his consideration for the
Special Agent position.

BASIS FOR CONSIDERATION: LARSH has an SAEE score of 35.28 and
PRG of 87.53. He possesses a Bachelor of Science degree in
Political Science and has the necessary three years work
experience to be considered under the Diversified Program
(33.75/80.00).

EDUCATION: LARSH attended Essex Community College, Baltimore,
Maryland, from 1/81 to 8/81. He earned a GPA of 3.71 on a 4.0
scale. From 9/81 to 6/82, he attended University of Georgia,
Athens, Georgia, earning a GPA of 3.82 on a 4.0 scale.

    LARSH attended Towson State University, Baltimore,
Maryland, from 9/82 to 5/84. He graduated on 5/27/84 with a
Bachelor of Science degree in Political Science. He earned a GPA
of 3.65 on a 4.0 scale and graduated Magna Cum Laude.

CREDIT AND CRIMINAL: All credit inquiries were satisfactory.

    Criminal checks on all of LARSH's relatives were
negative. Criminal checks on applicant verified the charge of
failure to obey yellow signal in 1984. There was no record to
verify the speeding charge from 1982.

67-85-2364 32

MILITARY: LARSH has had no military service. LARSH is in
compliance with the requirement that he be registered in the
Selective Service System.

16

10-11-87

PHYSICAL FITNESS: The following information was obtained during
the administration of the Firearms Proficiency Indicator Test on
10/2/87: double action trigger pull – strong hand (72) and weak
hand (68). He was able to hold the M-16A1 in position and reach
and operate the Remington Model 870 with his trigger finger.

1 – ▮▮▮▮ (Quantico)
    (3)

▮▮ 67C

(CONTINUED-OVER)

FBI Memorandum (p. 1), dated 10/8/1987, with results of my background
investigation and recommendation for appointment as a Special Agent.

Memorandum from D. Rarity, Jr. to Mr. Sharp
RE: WILLIAM ALAN LARSH
     BUAP - SPECIAL AGENT (DIVERSIFIED)

        On 9/24/87, LARSH was afforded the Preemployment
Physical Fitness Test and received the following results:
percent of body fat: 4.6% (5 points); sit-ups (2 minutes):
78 (6 points); push-ups: 71 (10 points); pull-ups: 9 (4
points); and 2 mile run: 13:24 (7 points). Total points:
32. His flexibility measurement was 19".

PHYCIAL EXAMINATION: Results of physical examination were satisfactory including his vision, color vision, audiometer examination
and EKG. He was found to be 5'9 1/2" tall and weighs 157 1/2
pounds in a medium frame (desirable limits 144-174 1/2). LARSH
has been certified for strenuous physical exertion. Applicant
had an orthopedic evaluation regarding his scoliosis. The Dr.
stated that he saw no significant scoliosis but a possible slight
curve. This curve would never cause him trouble in any way and
the patient has no limitation because of the curve.

DRUG TESTING: The specimen was forwarded to FBI Laboratory for
analysis. Results were negative.

BOARD INTERVIEW: (52.25) Applicant was interviewed on 6/18/87 by
the interview board of the Washington Field Office and favorably
recommended. It was the consensus of the panel that

K6, b2

SPOUSE INTERVIEW: Applicant's spouse was interviewed on 9/23/87
with very favorable results.

EXPERIENCE: LARSH's past employments with Friendly's Restaurant,
Baltimore, Maryland, 2/81 to 5/81; Western Electric Company,
Baltimore, Maryland, 5/81 to 8/81; Metropolitan Security International, Baltimore, Maryland, 11/82 to 3/83; and Perry Hall
Brunswick Bowling Lanes, Baltimore, Maryland, 6/83 to 3/84; were
all verified and favorable during employee's initial background
investigation.

        LARSH entered on duty on 9/10/84 as a GS-3, File Clerk
in the Criminal Investigative Division at FBIHQ. He was promoted
to GS-7, Program Analyst on 3/3/86, laterally transferred to
GS-7, Intelligence Research Specialist on 11/26/86, and promoted
to GS-9, on 3/29/87. He has received one exceptional and one
fully successful performance appraisal. There were no awards,
commendations or derogatory information located in employee's
file.

                        - 2 -

                                    (CONTINUED-OVER)

FBI Memorandum (p. 2), dated 10/8/1987, with results of my background
investigation and recommendation for appointment as a Special Agent.

Memorandum from D. Rarity, Jr. to Mr. Sharp
RE: WILLIAM ALAN LARSH
      BUAP - SPECIAL AGENT (DIVERSIFIED)

Special Agent FRANCIS J. STOREY, Section Chief, advised that LARSH is a dedicated, conscientious, and extremely bright employee who has contributed significantly to the work being performed. He can work under pressure, and has never had any difficulty following instructions or getting along with his fellow employees. He has demonstrated the ability to initiate projects on his own that are directly related to his responsibilities. He has prepared written communications and reports in a clear, concise, and articulate manner. He has also delivered oral reports and briefings in a similar manner. STOREY recommended LARSH for the position of Special Agent and considers him to be one of the most outstanding candidates that STOREY has observed in recent years.

Special Agent BRIAN R. LOADER, Acting Unit Chief, stated that LARSH has performed his duties in a highly professional and responsible manner. He is a self motivator and has initiated important projects with little supervision. LOADER highly recommended LARSH for the position of Special Agent and considers him an exceptional candidate.

SA EDWARD J. BODIGHEIMER, SA J. PATRICK CUNNINGHAM, SA WALTER SCHUPLEIN, JR., and JANE E. WHITMORE, co-workers, stated that LARSH is a thorough, dedicated worker, who is very conscientious. He is a self motivated individual who responds immediately and follows through with minimal supervision until a project is completed. They all highly recommended LARSH for the Special Agent position.

RECOMMENDATION: That LARSH be offered an appointment as a Special Agent with no contingencies.

APPROVED

Adm. Serv.	Laboratory
Crim. Inv.	Legal Coun.
	Off. of Cong.
Director	Off. of Pub. Affs.
Exec. AD-Adm.	
Exec. AD-Inv.	Training
Exec. AD-LES	

b7C

NAC: 11/2/87

- 3 -

FBI Memorandum (p. 3), dated 10/8/1987, with results of my background investigation, and recommendation for appointment as a Special Agent.

CHAPTER 2

MY NEUROTIC ROOMMATE

I will never forget my first day arriving at the FBI Academy located on the United States Marine Corps Base in Quantico, Virginia, on early Sunday evening, November 1, 1987. I reported for New Agent Class (NAC) 88-1, the first new agent class in the 1988 fiscal year. The fiscal year in the federal government began October 1st. I had an easy trip traveling to the FBI Academy, unlike most of my classmates. Since I lived in Lisbon, Maryland, I only had to drive seventy miles, less than an hour and a half from my home. The vast majority of new agents had to fly into either Washington National Airport (now called Reagan National Airport) or Washington Dulles Airport, and take a shuttle to Quantico.

The rules at the FBI Academy for new agents included a midnight curfew for the first six weeks. This meant I could not go home on the weekends, but Cindy could visit me as long as I got back to my room by midnight. Cindy stayed at a hotel in the town of Quantico off the base the first six weekends. We spent every Saturday and Sunday together until midnight. After six weeks, I was allowed to leave every Friday night at 5 p.m. and drive home, returning Sunday night before midnight. Cindy and I were never separated for more than five days at a time during my training, but I did not make a lot of friends in the class as a result. The other agents in the class did not have the luxury of seeing their loved ones regularly. Most of them left their families, spouses, children, girlfriends, or boyfriends, for the fourteen-week duration of the class, with the exception of Christmas, which luckily fell on a Friday that year. Otherwise, they did not have a sufficient amount of time to fly home for a weekend, even after the six-week curfew was over.

I arrived that first night, checked in at about 6 p.m. and was given my room assignment. The rooms consisted of two agents to a room. A bathroom was shared with the two agents in the room next door, known as your suitemates. My roommate had not arrived yet, but my suitemates had already checked in. I met them briefly and they seemed nice. It was all a bit intimidating. I hung up my suits, my white shirts, and some ties. I did not know how often I might need the suits. We were required to wear uniform clothing throughout training, consisting of khaki pants and a light blue polyester golf shirt, as well as a blue and gray sweatshirt. We wore gray sweat pants and a sweatshirt in the gym. We were required to purchase the uniform clothing with our own money from the FBI Academy store.

I put the rest of my clothes, pajamas, socks, and underwear in dresser drawers, leaving two empty drawers for my roommate. Surprisingly, I was the only agent in the class who wore pajamas. Everybody slept in their gym shorts, t-shirts, sweat pants, or their underwear. I took a lot of kidding for my old man pajamas. They couldn't shame me though. I told them all that I couldn't understand why nobody wore pajamas. I thought they were the oddballs.

My roommate showed up about ten minutes before 7 p.m. in the dorm room. He was a few years older than me, short in stature, but very muscular. He seemed very anxious upon his arrival. As I hid my nervousness rather well, my roommate wore it like a woman whose slip was showing. He made me look as relaxed as Perry Como. Our introduction to one another was short since he was so late arriving. He told me where he was from and then made a highly personal remark as he put an 8 X 10 photograph of his wife on the dresser, stating that his wife was going to divorce him for coming here. I said nothing to him except that I'd see him in the classroom and that he should hurry.

We were scheduled to be in the classroom at 7 p.m. The FBI Academy buildings were all connected and you never had to go outside to get from one place to another. Window-lined hallways connected the dorms to the cafeteria, the library, the classrooms, the auditorium, and to the gymnasium. It was a unique and exciting place to be, but after fourteen weeks of training, it seemed more like a prison, albeit a very nice one.

I was extremely nervous the first night, particularly as I entered the classroom. I wanted to make a good first impression. The FBI Academy was like living in a goldfish bowl. The FBI instructors and class counselors were there to test you and judge you constantly. I had confidence in my abilities, but it was still a bit off-putting. I knew I was smart enough and athletic enough to handle any situation, but I also recognized everyone was always watching you. I suffered a real panic deep down inside that someone might find me out. Why were they going to make me an FBI agent? They might come to the conclusion that they had made some sort of mistake in selecting me. I was scared of blowing this opportunity. This was my big chance in life. The possibility of failure was real and I felt it. As nervous as I was though, nobody knew it.

As I entered the classroom, it was filled with almost forty professionally dressed men and women. We had assigned seats in alphabetical order, the same as the dormitory assignments. The classroom was very large with no individual desks. It consisted of four rows of slightly curved desktops extending from one side of the room to the other. Each row was a little higher and longer than the next. The front of the room had a series of three built-in chalkboards extending the width of the room. I was assigned a seat in the third row, second from the end. I had been hoping for an end seat or a seat in the back. My roommate was seated to my right. We were brought together by virtue of our last names falling in line alphabetically. Unfortunately for me, this happenstance of our names being connected by the alphabet would keep us paired together in nearly every aspect of training.

At 7 p.m. sharp, everyone was quiet with our undivided attention directed to the front of the classroom. My roommate managed to make it on time. The class counselors were very welcoming and asked us to introduce ourselves. When my turn came, I said, "My name is Bill Larsh. I am twenty-five years old. I'm from Baltimore, Maryland. I previously worked at FBI Headquarters as an Intelligence Research Specialist."

The class had three other former support employees, one of whom I had met previously at FBI Headquarters after we received our appointment letters. He had worked in an administrative position in CID. Another FBI employee worked on the Special Surveillance Group (SSG) at WMFO. SSG was a surveillance team consisting of support employees who followed foreign counterintelligence (FCI) targets. I had considered putting in for SSG the year before, as the FBI was expanding the program in more offices, such as Houston, Chicago, San Francisco, Los Angeles, New York and Washington, D.C., all places where foreign consulates, missions, or embassies were located. The FBI also had what was known as Special Operations Groups (SOG), surveillance teams consisting of agents. The FBI figured out that support employees could be trained to follow around diplomats or foreign visitors, while agent resources could be better utilized on criminal cases and other more dangerous matters. The third former support employee was a black female from WMFO married to an agent.

The remainder of my classmates had varied professional backgrounds ranging from accountants, lawyers, engineers, police officers, bankers, to military officers. The youngest new agent was a twenty-four-year-old graduate from law school. I was twenty-five years old and the second youngest in the class. The oldest agent was a thirty-six-year-old former banker who left behind five kids and a wife in Salt Lake City, Utah.

My roommate made an introduction to the class notably different than everyone else's. He first said he had a Master's degree. He said he was from one city, but then said he worked as the manager of a gym in another city in another state. He also mentioned that he had previously been a correctional officer in the military. Frankly, it was all very confusing. What struck me was why anyone would be a prison guard if they had a Master's degree. I thought certainly that I must have been mistaken on what I heard, but I later determined I was not.

After the introductions were made and instructions from the counselors were given with regard to expectations, the next step was being sworn in as Special Agents of the FBI. We all raised our right hands and swore the oath to uphold the Constitution of the United States and enforce all laws passed by Congress in our duties as FBI Special Agents. I never felt more important or more proud in my life. It was almost surreal. I could not believe they wanted me to fill this prestigious and important position. Surely they had made a mistake. I was just some kid from Perry Hall, Maryland, slightly obsessed with chasing a little white ball. It was truly happening though and it was all very exciting.

My roommate's odd behavior made me more self-assured. In the days to come, I learned more about him and it was all very weird. When we got back to the room that first night, he had the picture of his wife on top of the dresser, as well as a picture of himself as the winner of a bodybuilding competition wearing a sash around his muscular, sculpted body. He was evidently quite proud that he was a bodybuilding champion, but I thought to myself, "Wow, who does this?"

It became even more awkward when he began telling me his wife looked like the singer, Cher. He went on to describe to me how much he loved Cher, and how much he loved his wife, too. I only saw a slight resemblance to Cher, but he apparently thought she was the spitting image of her. The sad part of the conversation was that he was very upset because his wife evidently told him that she was not leaving home. According to my roommate, if he got assigned anywhere else, she would divorce him. I didn't say anything, but I wondered why he and his wife did not undergo the spousal interview as Cindy and I had. If his wife would have revealed that she had no intention of leaving her home, his application process would unquestionably have been terminated. However, this was clearly not the case.

The first morning of training cemented my low opinion of him. I awoke at 6:30 a.m. and saw him posing in front of the mirror, flexing his muscles like he was a contestant in a bodybuilding competition. I just rolled over pulling the pillow over my head. I waited for him to take his shower and get the hell out of the room before I got up. I also had to wait for our two suitemates to finish in the bathroom, too, since they shared it with us. I waited for the three of them to leave before getting up at 7:30 a.m. I brushed my teeth, took a quick shower, shaved, and then dressed in my khaki pants and sky blue short-sleeved polyester shirt with "FBI Academy" printed on it. I went to breakfast in the cafeteria at 7:45 a.m., quickly inhaled a plate of scrambled eggs, toast, orange juice, and chocolate milk, and proceeded to class which started at 8 a.m. This would become my morning routine. Everybody came to the conclusion that I was unable to get out of bed in the mornings. I did not reveal the fact that it was due to my crazy roommate and my concerted effort to avoid him.

He told me a couple peculiar stories that I was never sure were true or not, though it really didn't matter. The mere fact that he divulged them without any hint of embarrassment proved to me he was unbalanced. The first story involved agents who he said came to see him at his work to inform him that he was selected to go to the FBI Academy. He said he had a rattail hairstyle and wore an earring. He claimed he was later called into the FBI office to meet with the Special Agent in Charge (SAC). He said the SAC asked him if he was planning to go to the FBI Academy looking like he did. My roommate said the SAC himself cut off his rattail. I seriously doubted that the SAC cut off his hair, but it seemed plausible that he might have been called in to the SAC's office to be warned or advised to lose the rattail and earring. It was always confusing talking to him. Nothing ever made sense.

The other story that cemented my low opinion of him was when he described his background in the military. He said that although he had a Master's degree, he signed up as an enlisted man. This sounded stupid, but it was not the most troubling part of the story. He said he worked as a prison guard. I told him that must have been a tough job. I then asked, out of curiosity, what was done at the prison with regard to rapes. I had always thought to myself that if I were 6 feet 4 inches tall, I would probably be able to survive in prison. However, at 5 feet 9 ½ inches tall and only 154 pounds, I am sure I would have been raped or killed in jail. My roommate's response to my question sickened me. He said, "We just watched and laughed." I knew by the way he responded to me that he was one sick son of a bitch. I tried to say as little as possible to him from then on.

As stated previously, attending the FBI Academy was very much like living life in a goldfish bowl. I tried to stay acutely aware of this fact at all times. I was not going to say or do anything to bring attention to myself. I definitely was not going to say to anybody that I thought my roommate was a nut. As it turned out, I did not have to. After about only a week or so, my classmates began approaching me to advise me that they thought my roommate was neurotic. I said, "Yeah, no kidding, I figured that out within two minutes of meeting him." The problem was I was stuck with him in every aspect of training. He roomed with me, sat next to me in class, and was assigned with me on every training exercise.

When we had any practical training, he was my partner. One night on a physical surveillance training exercise that took place in the town of Dumfries outside the marine base, we were in a car together following actors portraying bad guys. I was assigned to be the driver and my roommate was assigned to operate the radio. He was very upset he was not driving and immediately began whining about it. I said, "Sorry, but those are our assignments." We followed the subjects on the surveillance to a convenience store in Dumfries. I told my roommate to stay in the car while I went inside to get a better view of the subject.

While in the store, I heard the yelping sound of a police siren coming from our FBI vehicle in the parking lot. I immediately departed the store and found my roommate now in the driver's seat of the small compact Oldsmobile Calais. I opened the door of the passenger side and flicked the siren switch to the off position on the console between the seats. I asked my roommate, "What are you doing?" to which he replied, "I wanted to drive and accidently hit the siren switch climbing into the driver's seat and then couldn't find the switch to shut it off." I thought, "Why me, Lord?" Unfortunately, this was only the tip of the iceberg of his idiotic behavior. He continued demonstrating his weird ways throughout training.

He would scream at instructors in the classroom repeatedly over the next several weeks. After only two weeks into training, we had a review in class for our first major test, a legal exam. My roommate asked a question about some legal point he did not understand. The instructor spent the next fifteen minutes providing him and the entire class with a clear, pointed, and complete explanation to his question. The instructor politely and calmly asked my roommate, "Do you understand now?" He responded in a slightly agitated manner, "No, I don't." The instructor then asked, "What part of it don't you understand?" He then exploded, screaming at the instructor, "I don't understand any of it!" The instructor looked flabbergasted and the entire class snickered and looked at each other in astonishment. This type of behavior became the norm for him.

About a week later, we were participating in a firearms exercise in the evening clearing dark hallways. Actors posing as armed criminals were hidden around every corner. A DEA firearms instructor observed and critiqued our every move. The FBI Academy also served as the training site for new DEA agents. The FBI and the DEA were both agencies within the Department of Justice. This particular DEA firearms instructor was an older, gruff, no-nonsense type of guy.

On my roommate's turn to clear the hallway, the DEA instructor followed him down the hall. He turned the corner of the dark hallway. Upon seeing a silhouette of a man, he began clicking the trigger on his red-handled training revolver (training revolvers had no firing pins). He had repeatedly shot the unarmed man hiding in the hallway. The instructor calmly turned to him and said, "I want a memo on my desk tomorrow morning on why you shot that man." My roommate blew up and began screaming at the instructor, "He had a gun. His hand came up," as he motioned with his own hand, mimicking how the actor had apparently pulled a gun from his side.

The instructor was as cool as a cucumber and merely repeated to him to do a memo and have it on his desk in the morning. My roommate was beside himself and continued screaming at the instructor, adamant that he believed the actor had a gun. They went back and forth saying the same things. The contrast in their personalities and how they handled themselves was as much a training exercise as the exercise we were doing. My roommate stood face to face with the instructor, yelling, overly defensive, neurotic, and animated. The DEA instructor was like an oak, strong, calm, steady, and resolute, never getting upset or emotional. It was very odd, but not at all unusual when it came to my roommate.

Studying for tests was always a very stressful event for my roommate. The written tests started coming fast and furious after a couple of weeks into training. He would stay up half the night studying in the library, a complete nervous wreck worrying about the test. The irony was that he scored very well on the tests. I was always a bit nervous, too, because I wanted to do well, but the fact was that the tests were not all that difficult. The subject matter on the tests was reviewed by the instructors ad nauseam, and the tests were not tricky. The FBI training was not set up for failing the student. It was at great expense to the FBI and to the government in selecting applicants to the FBI Academy. It was a long, drawn out process involving testing, interviews, background investigations, and medical examinations for each student. A lot of time, money, and resources were utilized to select and finally send new agents to the FBI Academy.

Nobody in the FBI wanted a student to fail, not even if the student was as nutty as my roommate. At the time, though, I could not understand how he ever got through the application process. I was convinced he was mentally ill. It was only a matter of time, I thought, before he cracked. The first real sign, besides his usual defensive outbursts, came six weeks into training during a slightly formal ceremony in the classroom where we received transfer orders to our first office of assignment. Although it was serious business finding out where we would be going after uprooting our lives and family following training, it was done in a light-hearted, fun, and entertaining way. Our class counselor dressed in a Santa outfit as she handed out orders, randomly picking envelopes from her Santa bag.

Our class had a pool to guess which office we thought we might be assigned. A couple weeks before, I had gotten a call from the SSA from the Colombian/South American Drug Trafficking Unit who had given me the advice about knowing my current events for my agent interview. This SSA told me he had received orders for a transfer to the Tampa Division to be the SSA on the drug squad there. He made mention of how he would get me to Tampa to work for him on his squad, but I did not give much credence to his statement. He was usually full of bravado; however, when it came time to make a guess for the pool, I thought I might as well pick Tampa. It cost all of $1 and the prize was $39. The class was originally comprised of forty new agents, but an attorney decided after the first day he had made a mistake and subsequently resigned to return to his family and home in Los Angeles.

When the class counselor picked my envelope out of her Santa's bag, I went to the front of the classroom to retrieve my orders. Before opening the envelope, we had to state where we were from, what office we would like to go to, and what office we expected we might get orders to. I said, "I am from Baltimore, Maryland. I'd like to go anywhere south of the Mason-Dixon Line, and I expect I'm going to Tampa." I then quickly slid the file across the envelope and pulled out my orders. I read the letter, which said I was being transferred from Washington, D.C. to Tampa, Florida. I blurted out in genuine total surprise, "Tampa!" The class cheered and I heard my classmate who was running the pool say, "How does he do it?" I heard another classmate say, "Way to nail it, Bill." Everybody in the class knew I had worked at FBI Headquarters and had a lot of friends there. Many suspected it was a fix. However, I was completely caught off guard and honestly shocked at receiving orders to Tampa. I never dreamed the SSA would have managed to have such pull. I was very pleased to have won the $39 pool, too!

THE FBI – THEY EAT THEIR YOUNG

My orders to FBI Tampa.

When my roommate's turn to read his orders came, it turned to the bizarre and absurd, as it usually did with anything involving him. As a preface to what happened next, my roommate had apparently told a fellow student the night before that if he did not get assigned to a certain office, he was going to kill him. This particular classmate was a former accountant from South Carolina, who I would describe as mild-mannered, soft-spoken, and probably the nicest guy in the entire class.

My roommate stood before the class with his orders in his hand. He was clearly nervous and ill at ease. He muttered, "I really don't know where I'm from." He then indicated several cities where he wanted to go, but said he hoped to return to his hometown. Then, as he opened the envelope and pulled the letter out to read, he sighed and turned away. He stood there stunned for a few seconds. He was obviously not happy. His expression and his beet-red face revealed utter disgust. He pointed to the classmate he previously threatened at the back of the room and sprinted up the steps toward him. The classmate jumped from his seat and made a mad dash across the back of the room and out the door. Class members yelled, "Where are you going?" My roommate then said in the most exasperated way, "I'm going to Memphis, Tennessee!"

The entire class erupted into a spontaneous uproar of laughter at the strange incident. Later that night in the weight room, my roommate was throwing around weights and quite beside himself at the thought of being assigned to Memphis. He never told me personally, as we said virtually nothing to one another by this time, but the word was that he was convinced his wife would divorce him and would never go to Memphis.

Later on, ten weeks into training, when things were getting a little more relaxed for me and everybody else, everything came to a head concerning my roommate. One afternoon, the entire class was milling around the gymnasium waiting for the instructor to arrive for our defensive tactics class. Suddenly, my roommate sprinted across the gym floor toward a female classmate, a young woman who previously worked as a stewardess for the now defunct Peoples Airline. He charged her and hit her in what I could only describe as a "Dick Butkus" shot. Dick Butkus was arguably the toughest and one of the most feared, hard-hitting middle linebackers ever to play in the NFL. The only thing that prevented her from being forcefully knocked to the ground was my roommate grabbing her around the waist as he rammed into her. He knocked the wind out of her and she understandably began crying. Nearly everyone witnessed his inexplicable behavior, including other defensive tactics instructors and counselors who were also in the gym. I remember one of my classmates incredulously asking my roommate, "What did you do that for?" His embarrassed reply was, "I don't know."

Later that evening in our dormitory, we were summoned from our rooms into the hallway for an announcement from one of our field counselors. He announced to everyone that my roommate had resigned, as if it were a very solemn occasion. I was about ready to bust. This was the best news I had heard in ten weeks. The field counselor departed the hallway and everyone was quiet until I began high-fiving my close friends. My roommate's closest friend witnessed my jubilation. He was clearly not pleased with my reaction, but I could have cared less. I figured something was definitely wrong with his judgment if his best friend in the class was the neurotic. All I knew was that I would have my room all to myself for the remaining four weeks of training. I would not have to watch any more muscle flexing or wait to get out of bed every morning. The ten miserable weeks of living and training with the nut were over. It was such a great relief.

I found out years later from a classmate that there was much more to the story regarding my roommate. When I ran into this agent, we discussed the only thing we had in common, our experience going through the FBI Academy together. I recalled that this agent had the reputation at the FBI Academy for having an objectionable body odor. During our chance meeting, thankfully, I smelled nothing. When I mentioned how elated I was when my roommate resigned, he told me the story behind it. Our field counselor had relayed the entire story to him.

I would occasionally run into our former field counselor at WMFO firearms training held at Quantico. He was a very friendly guy with a laid-back, pleasant personality. He apparently volunteered as a counselor due to the fact that he was going through a divorce and wanted to get away for fourteen weeks. He really did not do very much as our counselor. His role was to provide a field perspective to new agents. The problem was that he had worked foreign counterintelligence his entire career and never made an arrest, executed a search warrant, or even testified in court. He really had no interesting or exciting work experiences to share.

He provided the scoop to my classmate on what really happened with my roommate. My roommate had been warned repeatedly about his outrageous behavior throughout his tenure at the FBI Academy. After his Dick Butkus shot to the former stewardess, he was reprimanded for his conduct. During this admonition, however, he admitted that he was on Valium or some other type of tranquilizer to help calm him down and improve his behavior. After his admission of taking anxiety medication, he was asked to resign.

Twenty years later when I was assigned to Oklahoma City, another classmate called me. I had not spoken to him since 1988. We had become best friends at the FBI Academy. I found him to be hysterically funny and laughed at all his antics. We played pool for hours in the evenings in the final weeks of training. I can still picture my crazy friend at the end of the pool table with his head behind the pocket trying his best to distract me during my turn. My friend and I got along so well that I invited him to stay with me at my home one weekend toward the end of training. My friend, my wife, and I spent a day sightseeing at the Baltimore Inner Harbor. He even attended my going away party at my parents' house in Perry Hall, Maryland. My wife thought he was a bit obnoxious with his crazy sense of humor, but I was genuinely amused by everything he did. She never liked the Marx Brothers or W.C. Fields, my favorite comedians, so she could not have appreciated his humor. I thought he was one of the funniest people I had ever met. His humor was a welcome contrast to the seriousness at the FBI Academy. He was assigned to New York after training. I got orders to Tampa, later amended to the Orlando Resident Agency (ORA) in the Tampa Division.

My hilarious friend and me.

In the spring of 1988, my wife and I moved into a new housing development east of Orlando. My hilarious friend called me requesting to visit us for a week in the summer. I was all for it, except that he wanted me to take off to hang out with him. I told him I couldn't do that since I was married and I was also busy at work. I told him he could come, but I could not take off work. I was saving my leave to visit home at Christmas as well. As federal employees, we only accrued four hours of annual leave every two weeks. It took one year to accrue thirteen days. After three years of service, the rate increased to six hours per pay period. After fifteen years, it increased to eight hours per pay period or twenty-six days per year. When I told him I couldn't take off work for his visit, he didn't come. I did not hear from him again for twenty years.

On the 20th anniversary of NAC 88-1, members of my class sent a flurry of e-mails over the Bureau computer. Many of them wrote about their careers, i.e., where they had been, what they had done, etc. I was curious to read about some of the older classmates who were at retirement age. I was only forty-five and had to wait five more years to be eligible to retire. Agents could retire at the age of fifty with twenty years of service. Mandatory retirement for agents was at fifty-seven years of age.

I had not maintained contact with any of my classmates after graduating. Many new agents were close with their roommates, but that was obviously not the case with me. I was not even close to my two suitemates. I never engaged them in any meaningful conversation, probably because of my avoidance of my roommate. I rarely even ran into these guys in our shared bathroom. My one suitemate seemed quite full of himself. The instructors would normally ask the class who had been in certain professions. Whenever an instructor asked if anyone was previously in law enforcement, or an accountant, or an attorney, or even a Rhodes Scholar, my suitemate raised his hand every single time. He was somewhat difficult to believe. He only lasted one year in the Bureau. The story was he had a fiancé who refused to go with him to his first assignment. He then apparently confronted his SAC, giving him an ultimatum that if he did not get a transfer back home, then he would have to quit. The SAC did not oblige him and he indeed resigned from the Bureau.

My roommate's best friend in the class was a fellow from Arkansas. After my roommate resigned, his friend became unfriendly toward me. Somebody in the class told me that my roommate's friend thought I had gone to the counselors and was the cause of my roommate's trouble. Nothing could have been further from the truth. I purposely said nothing to anyone, except to my few friends. They witnessed his manic behavior, as did everyone else in the class, except, mysteriously, this guy from Arkansas. If my roommate's best friend actually thought I was responsible for getting him kicked out, then he must have turned out to be the worst investigator. He never spoke to me the last four weeks of training. I saw him at a training conference a few years later, but we did not speak there either. Then I saw him about ten years later at a health care fraud conference in Las Vegas and we finally spoke, but just the normal pleasantries. I would have loved to have mentioned my roommate to him and asked, "So why were you best friends with that psycho at Quantico?"

CHAPTER 3

❦

THE 120-YARD SHUTTLE RUN

During the second half of my new agent training class, I became preoccupied with my desire to leave my name on the board in the gymnasium that displayed the FBI Academy records for new agents. It had the record holders for sit-ups, push-ups, pull-ups, the two-mile run, and the 120-yard shuttle run. In junior high school, I had broken the school records in the 100-yard dash and the long jump. My name was prominently exhibited in the lobby of the Perry Hall Junior High School on the track and field records board.

In high school, I made the varsity indoor track team as a sophomore and was beating the senior classman who ran the 50-yard dash. My best time that year was 5.8 seconds. The school record was 5.7 seconds. I figured it was only a matter of time before I broke the record and got my name on the board outside the high school gymnasium that displayed the track records. By the time I became a senior, my name appeared on the board with records in the sprint and mile relays in indoor track. What I coveted, however, was the individual sprint records. The 60-yard dash record was 6.6 seconds. I never ran outdoor track because I played on the golf team in the spring.

Most of the indoor track facilities were only large enough for a 50-yard dash. The only facility large enough for a 60-yard dash event was at the United States Naval Academy in Annapolis, Maryland, the site of the Maryland State High School Indoor Track Championships. At that time, the track at this facility was state of the art. The track consisted of a rubbery-type spongy material, wherein spiked shoes could be worn, the only indoor track of its kind on the east coast. None of the other track venues during the regular season had anything close to this type of track. The Fifth Regiment Armory in Baltimore, where we usually had our regular season track meets, and Essex Community College, where the Baltimore County Indoor Track Championships were held, had normal wooden floors where spikes could not be worn.

I was thrilled in my sophomore year to have finished third in the 50-yard dash at the Baltimore County High School Indoor Track Championships. The top three finishers qualified for the state meet. The first and second place finishers were both black. My time was 5.8 seconds, only a tenth of a second short of tying the school record. I figured that I would undoubtedly obtain the school record at the Naval Academy on the fastest track on the east coast. I later learned that because of the large facility there, I would be running a 60-yard dash. I had not run the 60-yard dash all season, but I figured I would have a good chance to break the record on such a fast track. I never thought I would have any chance to be state champion, but I was sure I could break or at least tie the school record using spikes.

At the state meet that year, I was a skinny fifteen-year-old preparing to race all black boys, most of whom looked like NFL running backs. I ran in the first heat against five other boys and finished dead last. Only two sprinters in each heat advanced. The sad part for me was that only the first two sprinters in each heat received a time. These boys were running about 6.3 seconds. I not only lost the race badly, but no official time was recorded for me. I would never know if I had run a fast enough time to break the Perry Hall Senior High School record.

The exact same scenario played out in my junior year. I finished in third place in the Baltimore County Indoor Track Championships behind two black runners. I ran the same time in the 50-yard-dash as the year before, 5.8 seconds, still a tenth of a second from tying the school record. I returned to the Naval Academy for the second straight year as the only white kid in the state competing in the 60-yard dash. Sadly, I finished last again in the first heat and did not receive a time. In my senior year, I was surprised when I finished out of the top three in the county. I qualified for the state meet as part of the sprint and mile relay teams, but not in the dash. No white boys at all competed in the 60-yard dash at the Naval Academy that year. By my senior year, I had become known as the "great white hope." I was arguably the fastest white boy in the state of Maryland. However, I never did break the 50-yard or 60-yard dash records for my high school.

When I got to the FBI Academy, we were tested in all areas of physical fitness, to include a 120-yard shuttle run in the gymnasium. It involved starting the run lying on your back next to a cone, and then when the whistle blew, you jumped up and sprinted around numerous cones, requiring sharp turns for a total of 120 yards. We were scored on a ten point scale. For instance, if you could complete 72 push-ups, you scored the maximum of ten points. We needed to do 20 pull-ups and 120 sit-ups in two minutes to get the maximum ten points. The two-mile run maximum for ten points required running it in less than twelve minutes. The 120-yard shuttle run was at 22.0 seconds to max out. I easily did 72 push-ups, as I was doing a lot of bench-pressing at the time. I managed only about nine pull-ups. Sit-ups were painful for me, although I had been training prior to coming to Quantico. I managed 75 sit-ups in two minutes on my first test. My two-mile run time was satisfactory at about thirteen minutes and fifty seconds. It was the 120-yard run, however, where everyone took notice of my time.

Several of the agents were maxing on their first try on sit-ups, pull-ups, and push-ups, but only one person maxed on the two-mile run, an American Indian. He ran like a deer in under ten minutes. Only one person maxed on the shuttle run, and that was me, obliterating the 22.0 second mark with a 20.1 second time. Everyone was impressed with my speed. The record board in the FBI gym on the wall above the entrance indicated that the 120-yard shuttle run record was 19.4 seconds, held by an agent in NAC 86-7. Another board listed the DEA training agents' records, and another listed the National Academy (NA) records. NA attendees were from local police departments all over the United States and around the world who trained for sixteen weeks. Most NA graduates usually required this training for promotion within their police departments, although many attended merely for the prestige. Had I been a new DEA agent or an NA graduate, I would have broken their respective shuttle run records. I was curious as to why the FBI record was so much better than the DEA and NA records.

Our defensive tactics instructor told me the reason. He was my favorite instructor at the academy. He was a middle-aged Hawaiian native and a judo expert who reminded me of the late

Bruce Lee. Our class did not have boxing matches as part of training, as other classes did, since he said that fights might consist of one or two punches, but they would always end up on the ground. Before demonstrating apprehension and arrest techniques, he would always mimic a bad guy by saying, "Not today FBI." He would then demonstrate judo-type moves in order to subdue and handcuff a non-compliant subject. The class always grappled and wrestled instead of boxing. He also provided outstanding advice with regard to any knife-wielding assailant. He said, "If anyone pulls out a knife, do not hesitate to shoot them or they will kill you." He was of the opinion that you could assume they were an expert with a knife. The instructor told me that the agent holding the FBI shuttle run record was a black sprinter who ran the 100-meter dash in the 1984 Olympic trials. He did not make the Olympic track team, and unfortunately for me, he became an FBI agent.

A few years later when I was assigned to WMFO, a similar set of unlucky circumstances would haunt me again. I had come close, but failed to win the WMFO Thomas E. DuHadway Memorial Golf Tournament two years in a row. Finally, in 1995, I had a great round and shot 75 at the tournament, held for the third year in a row at the Andrews Air Force Base golf course. After finishing, I was certain of victory, as this would have been the winning score the two previous years. However, it was not to be. The first place score was a sizzling round of 65, a score I was not even capable of shooting. The winner was a new agent at WMFO who had previously competed in the PGA Tour Qualifying Tournament. He had failed to obtain a PGA Tour Card and instead became an FBI agent.

In the second physical fitness test at the FBI Academy, I wore new Nike court shoes and improved my time in the shuttle run three tenths of a second. I believed if I trained and practiced getting up off the floor faster on the start, I might be able to break the record. My high school track coach told me he had never seen anybody get out of the blocks faster than I had. I was determined to get my name on the record board. It became my mission for the remainder of my time at training. I even borrowed a pair of indoor track shoes from a high school friend in hopes of improving my time. I made it known to the instructor that I wanted to try to break the record. My best friend in class worked with me and even cheered me on when I tried to officially break the record before class one morning. Three instructors timed me at 19.79 seconds.

I was disappointed, but still thought with a little more practice over the next couple of weeks, I might get lucky and improve four-tenths of a second. About three weeks later, I tried again in the gym before classes started. I felt confident since I was in the best shape of my life. My friends from class came to support me. My time was 19.74 seconds, still over three tenths of a second shy of the record. It was apparent that this was as fast as I was going to run the course. My favorite instructor said to me, "Agent Larsh, I do not believe you are going to break this record, but I must say, you are the fastest white man I have ever seen." I would never forget what he said and I proudly retold this story for years to come.

Trying to break the record...my favorite instructor on the far right.

Not fast enough....0.34 seconds off the record.

Fastest white man in the bureau

The back of the previous photo with a note from my funny friend.

CHAPTER 4

FBI ACADEMY GRADUATION

At the end of our training, two agents collected money for various purchases. First, they announced that the class was getting sweatshirts with the FBI logo on it with "NAC 88-1" and our class motto "So Much to Remember," which an instructor repeatedly had said throughout training. He most likely said this to every class that went through the academy, but these two decided they wanted it on a class sweatshirt and collected $25 from each person to order them. We had already been required to buy FBI Academy sweatshirts as part of our uniform at the academy. We had to buy hats, shirts, and khaki pants as well, all out of our own pockets. We even had to purchase handcuffs. The only items given to us were our service revolvers, credentials, and badges. These items, however, were Bureau property to be returned upon retirement or separation from the Bureau. If these items were ever lost or stolen, an agent might be suspended without pay, depending on the circumstances.

Also at the conclusion of training, flowers, token gifts, and plaques were provided to our two field counselors and our staff counselor. The two agents collected another $20 from all thirty-eight agents. I was perplexed at how these gifts added up to $760. It was not as if Waterford Crystal or gold-plated watches were being given.

As I stood up to leave the class following the presentation of gifts, the two self-appointed treasurers happened to be standing next to me, so I casually asked how those gifts cost $760. For some reason, both were highly insulted at my inquiry. They provided no explanation, saying absolutely nothing to me. The highly indignant looks on their faces said it all. I made no accusation, but I was genuinely mystified. All I managed to do was alienate two individuals who would not look at me or speak to me for the remaining days of training. To this day, I would love to know how that money was spent. I would like to think they threw a big party, one that I was obviously not invited to attend.

I had occasionally run into classmates over the years at various training or conference sites, but I did not maintain contact with any of them. I was pleasantly surprised when I heard from my hilarious friend on our 20th anniversary. We reminisced fondly of the good times we had together at Quantico. He sounded exactly the same. I found him just as humorous as he was twenty years ago. He told me he wanted to stay in touch and then talked about visiting me when I moved back east after retiring. He had spent most of his career in New York, but then took a promotion to FBI Headquarters late in his career. When I spoke to him, he was the Unit Chief of the Photography Unit in the Special Projects Section. He worked as a professional photographer prior to becoming an agent. He showed me some of his photographs at Quantico, which were mainly from sporting events. He had some great shots of horse racing. One stood out that I would have liked to have had framed, a close-up shot of several horses within a nose of each other in a race.

About a year later, the FBI intranet revealed that my former favorite classmate had been selected as an SSA in the Los Angeles Division. I immediately sent him a congratulatory e-mail on his new job. I then received a call from him with an open invitation for my wife and me to visit him in Los Angeles. I thanked him for the invitation, but I knew we would never actually go. Unfortunately, I never heard from him again.

He did, however, inform me of something very surprising about my former demented roommate. He told me that on the first day of training class, he and my roommate happened to be in the men's room together on their way to getting breakfast in the cafeteria. He said my roommate was flustered and muttering to himself. My friend, in his usual carefree and extroverted style, asked him if everything was all right. My roommate responded in his typical disturbed manner that he shouldn't have come and should go home. He unashamedly said that his wife was probably going to leave him if he was not at home and that he didn't think he could go through with this. My friend told him, "Why don't you go get some breakfast and then give it a try? You just got here. Give it a chance and see what happens." I told my friend, "Thanks for nothing. Because of you, I had to live with this deranged person for ten weeks."

We laughed and reminisced some more about our time at the FBI Academy. He gave me the low down on a classmate and mutual friend who I had heard was fired from the Bureau. My friend explained that the classmate had previously applied to the Central Intelligence Agency (CIA) prior to being hired with the FBI, failing a polygraph examination. When his failed CIA polygraph examination came to light after his graduation from the FBI Academy and his first assignment, an administrative inquiry was initiated by the Office of Professional Responsibility (OPR), the internal affairs branch of the FBI.

Apparently, the reason he failed the CIA polygraph was because he did not disclose that his brother served in the Israeli Army and in Israeli intelligence. He was terminated from the FBI following this admission. He was not only perceived as a national security threat, but he demonstrated a lack of candor by not divulging this information, thus falsifying his FBI application.

Graduation from the FBI Academy occurred Friday, February 5, 1988. I was very proud and wished that my entire family could have come to see me, but due to space constraints in the auditorium, each new agent was only allowed to invite four people. Cindy attended with her seventy-nine-year-old grandmother with whom we had resided since marrying, and of course, my mother and father. I had hoped that the rest of my family could have attended. I don't think I had ever been more gratified. I was beginning a new life and career on a path I was hoping to be much more meaningful and satisfying than any other job I could have imagined.

I really wanted to make a difference in the world and work in an important occupation, as opposed to simply making a living in order to pay the bills. My wife was fully supportive and planned to look for a teaching job in Florida. I felt great and was happy to have made my mother and father so proud, too.

New Agent Class 88-1

Acting Director John Otto presenting my badge and credentials.

My family at my FBI graduation, 2/5/1988.
From left to right: Ed Larsh, Lucille Larsh, me, Cindy Larsh, Elsie Davis.

Photo taken December 1987, the first photo on my FBI credentials.

CHAPTER 5

ORLANDO RA

The FBI paid nearly all my expenses on my transfer to Orlando, Florida, including temporary quarters, closing costs and real estate fees for the purchase of a new home. My classmates who were not already in the FBI were not as fortunate, as they bore transfer expenses and housing costs themselves.

On Thursday, February 11, 1988, I arrived on my first day of work at the FBI Orlando Resident Agency (ORA), located in the federal building, north of downtown. It was not a very impressive office. It was small and cramped. There was an interview room adjacent to the lobby. The office consisted of two large rooms and the Senior Supervisory Special Agent's (SSRA) private office. About a year or so later, the ORA moved its office about eight miles north of downtown Orlando to the Maitland Business Center, a newer and more upscale office building where agents shared two-man offices. The ORA was comprised of ten criminal agents and four FCI agents upon my arrival. The FCI agents' presence was due to a large number of defense contractors in Orlando and near Cape Canaveral on the Atlantic coast, a hot bed for counterintelligence work. The ORA did not have a sufficient number of criminal agents at the time to deal with the amount of crime occurring in the largely populated Orlando metropolitan area. The office grew in manpower over the years and expanded its space in its new accommodations, but this occurred after my transfer.

In my first meeting with the SSRA, he reviewed my file from the FBI Academy. Apparently, the only issue he felt the need to mention was my effort at Quantico to break the 120-yard shuttle run record. It was very odd to me that in my first meeting with my new supervisor, this was the only topic discussed. My reason for trying to break that record was personal. It had nothing to do with my performance at Quantico or my abilities as an agent, except maybe it demonstrated my motivation and initiative. All new agents were supposed to be formally assigned a "training agent," a veteran field agent to help them learn the ropes. The SSRA advised he would be my training agent, which was not according to FBI policy.

Luckily, many of the ORA agents were very helpful to me. The office was so busy that I quickly gained experience in a whole variety of matters. I became friendly with most of the agents, particularly the other first-office agents. We asked each other for assistance on cases and frequently ended up at a bar to wind down after an arrest. However, we did not really need to make an arrest for an excuse to visit the bar. Nearly everybody in the office stopped at the happy hour every Friday night after work at a nearby Hilton Hotel.

One evening, after stopping off at my friend's apartment following an evening drinking at a bar, the agent confided in me a shocking story that happened to him. He told me that after arriving home one night after having a few drinks, his revolver accidently fired as he placed it on his dresser. The bullet went through his apartment window located on the second floor of his building. He said the shot went straight toward an identical apartment building in the complex. He was terrified he might have killed someone. He went outside to inspect the building and saw where the bullet entered above the second story window into the wood siding just below the roof.

He knew an accidental discharge resulted in a shooting inquiry, but he said he did not report it since nobody ever knew about it and no harm was done. I told him I would never tell. I think the statute of limitations has passed, especially since the agent retired years ago. I wonder if that bullet hole can still be seen above the second story window!

One of my fondest memories in the office was when a discussion ensued regarding proper dress. Somebody started up a conversation about wearing striped shirts with striped ties. Some of the agents were of the opinion that it was acceptable to wear a striped tie with a striped shirt. I chimed in merely to say that my mother always told me, "If you wear a striped or plaid shirt, you must wear a solid tie. If you wear a striped tie, you must wear a solid shirt, otherwise you'll clash." Opinions differed on this point until an agent retrieved a book from his desk entitled, *Dress For Success,* to find a definitive answer to this pressing issue. As he approached the group with the book open, he loudly proclaimed, "Mrs. Larsh was right, Mrs. Larsh was right," and then read a passage from the book matching my mother's opinion practically word for word. I was quite pleased with this confirmation of my mother's rules for proper dress.

An older agent tried to entice me to join the Federal Law Enforcement Officers Association (FLEOA) shortly after my arrival, which would not have been so unusual, except for his sales pitch. Another similar group, which most agents were members, was the FBI Agents Association (FBIAA). The FBIAA was a lobbying group strictly for FBI agents and also provided attorneys for agents under OPR inquiries. FLEOA was similar in its function to the FBIAA, except FLEOA represented all federal agents. The older agent tried to persuade me to join FLEOA for the sole reason that under FLEOA, an agent could sue the FBI, but as members of the FBIAA, they could not. I just laughed at him and said, "I've only been an agent for less than two weeks, I have no interest in suing the Bureau. That is the farthest thing from my mind!"

A couple of years later, the FBIAA gained stature after they were credited with successfully lobbying Congress to gain overtime pay commensurate with an agent's salary. All agents had overtime pay included as a part of their salary, called Administrative Uncontrollable Overtime, or more commonly known to agents as AUO. Agents had to work ten hours per day on average at a minimum in order to keep the overtime in their salary. However, prior to 1990, the AUO was calculated at twenty-five percent of an agent's starting salary. For instance, my starting salary in 1987 was $24,732 as a GS-10 Special Agent, with $6,183 in AUO for a total salary of $30,915. After seven years (later changed to five years), agents were promoted to GS-13 pay. The problem was that although the agent's base pay doubled in seven years, the AUO remained the same.

The FBIAA lobbied to get the AUO increased commensurate with the agent's grade raises. Congress passed legislation in 1990 to increase the AUO by making it twenty-five percent of the base pay commensurate with the agent's current grade. This act of Congress virtually doubled the AUO pay for the higher-grade agents. I did not immediately see a large increase in my paycheck as I was only a GS-11 at the time, but I would reap the benefits of this extra pay for the next twenty-two years.

One of the senior agents in the office was not impressed with the FBIAA. He maintained that the FBIAA was not really responsible for getting this accomplished. He said it was fortuitous that an agent in the FBIAA had gone to college with a Congressman who was on a committee having responsibility over the budget. The agent met his old friend for lunch and convinced him of the need for legislation to fix the inequity of the AUO provision in agents' salaries. The Congressman agreed it was unfair and effected the change through subsequent legislation. This ORA agent thought it was hilarious that the FBIAA took credit for it.

After arriving in the ORA, I was assigned to work drugs. Two other agents were already assigned to work drugs. They were not exactly unfriendly toward me, but they did not seem to want to help me or work with me either. The SSA I had known from FBI Headquarters, who was now the SSA of the Tampa drug squad, wanted me assigned to his drug squad in Tampa. I had figured this SSA had something to do with my getting orders to the Tampa Division, as it seemed too big of a coincidence. The SSA had told me on the phone at Quantico when I called him after getting orders that he would get me on his squad. When I asked him if he had anything to do with my orders to Tampa, he laughed and said, "I might have." I did not believe him since he always spoke with such boastfulness.

I learned the real story from an ORA agent. Seemingly, everybody knew what the SSA had said and done. The SSA had been talking about me before I had arrived, claiming that he got me into the FBI, taught me how to play golf, introduced me to my wife, and was responsible for my transfer to the Tampa Division. The first three assertions were completely false. I only first met him in 1986 when I began working in the Colombian/South American Drug Trafficking Unit. The only truth to his outrageous statements was that he somehow fixed it for me to get orders to Tampa by influencing his Assistant Special Agent in Charge (ASAC), the second in command in the division. The ASAC was a little man with a Napoleonic complex with a less than impressive resume, I was told. I had never met him, but his reputation preceded him. At any rate, he was the man with power in the division, second only to the SAC.

The SSA evidently told the ASAC what a brilliant guy I was and that I had extensive knowledge of drug investigations, having previously worked in the Colombian/South American Drug Trafficking Unit. The SSA tried to convince the ASAC that the only logical place for me to be assigned was on his drug squad. He evidently bragged so much about me that the ASAC decided that if I was so smart and knew so much about drugs, then he would assign me to the ORA where, in his opinion, the two current agents assigned to drug matters were not doing a sufficient job. These two ORA drug agents became aware of this entire story long before I arrived, as apparently everyone in the division had too, due to the SSA's big mouth and complete lack of discretion. The ASAC did indeed have my orders changed to the ORA, and as far as the ORA drug agents were concerned, I was some hot shot from FBI Headquarters coming in to rescue the drug program. After hearing this story, it all made sense why they were somewhat indifferent toward me. They certainly built up resentment before they ever even met me.

During my first week in the ORA, one of the agents was arresting a subject in a murder-for-hire case. The subject hired a hit man to kill his wife. Luckily for the wife, the hit man ultimately hired was an FBI undercover agent introduced by a confidential source. The case was solid against the subject and an arrest warrant was obtained. I was in the car with the arresting agent when he communicated by radio to another agent the plans for the arrest the next day. I immediately asked if I could assist. The arresting agent then radioed signal 401, the SSRA, and told him that 428 (my signal) had expressed interest in assisting on the arrest. The SSRA said I could participate. I was very excited about it, as this would be the first arrest in which I was involved.

The arrest turned out to be a memorable experience. It was only my first week on the job so I was thrilled to be involved in any arrest. I even got to draw my weapon for the very first time on a criminal. The arrest plan was fairly simple. We waited for the subject to leave his house in the morning, and then conducted a car stop to effect the arrest. The plan was to draw weapons on the subject after the car stop, as he was believed to be armed and dangerous. I rode with another new agent who had arrived a few months before I had. We parked down the street from the subject's house. Three or four other FBI vehicles were parked in the neighborhood.

As the subject made a right turn out of his cul-de-sac, four FBI cars converged on him, one from the front head-on, one from the side perpendicular, one immediately from behind, and our car from about a 45-degree angle at the left rear of his vehicle. Eight agents jumped from the four vehicles with their guns drawn. The case agent gave commands to the subject on his car radio loudspeaker, "FBI, you're under arrest. Get your hands where we can see them. Get out of the car with your hands in the air." Luckily, the subject complied, was handcuffed, and taken into custody without incident. It was really quite uneventful and routine, but exhilarating nonetheless, particularly for a new agent a week out of the FBI Academy.

The subject had a MAC-10 machine gun in the back seat and we were all quite relieved that he had given up. I could not help but think that if he had decided to go for the gun, we would have all been caught in a horrible crossfire. When I jumped out of the car and drew my weapon on the subject, the two agents in the vehicle in front of the subject's car had done the same thing. We were all pointing our weapons at each other creating a crossfire situation.

I was very cognizant of arrest procedures having just come from training, but I was not going to be presumptuous and criticize the arrest scenario to anyone afterward. Only weeks before, the instructors at the FBI Academy had cautioned time and again against creating any crossfire situations. It was still fresh in my mind. The firearms instructors also taught us that car stops should be conducted only as a last resort. An arrest situation was far more volatile with the bad guy behind the wheel of a car. The instructors constantly warned of a car stop easily turning into a dangerous high-speed chase or providing cover for the subject in a shoot-out. I never said a word to anybody, except my wife, about the flaws and unsafe practices I observed during this arrest. I was far too new to express any critical opinion. It was a good thing I never did. Unbeknownst to me, I was already viewed as some kind of a smart guy, thanks to the SSA of the drug squad in Tampa. I actually had very little confidence in making a drug case. I literally had no clue how to initiate a drug case, or any other case, for that matter.

When I first arrived in Orlando in February 1988, I was assigned simple leads, such as serving subpoenas or conducting background investigations for applicants. In March, I was sent to Clearwater/St. Petersburg to sit on a Title III wire intercept on a drug case for thirty days. Another agent from the ORA was also assigned. I learned very quickly that this agent was sent because the SSRA did not like him. I was sent because I was the new guy. The other agent had no affinity for the SSRA and made it known to me what he thought of him. He and I monitored the wire together on the same shift for thirty days, but there were never any conversations on the wire concerning drugs. We had to continually minimize, meaning that when the conversation was clearly not about drugs, we had to stop listening. It was a bit slow, and at one point, one of the local police officers assisting on the joint case actually brought in her collection of John Wayne movies to watch during the shift.

The ORA agent had plenty of time to tell me his dislike for the SSRA. This agent had been an SSRA in the Midwest earlier in his career, but had stepped out of management to get an Office of Preference (OP) transfer to the ORA. An OP transfer was awarded based on seniority and the need for personnel in a particular office. He said he intimidated the SSRA because he had done his same job in the past and was much better at it. He had called out the SSRA on his bad decisions and the SSRA hated him for it, which was why this agent, the most senior agent in the ORA, was sitting on the wire one hundred miles away from Orlando with me, the newest agent. He was very friendly to me, but he clearly had issues with the SSRA.

At the end of March, I was taken off the wire, but the senior agent was assigned another thirty days when they renewed the wire. He was angry, believing that the SSRA kept him on this tedious assignment out of spite. The agent put in his retirement papers immediately and was gone in two weeks. I could tell he really did not want to retire, but he clearly had had enough. On his last day, he gave me a stack full of his paperwork as examples for my investigations, or what the FBI referred to as "ponies." He was quite proud of his reports and they actually came in handy for my future applicant reports, civil rights investigations, and on numerous other investigative matters I was assigned through the years. He kept in touch with many of the guys in the office after he retired.

I would occasionally see this retired agent in the years to come in social settings, but my relationship ended sourly in 1995 while attending an ORA agent's wedding in Cape May, New Jersey. When Cindy and I were leaving the wedding reception, this agent attempted an open mouth kiss unsuccessfully with Cindy. She did not tell me until after we departed, being afraid that I would make a scene and possibly punch him in the face. She was right on that point. Cindy said he was drunk and she pulled away as he opened his mouth for the kiss. I never saw him again. I was told many years later that he had been arrested for shoplifting in his old age.

The ORA was a very busy place during my tenure there. It seemed as though fugitives from every part of the country fled to Florida. We had a teletype machine in the middle of the office that was going all the time generating leads for immediate attention. Many of these leads were to arrest fugitives believed to be in the Orlando area. I participated in many of these arrests during my first year, but they were seldom assigned to me. The SSRA did assign me some fugitive leads, but they were not solid leads, such as the immediate leads coming in over the teletype. For example, a fugitive might be featured on the television program, *America's Most Wanted*, generating thousands of calls from the public. Invariably, a lead would come into the ORA from a television viewer who believed they saw the fugitive depicted on the program. These leads were straightforward with instructions to "locate and apprehend the fugitive." The FBI agent assigned had to locate the person, identify the suspect as the fugitive, and arrest them. I was often given these types of leads, but they never turned out to be the actual fugitive, at least the ones I was assigned.

When I arrived at the ORA, the best fugitive leads seemed to be assigned to the same two agents. The reason was that these agents were constantly checking the teletype machine. They would determine if the lead looked like a good lead and then take it directly to the SSRA for him to assign it to them. These leads originated from the FBI office where the fugitive was wanted. It was not until I had been in the ORA for several months before I was assigned a decent fugitive lead. This occurred only because the two agents getting all of the best leads were on annual leave on a cruise together with their wives. The lead was from Tampa to effect the arrest of a drug trafficker federally indicted in an FBI Tampa case. I was assigned the lead and would be credited with the arrest. However, the case agent and his partner from Tampa traveled ninety miles to Orlando to participate and transport the subject back to Tampa to appear before the United States Magistrate. It was not really my arrest, but since it took place in ORA's territory, the SSRA insisted it be assigned to an ORA agent.

It was very uneventful. We went to the subject's house and knocked on the door at about 6:30 a.m. A Hispanic woman answered the door. We identified ourselves as FBI agents. The case agent asked her where the subject was. She said he was in the bedroom. One agent stayed with her while the case agent and I rushed back into the bedroom. The subject was still in bed. We identified ourselves as FBI agents, handcuffed him, and read him his rights. The two Tampa agents then transported the subject back to Tampa. The first arrest technically credited to me was not only routine, but I felt like I was minimally involved.

As time went on during my four and a half years assigned to the ORA, I would be assigned so many fugitive leads, make so many arrests, assist so many other agents with their arrests, as well as arrest subjects I indicted in my own cases, that I would forget the vast majority of them. My best guess was that I was probably involved in more than 150 arrests during that time period.

By the end of 1988, the SSRA stepped down from management to take an OP transfer. Many of the first-office agents left within a year of my arrival, while others arrived from Quantico. The transfer policy at that time for new agents in small to medium-sized divisions, such as Tampa, was to transfer after three to four years to a Top-12 office, i.e., New York, Boston, Philadelphia, Baltimore, Washington, D.C., Atlanta, Miami, Cleveland, Chicago, Houston, Los Angeles, or San Francisco. Within a couple of years in the ORA, I would have more seniority than half the first-office agents due to this transfer policy.

Our new SSRA transferred from the Colombian/South American Drug Trafficking Unit at FBI Headquarters, the same as the SSA of the drug squad in Tampa had the year before. I had worked in the unit with him before going to the FBI Academy. While he was on his house hunting trip to Orlando, he attended his predecessor's going away party at the Walt Disney World Resort. The former SSRA's best friend and neighbor was the head of security at Disney. Everybody from the office attended. This connection with Disney security had proved to be a great perk for everybody in the ORA. We were able to get into Disney World for free. I would not only get into Disney free with my immediate family for the next several years, but so would our family from Maryland when they visited us.

From the moment the new SSRA saw me at the going away party, he gave me an enthusiastic greeting and said, "Hey, Billy Boy" in front of everyone. Although this was a trifle embarrassing, it went a long way to improve my standing in the office. It was obvious to everyone that he knew me and liked me. Agents in the office began to kid me, calling me "Billy Boy" the following week at the office. I began getting much better leads after his arrival. Through some good luck, I started making some decent cases on my own, too.

The goal for each agent was to get statistics for the office. Arrests, complaints, indictments, informations and convictions were the name of the game for keeping in good standing. A complaint was a federal charging document supported by a sworn affidavit for review by a United States Magistrate to determine if probable cause existed to issue an arrest warrant. An indictment from a Federal Grand Jury (FGJ) proceeding was another way to obtain an arrest warrant. Judges in federal districts selected 16-23 potential jurors to serve for eighteen months on a FGJ, usually convening two days per month. In most districts, more than one FGJ sat at a time. The FGJ heard evidence in order to determine if sufficient probable cause existed for a felony charge. Evidence was presented to the FGJ in secret by an Assistant United States Attorney (AUSA) through testimony from witnesses and federal agents. A minimum of twelve votes was needed for an indictment. An information was yet another method to obtain an arrest warrant, but was seldom used. An information was a federal charging document generally used by the United States Attorney's Office (USAO) when subjects plead guilty prior to an indictment by a FGJ. If agents racked up statistics, then the ORA and the SSRA looked good in the eyes of the Tampa executive management. A quarterly statistical sheet was disseminated in the office listing each agent's statistics.

The ultimate objective on the stat sheet was to avoid having goose eggs by your name. Not only was it a matter of pride, but also a lack of statistics would gain the attention of the Tampa front office, obviously not in a good way. One veteran ORA agent always repeated his advice to new agents that if the ASAC did not know you existed, you'd be better off. In other words, you definitely did not want to be known for anything bad, such as having little or no stats. However, he also said you did not want to stand out for anything good either, because you might be volunteered for something for which you neither had the time nor the interest.

Two ORA agents and me (on the left) with the Orlando Magic cheerleaders.

CHAPTER 6

DRUGS

After the new SSRA arrived, I started working a drug case targeting the owner of a fish store in west Orlando, a Jamaican who was reportedly dealing cocaine and marijuana. I opened the case and began conducting surveillance at the store. Without a source to purchase drugs, however, I could not make a prosecutable case. The other ORA agent assigned to work drugs determined from a supervisor at FBI Headquarters that a paid source in West Virginia had successfully made a case against Jamaican drug traffickers in Charleston.

I then asked the agent to work the case with me. The other drug agent had been transferred to New York. Only the two of us were now assigned drug cases in the ORA. I obtained SAC authority to install a pole camera across the street from the fish store. My partner arranged for the West Virginia source to come to Orlando. He made the arrangements to lease an apartment for the source and we directed him to frequent the fish store to try to introduce himself to the Jamaican target.

We observed the source's first entry into the fish store from a van equipped with a monitor to the pole camera. This proved to be a quick entry and exit by the source, a middle-aged black man who was not of Jamaican descent. The source took instructions well, but basically said very little. He responded to everything in the affirmative with an "Errrrright." My partner and I immediately began imitating him after each debriefing. A couple days later, we sent him into the fish store again, but the target was not there.

THE FBI – THEY EAT THEIR YOUNG

After about two weeks of his unproductive visits to the store, we sent him in one more time. The store was not really much of a store at all. It was a dilapidated single-story building in the worst part of town. On this last visit, the source went inside, but departed hurriedly. On his debriefing, he was quite upset and scared. The Jamaican target apparently threatened him and told him never to come back. If the source had not been so dark-skinned, I am sure he would have turned white from fright following this incident. We sent the source back to West Virginia, ending our joint effort to fight drugs in Orlando. We would continue to assist one another, but we were never again co-case agents on an investigation.

My partner would later be assigned to the DEA Task Force as the FBI representative. I would soon begin my first significant drug case on my own. My partner and I were both at our desks in the ORA when a call came into the office from a drug agent in the FBI Gainesville RA out of the Jacksonville Division. My partner was on the telephone when the secretary buzzed our office to advise that the Gainesville agent wanted to speak to a drug agent. This was the break I had been waiting for. The Gainesville agent told me he had convicted a drug dealer who was awaiting sentencing before a federal judge. The subject was expected to receive thirty years in prison under the federal sentencing guidelines. However, the judge stipulated that he could reduce his sentence by cooperating with law enforcement to make cases against other drug traffickers.

The case agent provided the names of a Jamaican couple and the owner of a car wash in Orlando who his subject identified as cocaine traffickers. He said the Jamaican couple lived together, but they were not associated with the car wash owner. I opened two separate investigations targeting these subjects. I conducted background checks with the local police and through the DEA's intelligence file, the Narcotics and Dangerous Drugs Information System (NADDIS). These subjects were known to law enforcement and were documented as being associated with other known drug traffickers.

Since the Gainesville source had made a purchase in the past from the Jamaicans, he was easily able to make a consensually monitored telephone call to them; meaning that the call arranging for the purchase of powder cocaine was recorded. Authority to make consensually monitored calls to purchase drug evidence was obtained from FBI management and with approval from an AUSA. The female AUSA with whom I discussed my case generally worked federal drug cases with the DEA. My first impression of her was not good. When I met her at her office, I said, "Hello Cindy, I'm Agent Bill Larsh with the FBI." She abruptly corrected me saying, "It's Cynthia." I said, "Sorry, my wife's name is Cynthia, but everyone calls her Cindy." She did not acknowledge my remarks, but she nevertheless approved the purchase of cocaine and consensual monitoring in the case. She authorized the recording of all telephone calls, as well as the use of a body recorder to be worn by the Gainesville source.

She advised that she would prosecute the case providing that at least a half of a kilogram of powder cocaine could be purchased. I was thrilled by this news. This was my first case wherein I would be investigating a case from its inception to prosecution. I was quite confident that the Gainesville source would be able to make the drug purchases. What better source could I possibly have had than a drug dealer trying to avoid going to jail for thirty years? After my meeting with the less than friendly AUSA, I documented our conversation in a letter from the FBI to the USAO regarding her authorization of consensually monitored recordings and her willingness to prosecute the case.

In the next few weeks, the Gainesville source made several recorded telephone calls under my supervision to the Jamaicans setting up a drug transaction. It was clear in their conversations that not only was the Jamaican couple working together, but there was no ambiguity that they were arranging for the sale of two ounces of powder cocaine. The only snag in the transaction was the availability of the cocaine. Fortunately, the delay in the transaction resulted in even more recorded calls and further evidence. The continued telephone conversations between them would also preclude any possible defense later that entrapment was an issue. The Jamaicans made it perfectly clear they were predisposed to sell cocaine. It became abundantly clear with each conversation that they had previously sold cocaine to the Gainesville source.

About two months after their first conversation, the time had finally arrived for the transaction to take place. The Jamaicans told the Gainesville source they would have two ounces of powder cocaine for $3,600 available Friday night at their house. I called the AUSA and advised her of the planned purchase. I obtained authority from the FBI and received the $3,600 check from the FBI draft office in the Tampa Division. I cashed the check and made copies of thirty-six $100 bills. This type of drug purchase by the FBI was known as "letting the money walk." I documented the serial numbers on the bills in case the money might be seized later and could be used as further evidence of the drug purchase.

This scenario for the drug transaction was a relatively easy one. I enlisted the assistance of about five agents in the office for surveillance of the transaction. The ORA agent assigned to the DEA Task Force was essentially my partner working drugs. He and I had our separate cases, but we always assisted each other. He opened up several drug cases jointly with the DEA and spent most of his time with the task force. However, when I needed help, he was always available.

He and I met the Gainesville source behind a shopping center in west Orlando and searched his vehicle thoroughly. I hid a Nagra body recorder on the source securing it in an ace bandage type of belt around his torso. The Nagra was a reel-to-reel tape recorder in a 3 X 5 inch metal encasement. I recorded a preamble at the beginning of the tape stating my name, the date, and time. We searched his vehicle and his person thoroughly to ensure he had no drugs or money of his own. We then counted the $3,600 and provided it to him. All of this was being done for court purposes to eliminate any reasonable doubt by a jury. The Gainesville source was then followed to the Jamaicans' residence. A transmitter had also been placed on the Gainesville source's person in order that all conversations could be monitored.

The transmitter was for his safety and security in case the subjects tried to rob or kill him. He was provided the code word "football" if he believed his life was in imminent danger and needed the FBI to rescue him. The distress call was not needed. The Gainesville source entered the Jamaicans' house and was back out in a couple of minutes. We followed him back to the rear of the shopping center and went through the same routine, searching him and his vehicle. He provided us with the alleged two ounces of cocaine in a sandwich-sized plastic Ziploc bag. He said he had no conversation in the house. They simply handed him the cocaine. I retrieved the evidence, the Nagra, and the transmitter, and headed back to the office with my partner.

In handling evidence, particularly with valuable evidence such as money or drugs, a witness always had to be present, not only for court purposes, but also to eliminate any appearance of impropriety. We initialed and dated all the appropriate packaging and forms and sent the alleged cocaine by Federal Express to the local DEA lab for testing, where all drugs seized by the FBI were sent. A section on the DEA form was checked to forward the packaging, the plastic Ziploc sandwich bag, to the FBI Laboratory Division, Latent Fingerprint Section, to test for prints. The Nagra tape was sent to the FBI Tampa office for copying, transcribing, and to be placed into evidence.

A couple of weeks later, I directed the Gainesville source to call back the Jamaicans to arrange for the purchase of a half of a kilogram of powder cocaine. It took several weeks to finalize this transaction. They finally directed the Gainesville source to come to their residence in west Orlando on a Saturday morning. Their price was $12,000, a little high for a half of a kilogram of powder cocaine at that time, but it didn't matter. All I wanted was the transaction to take place since we would not be letting the money walk this time. The $12,000 was "show" money. The plan was to arrest the subjects and seize the drugs during the transaction, commonly known in the FBI as a "buy-bust" scenario.

I called the AUSA to advise her that the case would culminate Saturday with the purchase of the half of a kilogram of cocaine. To my bewilderment, she said she could not prosecute this case, inasmuch as the amount of cocaine was insufficient for her office to proceed. I reminded her that three months ago she had expressed her willingness to prosecute the case. She responded that I would have to prosecute it at the state level. I wasn't even working with any other law enforcement agencies on the case. I could not believe it. She had done a complete one hundred and eighty degree turn, leaving me high and dry.

My SSRA was on leave so I called the SSA of the drug squad in Tampa, my former colleague from the Colombian/South American Drug Trafficking Unit. The SSA was incensed and said for me not to worry about a thing. He said it was ridiculous and that this AUSA worked cases with the DEA involving only ounces of powder cocaine. He called me later to advise that the USAO in Orlando would prosecute my case. He told me he had called someone at the USAO in Tampa who, in turn, called the Managing Assistant in Orlando. The SSA advised that a different AUSA, a new, young guy, would be handling the case. I thanked my old friend and was somewhat impressed with his handling of the matter. He may have been a bit obnoxious in the past and distorted his relationship with me to others, but that was all forgiven now. He obviously took the bull by the horns and came through for me when it counted. I had no idea why the female AUSA suddenly refused to take the case, but I was relieved that at least their office was willing to prosecute.

I called the newly assigned AUSA and brought him up to date concerning the details of the case. He made no mention of the other AUSA, the SSA, or his boss, and probably had no idea what had happened. He was assigned to prosecute the case and seemed happy to be doing it. I never made a remark either of how we came to be working together. I prepared affidavits for the AUSA's approval in order to obtain two criminal complaints and a search warrant to be executed Saturday morning at the Jamaicans' residence. I appeared before the United States Magistrate that Friday afternoon and obtained arrest and search warrants.

For the planned drug transaction Saturday morning, I enlisted the help of the entire ORA, at least all those who were available or willing to help. A couple of the older FCI agents had no interest in helping, particularly on a Saturday morning. The FBI policy for the $12,000 "show" money stated that it was never to leave the care, custody, and control of the FBI. I never really knew the exact meaning of that, considering I was giving it to a convicted drug dealer for a period of time. The Gainesville source had the money in his car and was instructed not to take the cash from his car into the residence. In other words, under no circumstances was he ever to give the subjects the cash.

My partner and I went through the same procedure behind the shopping center searching the Gainesville source and his vehicle, placing the Nagra recorder and the transmitter on him, and counting the money. I instructed the Gainesville source to make sure he saw the drugs in the house first before he showed the subjects the money. He was then to depart the residence, presumably to retrieve the cash from his car for the exchange, and/or possibly bring the Jamaicans outside to see the cash. After departing the residence and seeing the drugs inside, he was instructed to take off his ball cap as a signal to the FBI agents, confirming that the cocaine was in fact inside. If he took his hat off, FBI agents were to swarm the house to arrest the subjects inside and retrieve the drugs pursuant to the execution of a search warrant.

This was the plan, plain and simple. We followed the Gainesville source to the residence in my FBI vehicle, a white 1985 Dodge 600. I pulled into a driveway of a neighbor a few doors down and across the street, keeping the targets' front door in full view. About five other FBI vehicles were parked in the neighborhood which was flourishing with activity on a beautiful, sunny, and warm spring Saturday morning. The neighbors were taking notice of the unfamiliar FBI cars parked throughout the neighborhood.

We had only been there for a few minutes when an older couple out walking approached our car to ask what we were doing there. I flashed my badge and told them we were on police business. Just as this nuisance distracted me, I glanced back toward the house to see the Gainesville source taking his ball cap off as he left the house. I grabbed the radio and told all units to move on the house. I sped out of the driveway, leaving the startled old couple standing there. They undoubtedly figured out that law enforcement was involved in some type of operation after seeing cars converging on the front lawn of the Jamaicans' residence.

As I got out of my car and made my way toward the front door, the door was abruptly shut and I heard the dead bolt being locked. I announced my identity loudly, "This is the FBI, open the door, we have a warrant for your arrest." We got no response. The windows had steel bars on them. Agents who had gone to the back door radioed to advise that the back patio doors were barred as well. An agent immediately went to the trunk of his car and retrieved a sledgehammer. He took a big overhead swing at the front door, and then several more, until the door and the frame caved in, enabling agents to enter the house. The female Jamaican was in the living room with two small children. She was immediately handcuffed, read her Miranda rights, and placed under arrest. The male was not in the room.

Another agent and I made our way into the back bedrooms with our guns drawn. We found the male in the bathroom, kneeling at the toilet, presumably trying to flush drugs down the toilet. However, a large Ziploc plastic bag full of the alleged half kilogram of powder cocaine was found in the bedroom closet. After being placed under arrest, they were both questioned, but they were smart enough not to say anything. A search of the house was conducted, but no other drugs were found. The male had about $850 cash in his wallet and a 9mm semi-automatic pistol was found in the bedroom and seized.

The female asked if we could call her relatives to take her children rather than call local government social services. We obliged her request and later transported the Jamaican couple to the Seminole County Correctional Facility. On the following Monday, my partner and I picked them up at the jail and turned them over to the custody of the United States Marshals Service at the Federal Courthouse in Orlando for their initial appearance. They were not granted bail, in view of the fact that precedent had been set in the Middle District of Florida that drug traffickers were inherently dangerous to society. Both were from Jamaica and were illegal immigrants, making it more likely they would flee to avoid prosecution.

The recorded tapes from the telephone conversations made this a slam-dunk case, not to mention that more than a half of a kilogram of powder cocaine was purchased as evidence. Not much was recorded of substance on the body recorder during the actual transactions, but both drug purchases were sufficiently monitored electronically with physical surveillance, and the Gainesville source's testimony of the transactions would be corroborated by all of the above. The Jamaicans never cooperated by giving up their source of supply of cocaine, but they ultimately had little choice but to plead guilty to federal drug charges. They were later sentenced to federal prison for 72 and 60 months, respectively. Following the completion of their jail sentences, the United States Immigration and Naturalization Service (USINS) would deport them to Jamaica.

The Gainesville source had one more case to complete for me in Orlando against the car wash owner. This case would be more difficult, inasmuch as he had never met the car wash owner, but only knew of him. The Gainesville source had an associate who purchased from this individual more than a year ago. I believed he would have no trouble purchasing drugs from him. The source could not be mistaken for anything other than a drug dealer. He was a twenty-five-year-old black male with gold front teeth and gold chains around his neck. He possibly spoke the worst English I had ever heard. It sounded even worse than "Ebonics" if that was imaginable. He owned a record shop in the city of Gainesville in a black neighborhood and drove a BMW. I am sure other local drug dealers in Gainesville knew he had been arrested and were probably smart enough never to do business with him. However, Gainesville was about seventy-five miles north of Orlando. The car wash owner surely had no knowledge of his arrest.

Drug dealers were usually very careful to whom they sold drugs and were even more careful what they said on the telephone. This was not the case with the car wash owner. On the very first recorded call, the Gainesville source told him of their mutual friend and that he wanted to come to Orlando to make a purchase. The car wash owner then possibly made the most extraordinary statement ever heard from a drug trafficker, declaring, "Yeah, come to Callaway's, Callaway's. Ask anybody in Orlando, I'll get you all the keys you want!" I never got evidence like that before or since on tape right out of the box on a case. I figured all I needed to do now was just get the source to purchase enough cocaine for the USAO to be happy. The same young AUSA who worked on the Jamaican case was on board with this case.

The car wash owner was well known to local law enforcement. He had served fourteen months in the county jail on an assault and robbery charge three years previously. A check of NADDIS revealed a connection to a Haitian drug trafficker. He had a younger brother with no criminal history working with him at the car wash. The owner's right hand-man, however, was a hardened criminal having previously been convicted of attempted murder. He had a long rap sheet and was recently released from prison. He was a very scary looking individual, resembling a large Mike Tyson, but much meaner looking. Although the source had a very productive telephone call with the car wash owner, it was an entirely different story the first time he physically showed up at the car wash.

My partner and I went through the usual routine, searching him and placing a body recorder on him before sending him into the car wash. After his first meeting, the source was a little shaken. He said that the owner and his right-hand man threw him up against the wall and said they were going to search him for any tape recorders. The source said he told them, "Bullshit, nobody is searchin' me...I come here to do business and I ain't strippin' off my shirt for nobody!" If they had discovered he had been wearing a wire, it might have turned into a volatile situation, not to mention it would have ended the case. They did not search him though. Only a real drug dealer such as the source could have been able to avert this disaster. The car wash owner probably wished later that he had searched him. Instead, he told the source he had nothing to sell and he would have to come back in a couple of weeks.

Under my direction, the source returned two weeks later to the car wash unannounced and without wearing a wire. I had good tape already from their original telephone conversation so I didn't want to jeopardize the case. If he had been frisked again and discovered to be wearing a Nagra recorder, I would have had no case. Although the recorded telephone conversation of the owner bragging about getting him all the keys he wanted was potentially great evidence, by itself it was not enough to make a case or put anybody in jail. A cocaine purchase was needed to make a case. The prosecutors liked to say that they needed "drugs on the table." Without any cocaine being purchased, the USAO was not going to prosecute. When the source went to the car wash the second time, the owner told him he could get him three quarters of a kilogram for $15,000 to be delivered the following week. The right-hand man was present again, as well as the owner's brother. When the source told me they hadn't attempted to frisk him, I immediately regretted not placing the Nagra on him.

The next week I recorded the telephone call to the owner from the source. The owner instructed him to meet him at a busy intersection at 8 p.m. the next night in west Orlando to make the exchange. My partner and I went through our routine and provided the source with FBI money to purchase the drugs. In this case, I decided to allow the money to walk. I wanted to purchase the drugs and go for more on the next purchase in an attempt to determine their source of supply, and possibly go up on a wire on his telephone. I placed the body recorder on the source, as well as a transmitter, to monitor the transaction.

Everything went according to plan. I witnessed the entire transaction from my vehicle. A 1987 Mercedes-Benz, leased to the car wash owner, pulled up to the intersection with three black males in the vehicle. It was difficult to positively identify the individuals in the car. The sun was going down and it was getting dim. It was also raining. The source previously identified the car wash owner and his right-hand man after seeing mug shots of the two of them. The problem was that the mug shot of the car wash owner was from his arrest three years previously. He was 6 feet 7 inches tall in the photograph and slim. The source identified him in this picture as the same individual with whom he was dealing. The source failed to tell me that he had put on over one hundred pounds and was much fatter than he was in the three-year-old mug shot.

To complicate matters, his younger brother was the spitting image of him. I had a driver's license photo of the younger brother who was 6 feet 6 inches tall, 315 pounds, and appearing fat in the picture. The younger brother was believed to be involved in the drug trafficking, inasmuch as the source had advised that the younger brother was present at both meetings with the owner at the car wash, but the brother never said anything. At the intersection, I witnessed a large overweight black male getting out of the Mercedes-Benz with a brown grocery bag approaching the source's vehicle. I immediately thought I was seeing the younger brother, since I was under the impression that the owner was thin. This confusion in their identities caused me some minor embarrassment later, but it was nothing compared to the source subsequently jeopardizing the entire investigation.

The traffic was very heavy at the intersection. The source sped away very quickly and none of the surveillance agents saw where he went. This would not look good in court. I was not too worried since I believed at the time we would be making other drug purchases from the car wash owner and his associates. My partner and I went back to the prearranged meeting place, but there was no sign of him. Still, I was getting a bit nervous. It was bad enough we had no surveillance on him back to the meeting place, but now he was nowhere to be found. He was in possession of $15,000 worth of drug evidence.

About ten minutes later, the FBI Tampa office called me on my FBI car radio and advised me to call my wife at home regarding my source. I called her from a pay phone and she said the source had called her. He told her that my pager had obviously not worked as he had been paging me. This problem with pagers was not uncommon. Looking back on my experiences working drug cases, I cannot imagine how I ever managed without cellular telephones. Luckily, I had provided the source with my home telephone number just in case of such an emergency. Most agents would never have done this in a million years, but I was so motivated to make a case that I did not want to have any communication problems occurring, such as the one that happened that very night.

My wife told me she had an extremely difficult time understanding him, but that the source told her he was at a pay phone at the West Colonial Shopping Center in west Orlando. Cindy told me she was not one hundred percent sure if he said "Colonial" because he pronounced it many different ways, including "Conal," "Cowonal," and "Cowowonal." She said he never could enunciate Colonial. Cindy found it all very amusing. His mispronunciation may have been funny to my wife, but I was not amused by the situation at that moment. Losing him would have made for embarrassing testimony on my part were this to end up at trial.

We caught up with the source that evening and debriefed him. He said he thought he was being followed so he did not go to the prearranged meeting place. He said the car wash owner had given him the cocaine. I later sent it to the DEA lab and it amounted to just under three quarters of a kilogram of cocaine. The car wash owner's fingerprints were also later found to be on the brown grocery bag. I would not get these results from the lab for another couple of months.

My problem at the present time was that I believed it was his younger brother who I saw hand the bag to the source at the intersection. The AUSA suggested that I present a photo lineup to the source. I prepared a photo lineup with the brother's picture among the six photographs in the lineup, but not the car wash owner's. The source immediately picked out the younger brother's picture as the person who handed him the bag with the cocaine. I was happy with this piece of information because now I had a third person to add to the cocaine transaction. I had solid evidence on tape on the car wash owner; I witnessed his brother (I thought) making the transaction; and the right-hand man was present each time setting up the drug deal. The evidence, however, was weak against the right-hand man. I had no recorded tape on him, only the source's testimony. Within a week, though, I would find out that I might have no case at all.

The FBI agent in Gainesville called me to advise that the source was back in the drug dealing business and would be arrested very soon. The agent told me that the federal judge in the case gave him this chance, but if he ended up back in court for selling drugs again, the judge would put him away for life. This meant that my case against the car wash owner would be jeopardized. The Jamaican couple had already signed plea agreements, so the source would never have to testify against them. Any testimony he would give now would unquestionably be tainted if he was arrested again. A good defense attorney would be able to discredit him for being charged again for selling drugs, while at the same time he was supposedly assisting law enforcement. He would not have been the greatest witness in court anyway because of his obvious personal motivation to work off his sentence. He was also not really too bright outside of knowing the drug dealing business. As my wife quickly determined in her short telephone conversation with him, the man could barely speak English.

I met with the AUSA regarding the latest development concerning the source. I thought for sure he would discontinue his support of the investigation, but instead he said we had sufficient evidence to indict all three subjects. He thought we had a strong case against the car wash owner, particularly with his initial comments memorialized on tape, as well as the amount of cocaine involved. A FGJ was convening on Wednesday of the next week, he said. The AUSA believed that we should indict the case immediately. He thought we'd probably get a plea agreement and the case would never go to trial anyway. If it never went to trial, this would preclude ever having to use the Gainesville source as a witness. The AUSA still thought that if we did have to use the source as a witness, he could easily corroborate the recorded telephone call made to the car wash owner, which he said was irrefutable evidence. Then the AUSA said, "And you witnessed the drug transaction."

The next Wednesday, a sealed indictment was handed down by the FGJ and three federal warrants were issued for the car wash owner, his brother, and the right-hand man. I immediately drove to the car wash to look for the car wash owner's grey Mercedes-Benz. I didn't care about my car getting "burned" by continuously driving by there. In fact, I spent the next several days and nights driving by the car wash and conducting surveillance. My goal was to spot his car and then call in the troops for his arrest. After several days of not seeing his car, however, I decided to review some addresses from license tags at the car wash I had checked at the beginning of the case. One of the tags was registered to a twenty-four-year-old black female in west Orlando, who I thought might possibly be a girlfriend. I drove by her address at about 6 p.m. on a Tuesday evening on my way home, but I saw no vehicles. I then drove by the car wash, but did not see his car.

The next morning I got up early and headed out to west Orlando to the supposed girlfriend's address again. To my great surprise, his Mercedes-Benz was parked in front of her house. I radioed back to the office for some assistance. Nearly all of the criminal agents from the office responded to the scene. I also called the Orange County Sheriff's Office for some backup. I provided everyone with a rendezvous point a couple of blocks away and around the corner from the house.

Within about a half an hour, all the agents and officers had arrived. As I began to debrief them regarding the proposed arrest at the location a few blocks away, a well-dressed, middle-aged white male drove up in a new Mercedes-Benz four-door sedan and introduced himself as the car wash owner's attorney. The attorney advised that his client was at the residence and wished to give himself up. The approximately ten law enforcement vehicles, to include two uniformed Orange County Sheriff's Office vehicles, followed the attorney to the residence. The attorney went to the front door and escorted his client out of the house. The car wash owner proceeded across the front lawn with his hands in the air. The officers were closest to him and placed handcuffs on him. An agent directed them to put him in the back seat of an FBI car.

As I approached, the car wash owner asked the agent, "Who drives that white Dodge?" while motioning his head toward my car. The agent answered, pointing at me as I walked up to them, "The white Dodge belongs to Agent Larsh." The car wash owner then provided me with the greatest compliment of my career. He said very plainly and loudly for all to hear, "I been seein' that white Dodge for a week...Larsh, you're one hardworking motherfucker." I could not have been more proud. I had worked long hours, not only overall on the case, but particularly during the past week following his indictment. Nobody in the office knew how much time I had put in day and night to apprehend and arrest him. All my efforts to find him were done on my own. I could have given him a kiss for acknowledging my otherwise unknown diligent efforts in front of my boss, co-workers, and fellow law enforcement officers.

My inflated ego was short-lived though. Upon seeing the car wash owner on the front lawn, I quickly realized that the person I saw at the intersection handing the brown paper bag containing the cocaine to the source was the car wash owner, not his brother. He had put on at least one hundred pounds from the time his mug shot was taken three years before. He and his brother now had the exact same physique and looked almost identical, but I knew now it was not the younger brother who made the exchange. I had no evidence against the younger brother other than the source saying he was at the car wash on his two visits there. I had no taped conversation or any solid evidence to present in court against him.

Prior to the car wash owner's initial appearance before the United States Magistrate that same day, I told the AUSA of my error in identifying the brother and having no other evidence against him. The AUSA said it was not a problem and that we could dismiss the charges against the brother.

I was very embarrassed by this mistake, but the AUSA did not think it was in any way detrimental to the case. After testifying before the judge describing the mix-up, it did seem to be a very routine matter. I felt much better about the whole thing after testifying. The car wash owner's attorney said nothing to the judge about it. Following the hearing, the attorney was very appreciative of the dismissal of the charges against the brother. It made me wonder how much involvement the brother really had in all of this.

My next step in the case was finding and arresting his right-hand man. I checked all the addresses again from the license tags I had at the outset of the case. I found another car registered to a young, black female, whose address was a townhouse in Orlando. I went to the location and saw the subject's vehicle parked out front. I called for backup and four agents from the office showed up. I sent two to the back and three of us knocked on the front door with our guns drawn, but no one answered. The subject had a long criminal history, including jail time for armed robbery and attempted murder. He was obviously considered armed and dangerous.

The leasing office was a block up the street, so I left the agents at the front and back doors and went to check with the manager. I showed him the picture of the subject who he identified as living in the townhouse. He confirmed that his car was parked out front. I asked the manager if he had the key to the townhouse and if he could open the door for us. The manager agreed and walked down with me to the front door. As he unlocked the front door, I opened the door with my gun drawn, expecting the worst. I firmly believed that I would probably have to shoot upon entering, figuring that he was inside possibly armed and waiting for us. To my great surprise and relief, I instantly saw him seated on the couch bouncing a toddler up and down. I immediately announced we were the FBI and he was under arrest. I instructed him to get his hands in the air, which he did without hesitation.

Luckily for me, he did not say the words my former FBI Academy fitness instructor always said when demonstrating apprehension techniques in an arrest, "Not today FBI." It was even luckier that the subject did not just shoot at us as we rushed through the front door. This would not be the first time that I thought I'd be shot. I had always firmly believed in God. The expression, "There but for the grace of God go I," was quite applicable on this occasion and many others. I could have been killed on a number of arrests had the bad guy decided, "Not today FBI."

The case against my subjects was tenuous at best, considering that the main witness against them was going to be indicted on drug charges himself at any time. When the defense attorney told the AUSA that the car wash owner would plead guilty if we dropped the charges against his right-hand man, the AUSA jumped on the offer. We had no tape on the right-hand man anyway. I was not thrilled that a thug such as this would walk, but we had to take what we could get, considering the circumstances.

The car wash owner not only pled guilty, but also decided to cooperate with law enforcement to get his sentencing reduced. He met with me with his attorney. He was kind of funny and very prophetic about the whole situation. He was in no way resentful or bitter. The sentencing guidelines with his cooperation would put him in prison for at least 24 to 36 months. He stated to me that "going to jail was just part of doing business." His cooperation was only half-hearted, however. It was clear he was merely going through the motions in order to get credit to reduce his sentencing.

He gave up the name of his cocaine supplier in Miami, but two recorded telephone calls from him to the purported supplier produced nothing. NADDIS records/intelligence corroborated his supplier was indeed a documented Haitian cocaine trafficker. The Haitian clearly knew him, but told him he had no product and was not in the business anymore. Maybe he was aware of the car wash owner's arrest, but the bottom line was that no transaction was going to occur between the two. He got full credit for assisting law enforcement, even though he provided intelligence we already knew and he did nothing to help put anybody in jail as the Gainesville source had.

The Gainesville source had worked on numerous drug cases assisting law enforcement in the state of Florida. His impending drug charges affected all of them, as it had mine. Luckily, the car wash owner was convicted and sentenced to 30 months without him or his defense attorney ever knowing about the Gainesville source's circumstances. The Jamaicans received more considerable jail time. Both cases provided me with some much needed stats. I enjoyed getting the conviction stats, but it was personally more satisfying knowing that I was finally putting people in jail on a regular basis that deserved to be there. The Gainesville source, the most valuable cooperating witness I ever had, was handed to me as a gift on a silver platter. Unfortunately, he was about to get the proverbial book thrown at him.

The federal judge in the Northern District of Florida had originally given the Gainesville source probation for his widespread assistance to law enforcement. The judge told him, however, that if he ever saw him in his courtroom again, he would give him life. It only took a few months for him to be back in the judge's courtroom. He returned to the drug business at the same time he was assisting me and the other law enforcement agencies. He was convicted again and was given life in prison, as promised. He was stupid and a criminal, but I still could not help feeling sorry for him. He was only a couple of years younger than I was. I couldn't imagine spending the rest of my life in prison.

Around the same time I was working these drug cases, I had a memorable fugitive lead assigned to me of a Hispanic male wanted out of Howard County, Maryland, for attempted murder. He apparently shot at someone in the parking lot outside a bar in Columbia, Maryland. The lead indicated that the fugitive was staying in an apartment in Orlando. I solicited two agents, a married couple in the ORA, to help me. We went to the address at about 7:30 a.m. and saw a Hispanic female leaving the apartment with laundry. The three of us followed her and identified ourselves as she went back to the apartment. We asked her where the fugitive was and she told us he was in the back bedroom. The female agent stayed with her while the two of us made our way down the hall with our guns drawn. We opened the bedroom door and found no one. I opened the closet door in the bedroom expecting him to be hiding, but again saw no one. Another door was located on the opposite side of the walk-in closet. I figured he was either hiding or he was going to shoot at us. I was fully prepared to shoot if I saw he was armed. My finger was on the trigger and my mindset was to shoot quickly, if necessary. As I opened the door abruptly, the fugitive was standing in his underwear at the toilet, urinating. Luckily, the weapon in his hand could do us no harm.

My partner had some interesting cases with the DEA. They were much bigger in scope than the cases I had taken to prosecution. However, I did not have an entire task force working on my cases. One case in which I assisted was a Colombian drug trafficking case. Several FBI agents from the office helped with surveillance. A DEA source was in a position to purchase a kilogram of powder cocaine from a Colombian in Orlando. The Colombian indicated to the source that he could obtain the cocaine from his supplier in Miami and deliver it to the source the following day. The source met the Colombian at about 5 p.m. on a Friday evening.

The DEA decided to conduct surveillance to determine the identity of the supplier, should the Colombian agree to a transaction. Once the cocaine was in the possession of the Colombian, a uniformed officer would stop his vehicle, seize the cocaine, and arrest him. The DEA would then try to solicit his cooperation against the supplier. This type of scenario would keep their source out of the equation and not compromise him, enabling him to work further in the case as well as help in other cases. Surveillance was conducted of the meeting between the source and the Colombian. The Colombian went back to his house. The source met with the DEA case agent immediately following the meeting to advise that the Colombian said he would have the cocaine for him tomorrow. Surveillance was then set up on the Colombian's house. He left at 7 p.m. that same evening and headed south on the Florida Turnpike toward the Miami area.

He arrived in a Miami suburb at about 11 p.m. in an upscale neighborhood that only had one way in and out. I observed him going into the front door of the house and called it out over the radio with the street number of the house. It was decided that no surveillance vehicles would park in the neighborhood, but we needed to have someone on foot to watch the house. I volunteered since I was already in the neighborhood. I parked my white Dodge 600 a short distance away and hid in the bushes of a house across the street. I took my handheld Motorola radio and a pair of binoculars.

As I hid in the front bushes, a porch light came on. I thought, "Oh great, not only might I compromise the surveillance, but the owner of this house is going to shoot me." I kept quiet in the bushes and turned off my radio. I saw no lights come on in the house and no movement. The porch light turned off after about three minutes. I then moved deeper into the bushes and positioned myself a little better. As I moved, the porch light came on again. I realized that it was a motion sensor. The light turned off again in another three minutes.

I settled in and turned the radio back on to announce that the Colombian was still in the residence and that I would advise when he moved. I spent about two hours with my eyes peeled on the house, hoping that no neighbors, particularly the people in whose bushes I was hiding, would discover me. No one did and at about 1 a.m., the Columbian left the residence. I notified the surveillance agents of his movements and quickly made my way back to my vehicle. I wondered if he had the cocaine. Within a half an hour, the DEA agent announced over the radio that the Colombian called the source to tell him he went to Miami, but could not obtain any cocaine. We continued to follow the Columbian throughout the rest of the night as he traveled north on the Florida Turnpike, returning to his residence in Orlando at about 6 a.m. The Columbian had stopped at a rest stop on the way down and my partner called his wife to tell her we would be out all night. She was supposed to call Cindy, but apparently forgot. Needless to say, Cindy was very worried at not knowing where I was all night.

My partner and I had not been very close until we began working drugs together. He was funny and witty, and Cindy liked his wife, so we socialized occasionally. Our most memorable outing was attending a Paul McCartney concert at the Tampa Stadium in 1990. We were a bit apprehensive about what we might do if any concertgoers smoked marijuana in our presence. After all, over 60,000 people would be attending this rock concert, a venue where dope smoking was not only prevalent, but was a part of the experience. On top of that, McCartney was a renowned pot smoker who'd been busted on his concert tours periodically throughout the years. My partner and I discussed extensively on the ninety-minute drive from Orlando to Tampa what we were going to do as FBI agents if some idiots lit up next to us. At the very least, we decided we would badge them and extinguish their cigarettes. Cindy and his wife thought we were both crazy and both expected a ton of people to be smoking in our immediate vicinity.

I was relieved at the concert when I saw no one smoking marijuana, although the smell was potent. I swore there was a cloud of marijuana smoke over the entire stadium. Paul McCartney was fantastic though. When he performed the Beatles songbook, you would have thought you were in the middle of Beatlemania from the 1960s. I enjoyed everything he sang, including his Wings hits, and even the new songs from his latest album at that time, *Flowers in the Dirt*. In fact, I went out the week after the concert and bought the album, the last LP I ever purchased, as CDs were just becoming popular.

A four kilogram cocaine seizure in my partner's case in the ORA from the gas tank of a pick-up truck (me on the far left).

CHAPTER 7

FUGITIVES

Working in the ORA continued to be a pleasurable and gratifying experience. The only stress I felt was self-induced in trying to develop another drug case, but I was under no pressure from my SSRA. I had a sufficient number of stats. I was assigned many fugitive leads during this time and spent a considerable amount of time and effort to find them. I believed I gave a little extra effort than most agents on these cases. I was very thorough in conducting all my leads. The search for fugitives was enjoyable, and downright thrilling when finding them. It felt like hitting a home run when finally locating a fugitive. I loved the chase. I could work ninety-five percent of a fugitive case completely on my own. For the most part, only after pinpointing the whereabouts of a fugitive did I need help. However, on some occasions I solicited assistance from my co-workers for surveillance.

On one case, I was attempting to locate a convicted rapist, a twenty-six-year-old white male who had escaped from prison in South Carolina. The FBI's jurisdiction in the apprehension of escaped prisoners derived from federal statute, Title 18, United States Code, Section 1783, called Unlawful Flight To Avoid Confinement (UFAC). State or local authorities usually sought assistance from the FBI when evidence suggested that the fugitive fled to another state. Another federal statute giving the FBI jurisdiction to assist state and local law enforcement in the apprehension of fugitives was Title 18, United States Code, Section 1073, Unlawful Flight To Avoid Prosecution (UFAP), in which subjects fled their state after either being criminally charged or awaiting trial. The FBI called these UFAP warrants.

An inordinate number of fugitives seemed to have fled to Florida. They were relatively easy cases and the arrests of these fugitives often resembled something you might see depicted on television. The UFAC case of the rapist to which I was assigned was no different.

The escaped fugitive was believed to have gone back to his hometown, Sanford, Florida, where George Zimmerman over twenty years later infamously shot and killed a seventeen-year-old black male, Trayvon Martin, who was passing through Zimmerman's neighborhood on his way to his aunt's house. The escaped fugitive's parents' house was deep in the woods, several miles outside the town of Sanford. The back roads in the area were not paved and it was nearly impossible to conduct surveillance by myself. I drove by his parents' house twice, but it was difficult since there was only one way in and out on the dirt road to their house. At one point heading toward the parents' house on the main road, I thought I saw the fugitive in the back seat of a car that was going the opposite direction. By the time I turned around, I saw no trace of their vehicle.

I decided to get some help from a couple of agents to watch the house for a few hours early in the morning. One agent parked on the main road while my partner and I hid in the woods watching the house. Two cars at the residence departed, but it was the parents, each leaving separately. There was no indication that the fugitive was there. I discontinued surveillance after three mornings. I made one more drive-by of the parents' house about a week later, but saw nothing unusual.

A few days later, I received a call at home in the evening from the FBI switchboard operator in Tampa. The Sanford Police Department called the FBI indicating that the fugitive was holed up at a convenience store in Sanford. The fugitive indicated to the police that he wanted to speak with the FBI. I called the two agents who previously helped me on the surveillance and asked them to meet me in Sanford. When we got there, the police advised that the fugitive had entered the convenience store and threatened the clerk. He subsequently let the clerk go and locked himself inside alone. He threatened to kill himself, but surrendered a short time later after admitting to consuming an entire bottle of *No-Doz*, over-the-counter caffeine pills.

Since the fugitive was technically my prisoner, my partner and I went to the hospital in Sanford with the police where he had his stomach pumped. Several local police officers were present as we watched the doctors in the emergency room shove a plastic tube down his throat. He was gagging and appeared to be in great discomfort. The officers were quite amused at this sight. Personally, I found their reaction to his misery somewhat odd. When he started vomiting the *No-Doz*, the officers completely lost it. One would have thought they were watching some hilarious comedy.

I was responsible for the prisoner and believed I was going to have to guard him for the rest of the night. However, to my surprise, the Seminole County Sheriff's Office Commander advised that two of his deputies would take him to the jail when he was released from the hospital. I was thankful as it was getting near midnight and I really didn't want to stand guard all night. My partner and I went to the jail the following day to take the fugitive before the United States Magistrate. The judge remanded him to the custody of the United States Marshals Service and he was sent back to prison in South Carolina. I liked to think that my relentless pursuit of the fugitive was the reason he went a little crazy and was caught.

Another memorable UFAC case involved a convicted drug trafficker, a thirty-six-year-old white male who escaped from a federal prison in Louisiana. He was considered armed and dangerous, and possibly infected with the AIDS virus. Telephone records from the prison revealed calls to his mother in St. Cloud, Florida, and to another number in St. Cloud at the residence of a thirty-four-year-old white female, who I presumed to be his girlfriend. I interviewed his mother and warned her against violating federal law by aiding and abetting a fugitive. I also used my usual line to parents of fugitives that it was for their loved one's own safety to turn themselves in. I knew no parent was ever going to tell me where his or her child was. I liked to imply that if they did not give themselves up, the possibility existed for things to go badly for the fugitive when they were finally apprehended by law enforcement. Every word I said was true, but, of course, it never worked. No parent ever dimed out their kid to me, no matter how bad of a criminal they were.

I decided to conduct surveillance on the presumed girlfriend's house for a few days. I parked down the street from her house, but saw no sign of the fugitive. Her Suzuki was parked at the residence most of the time, except for an occasional trip to the store. On the second day of surveillance, a neighbor, looking like a typical housewife, approached my car. I drove away as she got closer, inasmuch as I did not want to divulge to her who I was and risk heating up the neighborhood. I parked outside the development where I still had a view of the Suzuki, but blocks away from the curious neighbor. A couple of hours later, the same neighbor drove past me in her car. Her daughter, who I guessed was about eight or nine years old, stuck her tongue out at me from the back seat of the car as they drove by. I was very amused, but realized I was becoming conspicuous in the neighborhood.

I then decided to end my surveillance. A week later, I interviewed the next-door neighbor, an elderly lady. She said she did not know her neighbor who she said moved in about a year ago. They had never spoken beyond saying hello. I showed her the picture of the fugitive and asked her if she had ever seen him. She said she thought she saw a man similar to the fugitive coming and going about a month ago. This would have made sense since he had escaped from prison over two months ago. I asked her if she would please call me immediately if she saw him again. She said she would.

A few weeks later, I had a file review with my SSRA. He suggested that I close this lead out and send back the negative results to the FBI New Orleans Division. I agreed, but decided to call the neighbor first to make sure she had not seen any sign of the fugitive. To my surprise, she said that although she had not seen the fugitive, the woman next door appeared to be moving. I found this very interesting and advised the SSRA of this new information.

The town of St. Cloud was about forty-five minutes to an hour southeast of Orlando, depending on the traffic on I-4 around Disney World. I drove to St. Cloud and saw the presumed girlfriend loading her Suzuki with chairs and a futon. I followed her to an apartment complex a few miles away. A man and a woman helped her unload the furniture and put it into their apartment. She then drove back to her house. A short time later, she came back out loading boxes into her Suzuki. I figured she would go back to the apartment where she had been earlier, but this time she went in the opposite direction to the Kissimmee RV Park about three miles away. She entered the RV park and drove to a large Winnebago. I proceeded directly to the manager's office and showed him a picture of the fugitive. He told me that the fugitive had driven the Winnebago into the RV park two nights ago. He didn't know if the fugitive was there now.

I immediately called my SSRA and advised him of the situation. He said he would send a couple of agents to my location to assist. About a half an hour later, I radioed the Osceola County Sheriff's Office for assistance. A uniformed officer arrived in about five minutes. I told him a couple of agents were about ten to fifteen minutes away. When they arrived, we all drove to the Winnebago. We knocked on the door and the girlfriend immediately answered. We barged in identifying ourselves and asked if the fugitive was there. She did not answer and the officer grabbed her by the arm and pulled her outside.

Another agent and I went further into the Winnebago. This would be another moment when I thought that things could go badly if the fugitive had the mindset, "Not today FBI." Our guns were drawn and within seconds we saw the fugitive in bed covered with a sheet. His ten fingers were exposed grasping the top of the sheet he had pulled up to his chin. We yelled "FBI, you're under arrest, get your hands in the air." He complied and shot his hands straight up. Then the other agent grabbed the sheet and pulled it completely off the bed. The fugitive was lying naked as a jaybird on the bed with his hands in the air, looking more frightened than I had ever seen any human being look before. We grabbed a hold of his arms and flipped him on his stomach, instructing him to put his hands behind his back. He was handcuffed and then rolled off the bed. I asked him where his underwear were and he motioned toward a drawer. I retrieved a pair of his Fruit of the Loom briefs. I had him step into them and then with my head turned away, I began gingerly pulling them up his legs, finally covering his privates. This was a first. I had never put anyone else's underwear on for them in my entire life. I then did the same with his trousers, located a shirt for him, and transported him to the Osceola County jail.

My favorite fugitive arrest involved another drug trafficker from North Carolina and a pair of Serengeti sunglasses. I was assigned a lead to locate and arrest a twenty-eight-year-old white male indicted on federal drug charges in Charlotte, North Carolina. The only lead concerning his whereabouts was a post office box he had used in the past in Maitland, Florida. The Maitland Post Office was conveniently located about five minutes from my office. I met with the Postmaster and explained the situation. I asked him if he would assist me in determining if any mail was being delivered or picked up from the post office box. After a week, I called the Postmaster. He advised that mail was picked up from the box on Thursday. The next week I called him again. The Postmaster said mail was retrieved again from the post office box on Thursday.

The following Thursday, I parked at the Maitland Post Office early in the morning looking for the fugitive. At about 11:30 a.m., I spotted him walking through the front door of the post office. I recognized him immediately from the picture that the FBI Charlotte Division had forwarded to me. I radioed the ORA asking for assistance to arrest the fugitive. I received affirmative responses over the radio from two other agents. I continued to call out my location as I followed the fugitive in his car from the post office to an apartment complex a few miles away in Altamonte Springs. A few minutes after I arrived at the apartment complex, the two agents reached the location.

I had not seen exactly which apartment the fugitive entered so we went to the manager's office. The manager recognized the fugitive. The fugitive had leased the apartment in his true name. We asked the manager to call him and tell him to come to his office. A few minutes later, he arrived at the manager's office and was placed under arrest without incident. We took him to the United States Marshals Service in Orlando. He was turned over to their custody prior to his initial appearance before the United States Magistrate scheduled later that day. The Marshals Service did not want any of his valuables. Before transferring custody over to them, they told us to remove all of his valuables, to include his watch, two gold rings, and a gold necklace. I removed them and placed them in an envelope, providing the fugitive with a receipt. The fugitive told me he would have his brother pick up the jewelry at the ORA.

I then met with an AUSA to handle the fugitive's court appearance. This was a routine matter. I testified that I apprehended the fugitive pursuant to the federal arrest warrant issued in the Northern District of North Carolina and described the circumstances. The fugitive was advised of the charges by the judge and remanded to the custody of the United States Marshals Service, who were responsible for transporting him to Charlotte. I returned to my office and called the case agent in the FBI Charlotte Division. I told him I was in possession of the fugitive's gold jewelry and that his brother was supposed to pick it up. I asked him if he was planning to forfeit the jewelry. The agent said he was not. He could not prove if his jewelry was purchased with proceeds from selling drugs so he gave me the green light to return it. I then sent a teletype to FBI Charlotte advising in writing of the details of the arrest. I received a telephone call at the office later that day from the fugitive's brother. The brother came into the office shortly thereafter and signed for the jewelry.

About a week later, I found a pair of Serengeti sunglasses in the back seat of my Dodge 600. I figured they must have belonged to the fugitive from Charlotte. No one else had been in my back seat since then. At the time, these Serengeti sunglasses cost about $150. I thought about returning them, but the fugitive was in jail in Charlotte. I also did not know how to get in touch with the brother. I asked my partner his opinion about what to do with the sunglasses and his response was "finder's keepers."

A few months later, my partner and I arrested another fugitive and were dropping him off at the Seminole County Correctional Facility. As I got out of the car, my Serengeti sunglasses, compliments of the last fugitive, somehow fell to the pavement, cracking the lenses. When I got back to the office, the SSRA asked how the arrest went. I told him everything had gone fine except for breaking the lens on my Serengeti sunglasses. The SSRA immediately said he had a friend at Corning Optics in New York, where they make Serengeti sunglasses. I said in complete surprise, "You do?" I could not believe the odds. He called his friend who said all I had to do was mail him the broken sunglasses. I did just that and a few weeks later I received a package from Corning Optics. I opened up the box to find not only a brand new pair of Serengeti sunglasses, but also a leather sunglass case to go with it.

Following this incident, a new agent arrived in the ORA. He was a former United States Army Ranger and proved to be an aggressive investigator. We hit it off and became fast friends. At some point, I told him the entire saga regarding the Serengeti sunglasses. I was transferred from Orlando in 1992, but we stayed in touch.

Years later, I was vacationing at the beach with my family in Ocean City, Maryland. I was wearing my Serengeti sunglasses while playing with my two small children in the ocean a few feet from the shoreline. The waves were hitting hard onto the shore causing a riptide. As I tried to catch an errant throw of a beach ball, my sunglasses fell off. Before I could even reach down into the water, the riptide had taken the sunglasses back out into the ocean. They were gone forever. I was really disappointed and mad at myself for wearing them in the ocean. I had been re-telling the Serengeti sunglasses story for years. Now it had an ending and not a good one. I told the sad story to my old friend, the Army Ranger, who was still assigned to the ORA.

Later that year, I received a package from the ORA while I was working at WMFO. I curiously opened the package to find an identical pair of the Serengeti sunglasses I had lost. This pair was in a black case. There was no note or anything to indicate why I was receiving these sunglasses. I suspected my old friend, the Army Ranger, had something to do with this. I immediately called him and he explained that he had evidence from an old Orlando bank robbery he had to destroy. The bank robbery evidence was only being held pending an appeal of the conviction. The prosecutor recently gave him permission to dispose of all evidence since all appeals were exhausted. The Serengeti sunglasses had been a piece of evidence in his case. He sent them to me rather than trashing them, knowing how much they meant to me.

My Army Ranger friend and I once had to transport a fugitive to Tampa following his arrest in Orlando. The United States Magistrate in Orlando was not available for some reason. The law required that arrested subjects had to be taken before the nearest United States Magistrate to be advised in court of the charges against them. I had recently been assigned a blue Dodge sports car that had once belonged to a drug dealer. The car had been seized by the FBI and put into the Tampa Division fleet. My SSRA was able to get the car assigned to the ORA. He subsequently assigned it to me so I would blend in better when conducting surveillance. The car had a great stereo. The excessive amount of stereo controls on the dashboard and the bucket seats gave the feeling of being seated in the cockpit of a plane. The back seat was small and cramped. FBI policy required an agent to be in the back seat with a prisoner. The Army Ranger sat next to the bad guy on this occasion.

On the 90-mile drive to Tampa from Orlando, I played a homemade mixed cassette tape on the state of the art car stereo. I loved old music. This particular tape contained some big band music, Bing Crosby, and Judy Garland, among others. After a short while, Judy Garland sang "Somewhere Over the Rainbow." The fugitive objected and said, "Do we have to listen to this...this is cruel and unusual punishment." Then the Army Ranger (the Benedict Arnold!) chimed in and said, "Yeah, can we listen to something else?" I said, "No, this music is great," and I turned it up.

Another memorable arrest occurred on a case investigated by the DEA Task Force. I had helped my partner occasionally on his joint DEA cases. On this particular case, I had filled in to cover some shifts on a Title III wiretap investigation targeting a Colombian family in Winter Park, Florida. Winter Park was a small, upscale city located northeast and adjacent to Orlando. As the case wound down and sufficient evidence had been obtained, the DEA indicted fifteen to twenty members of this large extended family on cocaine trafficking charges. The family was from Cali, Colombia. It was decided that an opportune time to arrest them would be at a college graduation party for the daughter where all were expected to attend. A huge party was scheduled at the Hilton Hotel following her graduation from Rollins College, a prestigious private college located in Winter Park. This had to be one of the most convenient arrests of a Colombian drug trafficking ring in the history of law enforcement. It was one of the most memorable, too.

A briefing for the arrest plan took place at the DEA office the day before. Although less than twenty people were to be arrested, several hundred guests were expected to be in attendance at the lavish party. It was important to have a large uniformed law enforcement presence for the safety of all concerned.

Another agent and I were quite astonished that we were assigned to arrest the daughter. We had no idea that every member of the family was involved in the drug trafficking. The picture we were provided revealed a strikingly beautiful, young woman. One of the DEA agents immediately ruined our image of this girl when he told us that on the previous night on the wiretap, she was overheard explaining to her boyfriend in excruciating detail of her problem with "the clap." She indicated to her boyfriend that they could not have intimate relations because "it was dripping like cottage cheese." Our anticipation of arresting this stunning girl quickly turned to complete repulsion. The following evening, the arrests at the hotel went off without a hitch. Law enforcement crashed the party and surrounded the hundreds of guests in the room.

THE FBI – THEY EAT THEIR YOUNG

We spotted the exquisite-looking guest of honor decked out in a sexy, red gown at a table up front. As we made our way to her table, a DEA agent took the microphone from the lead singer in the band on stage and announced our intention to arrest the co-conspirators present at the party. It was pretty cool crashing this extravagant party to take an entire drug trafficking family off to jail. We identified ourselves to the girl, advised her she was under arrest, handcuffed her, read her Miranda rights, and escorted her from her party. It was all very orderly. The hundreds of guests looked on in shock as we abruptly ended the festivities. The other agent and I were still grossed out knowing that this beautiful girl had the clap. We both glanced at her legs and then looked at each other with wry smiles, both of us thinking the same thing. We were relieved we saw nothing dripping down her legs.

On another occasion, my partner and I were assigned to destroy four 100-pound bales of marijuana. I don't remember the exact details as to why the ORA was in possession of these drugs. I recall that they were obtained from the FBI Miami Division, possibly to be used by the ORA in a case, but they never were. I only know that we were to take the bales to a local hospital incinerator for destruction. We loaded them into the surveillance van we used on our failed case against the Jamaican at the fish store. I took the van home filled with the four bales of marijuana and parked it in my driveway overnight. I showed my wife what four hundred pounds of marijuana looked like. They actually resembled bales of hay, only green. She was amused by the fact that this large amount of drugs was parked in our driveway all night.

The next morning, I picked up my partner at his house a couple of miles away on the way to the hospital. We dutifully unloaded the bales at the hospital loading dock. We made contact with the appropriate hospital personnel with whom we had prearranged the use of the hospital incinerator. We carried each bale of marijuana from the dock and placed them in front of the incinerator, and then hurled each bale into it. The maintenance personnel working in the basement of the hospital knew what we were doing. Anyone who had ever smelled marijuana smoke knew its distinct odor. Many of the maintenance people, who obviously smoked marijuana, were watching us, cringing and shaking their heads.

Cindy was astounded another time when I came home with a half of a kilogram of powder cocaine. I stopped to use the bathroom following a drug deal and was only at the house for a few minutes. I showed Cindy what a "half a key" looked like. She was duly impressed and never forgot it. In fact, I had completely forgotten about it while writing this book. She made me put it in after reading it and realizing I had said nothing about it.

On December 2, 1989, I was at home watching television with my eight-month pregnant wife and her sister, Betsy, who had traveled from Maryland the week before to attend two baby showers, and to bring gifts from relatives back home. The FBI agents' wives gave Cindy a shower at our house the previous weekend. The second shower was given by Cindy's co-workers at Gateway High School in Osceola County where Cindy had been teaching United States History the past year and a half. Cindy enjoyed teaching, but was ready to be a mother and had no plans to return to work.

As I fell asleep at the beginning of *Saturday Night Live*, I was awakened by Cindy calling my name from the bathroom in the master bedroom. I was a little groggy, but soon realized that Cindy's water had broken. I rushed Cindy to the hospital while her sister comforted her. It was indeed special for Cindy to have her sister with her. At 3:30 a.m., the nurse told me and her sister that we should go home and get some sleep. The nurse indicated it was going to be a very long labor. We subsequently went home to sleep. At 8:30 a.m. that same morning, I awoke to get ready to return to the Arnold Palmer Children's Hospital. I telephoned Cindy's room to tell her we were coming. Cindy proceeded to tell me that the baby was born at about 6:30 a.m. He was a healthy five and a half pound baby boy, despite being premature by a full month.

I was a bit disappointed that I missed the baby being born. I wanted to be there, although I had no desire to witness the actual birth. I saw myself as more of the Ricky Ricardo type, pacing back and forth in the waiting room. I did not want to see the gory mess of umbilical cords and the like. I was happy to view mother and baby after they were all cleaned up. However, I did want at least to be in the waiting room, but Cindy said she didn't want to wake me. We arrived at the hospital at about 9 a.m. I took a picture of her sister with our new baby and then took her to the airport to catch her flight home.

THE FBI – THEY EAT THEIR YOUNG

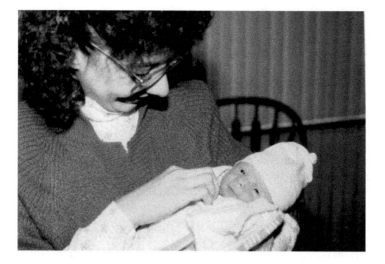

Aunt Betsy and Ethan at the Arnold Palmer Children's Hospital, 12/3/1989.

We had a wonderful day at the hospital. Cindy and I were completely smitten with our new baby boy. We took pictures and videos of him all day. We even watched a football game together. Basically, we felt more joy in our lives than ever before with our new creation, who we thought, like most new parents, was the most beautiful baby in the world. I left in the evening and got up for work the next day very early. I had planned to pick up doughnuts to take into the office in celebration of the birth. I left the house at about 6:40 a.m. I then heard FBI Tampa calling on the radio. I responded and was advised that a bank robbery had occurred on East Colonial Drive, right on my route to Dunkin' Donuts. I immediately responded that I would handle it. No other agent in Orlando was even on the air yet.

The agent who normally handled bank robberies in the office had more than eighty pending bank robbery cases. I was not about to call him at that early hour. I arrived at the bank to find that the local police had already been there for about fifteen minutes. Two white males wearing masks, one a pig's mask, had robbed the bank and left in a blue Ford pick-up truck with over $180,000. They switched vehicles at an IHOP restaurant and accidently threw away one of the bank bags of the stolen money into a dumpster there when they discarded the garbage can used in the robbery to haul off the money.

The only employee in the bank at the time of the robbery was an assistant manager who said she always came in early Monday mornings to empty the overnight deposit box. The robbers smashed in the glass front door, took the overnight deposits, and departed within minutes. She said that had the robbers looked in the vault she had just opened prior to their arrival, they would have gotten off with another $750,000. The night deposits were an unusually large amount due to all the local businesses making their deposits Saturday and Sunday nights. The bank video revealed very little information to identify the bank robbers since they were both wearing masks.

I proceeded to the ORA after gathering all the necessary information from the bank. I announced the birth of my son at the office and offered up my doughnuts. I then got to work on all of the paperwork required to open the case. The bank robbery case agent told me later that these two bank robbers were never seen previously in any other bank robberies. They obviously planned this heist carefully, and cleverly timed it with the early Monday morning collection of the night deposits. Bank robbers usually kept robbing banks until they were eventually caught. These two guys were smart enough to rob just this one bank for a substantial amount of money, and then apparently called it quits. He said they were never seen again in any surveillance photos from subsequent bank robberies.

CHAPTER 8

KIDNAPPING

When my son was about thirteen months old, I got a call from my partner late one night to assist him with a lead regarding the whereabouts of a kidnapped baby. A babysitter in Alabama kidnapped a six-month-old baby who she had watched regularly. A few days later, the babysitter was located at her sister's house in Georgia, but with no baby. After being interrogated at length, she admitted that she took the baby and went to Miami to meet her Iranian-born boyfriend. I don't know why she left the boyfriend and the baby to go to Georgia, but she told investigators there that the boyfriend and the baby were at a motel in Kissimmee, Florida. I met my partner, the SSRA, and a female agent in Kissimmee at the motel at about 12:30 a.m. My partner checked with the motel manager who gave us their room number.

The four of us knocked on the motel room door. A short, fat, balding Iranian male opened the door. We immediately saw the baby girl on the bed in her diaper. The male was about to change her. The baby wipes and baby oil were laying on the bed. He was handcuffed and advised that he was under arrest for being an accessory after the fact in a kidnapping. He immediately denied knowledge that this was a kidnapped baby. I was never on an arrest where I felt so irritated at somebody that I just wanted to smack them. All four of us had so much contempt for the man. I guess it was because we felt it was such an egregious act, stealing someone else's baby. My partner and I both had babies at home. The SSRA had children too. The Iranian's continued denials were infuriating.

The only good thing about the situation was that the baby had been well cared for. She was obviously being changed and fed. I had become an old hand at changing diapers since Ethan had been born. I finished changing the baby's diaper while the Iranian was being interrogated. He would not admit that his girlfriend had kidnapped the baby, even though she arrived in Miami the week before with a new baby. He said nothing more than that. The SSRA suggested that we call Osceola County Social Services to come get the baby, but this seemed a bit impractical given it was the middle of the night.

I immediately volunteered to take the baby home. I brought Ethan's car seat from home just in case we recovered the baby. The SSRA thought it was a good idea. My partner called the FBI in Alabama so they could notify the local deputies who were in contact with the baby's mother. He was told that the deputies would drive the mother to the ORA later that morning. The approximately eight-hour drive would put them in Orlando at about 10:30 a.m.

I arrived home with the baby at about 2:30 or 3:00 a.m. Cindy heard me coming in the door through the garage. She met me before I got to the bedroom and said, "What are you doing with a baby?" I told her how we recovered the kidnapped baby at the motel in Kissimmee and that the mother was en route from Alabama. Cindy took the baby from me and fed her. I immediately went to bed. I slept only about four hours. Prior to leaving for the office, Cindy bathed and fed the baby in preparation for the reunion with her mother.

I transported the baby safely strapped into Ethan's car seat to the ORA. Everyone was interested and excited about what had transpired in recovering the baby. My partner and I were in the office only a short time before heading to the jail to take the Iranian to his initial appearance. We missed all the hoopla that took place when the mother arrived with the Alabama deputies. It was apparently a joyous reunion and television and newspaper people were there to capture the event.

Abducted baby back in her mother's arms

By John Conway

OF THE SENTINEL STAFF

A two-week, 800-mile odyssey for an Alabama baby kidnapped from her home ended early Wednesday when FBI agents found the 6-month-old in a Kissimmee motel room.

Patricia Shaw, 24, a baby sitter for the child and friend of the family, was charged with abducting Dana Christine Holloway on Dec. 26.

Dana's mother, Sheena Holloway, speculated Wednesday after being reunited with her baby at FBI offices in Maitland that Shaw might have taken the child because she had lost custody of her own four children.

"Her crying just thrills me to death," Holloway said after a tearful reunion with Dana, one of her three children.

Agents found Dana unharmed in Room 218 at the Thrifty Inn about 12:30 a.m. Wednesday. Empty baby food jars and soda cans littered the room.

The baby was with Akbar Salemi, a 37-year-old Iranian national who had checked in with Shaw on Jan. 1. Salemi, who authorities say had lived in Miami with Shaw, was charged with being an accessory to kidnapping.

Please see KIDNAP, A-11

Six-month-old Dana and her mom, Sheena Holloway, are reunited after 2-week kidnapping ordeal.

The Orlando Sentinel, Thursday, January 10, 1991   A-11

Motel guests helped care for 6-month-old girl

KIDNAP from A-1

"The baby was just lying there on the bed, smiling away like there's no problem," said Eddie Bodigheimer, agent in charge of the FBI office in Orlando.

An Orlando agent took the baby home, where he and his wife cared for her during the night until Holloway arrived in Central Florida.

FBI agents arrested Shaw about 8 p.m. Tuesday at her mother's house in Columbus, Ga. Ursula Page notified authorities after

Salemi

Shaw called her and said she was coming to visit.

Page told The Columbus Ledger-Enquirer in an interview Wednesday that her daughter was mentally disturbed and "in and out of touch

with reality."

Shaw told FBI agents after her arrest where they could find the baby.

"She said the tremendous media coverage was bearing down on her," said Charlie Spaht, an FBI spokesman in Mobile, Ala. "She knew everyone was looking for her, and she had nowhere to hide."

Shaw was arraigned Wednesday morning in federal court in Columbus. U.S. Magistrate William L. Slaughter appointed an attorney for her and scheduled another hearing for 9:30 a.m. Monday. She is being held in the Muscogee County Jail.

Salemi appeared in federal court in Orlando Wednesday before U.S. Magistrate Donald Dietrich, who ordered U.S. marshals to take him to Montgomery, Ala. for trial. Salemi said through an interpreter that he will not fight extradition.

Court records show Shaw has been convicted of prostitution, forgery, theft and drug possession, and has used several aliases.

She has four children ranging in age from 2 to 6, but lost custody of all of them, her mother told the Columbus newspaper.

Page said two of Shaw's children are in the custody of an ex-husband in Louisiana, one is being raised by Page and the other's whereabouts are unknown.

The Immigration and Naturalization Service will seek to deport Salemi because he is suspected of entering the country illegally in 1977, said Assistant U.S. Attorney Daniel Brodersen.

Shaw faces life in prison if convicted of kidnapping, and Salemi could be sentenced to up to 10 years if convicted of being an accessory to the crime.

A nationwide search for Dana began after she was reported missing Dec. 26 from her home near Fort Mitchell, about 60 miles east of Montgomery.

Holloway told authorities that she had left the child with Shaw while she went out. When she returned about two hours later, Shaw and the baby were gone, along with diaper bags, toys, clothing and the baby's Christmas gifts.

Authorities tracked Shaw to the Miami area, where she had lived on and off for about a year.

FBI agents said they interviewed Salemi in Miami on New Year's Eve. When they went back for a second interview later that day, he was gone.

Motel records show Shaw and Salemi checked into the Thrifty Inn on Vine Street in Kissimmee on New Year's Day.

Motel guests and employees said the couple had told them they were married and the baby was theirs.

After Wednesday's jubilant reunion, Sheena and Dana Holloway were bundled into a car driven by a Russell County, Ala., deputy sheriff for the seven-hour ride home.

"We're going to throw her a little party at home," Holloway said. "Her grandma's probably baking her a cake right now."

Larry Lebowitz and Mark Andrews of the Sentinel staff contributed to this report.

Both Shaw and Salemi had lined up work within walking distance of their $133-a-week motel room. A manager at The Clock Restaurant said Salemi worked several days there as a short-order cook. Shaw was to start work Tuesday at a Taco Bell restaurant as a cashier, a manager there said.

On Tuesday morning Shaw told Salemi she was going to get breakfast and would be back soon. She never returned.

Motel manager Suzanne Huang said Salemi panicked when Shaw did not return.

"The man went crazy," Huang said. "He didn't know how to take care of a baby."

Because Shaw had taken the couple's money, Huang and her husband chipped in for baby food and formula. Motel guests took turns holding and caring for the child while Salemi nervously paced the balcony hallway most of the day, Huang said.

Guests and employees said the baby appeared well cared for.

"She [Shaw] was just so sweet. I don't believe it," Thrifty Inn maid Lillian Crespo said of the woman's arrest.

Orlando Sentinel, dated 1/10/1991, regarding kidnapping.

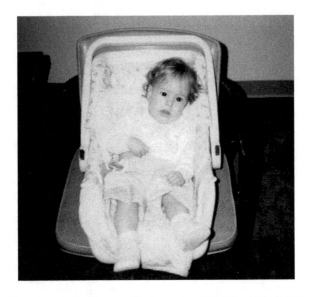

The recovered kidnapped baby at the FBI ORA, 1/9/1991.

U.S. Department of Justice

Federal Bureau of Investigation

Office of the Director   Washington, D.C. 20535

March 14, 1991

PERSONAL

Mr. William A. Larsh
Federal Bureau of Investigation
Tampa, Florida

Dear Mr. Larsh:

    You are certainly to be commended for your superior performance during the Kidnaping case involving Patricia Shaw and Akbar Salemi.

    When you received information about the kidnapers, you proceeded to the Thrifty Inn where the management confirmed that the victim and Salemi were in a room. Because of your quick response to the information, Salemi was arrested and the victim was returned to her mother unharmed. It is indeed gratifying to realize that we have employees with such a deep regard for the welfare of others. You have my profound thanks for a job very well done.

Sincerely yours,

William S. Sessions
Director

Letter of Commendation, dated 3/14/1991, from Director William S. Sessions.

CHAPTER 9

THE GOAT MAN

During the summer of 1990, I began working a drug case with a Bureau of Alcohol, Firearms and Tobacco (BATF) agent. BATF agents had the reputation in Orlando at that time of being "cowboys." They gained this reputation by having a penchant for making quick cases and then going in like cowboys on arrests, hence, the cowboy reference. They were not known for conducting extensive investigations; however, this was not the case in this instance. The BATF agent with whom I worked had been previously assigned to undercover work as a member of a biker gang. When we began working together, he maintained the appearance of a biker with long hair, a scraggly beard, and a moustache. He called the ORA to request the FBI to work jointly with him on a case he was developing. My partner was busy working with the DEA Task Force so the call came to me. The BATF agent had an informant known as "the goat man." The goat man, a white male, got his name from the Jamaicans in Orlando to whom he sold goat head soup.

The goat man had served time and was a convicted felon. The Jamaicans purchased a handgun from him on one occasion, knowing that he was a convicted felon. This was a violation of federal law, albeit a minor one. The BATF agent requested assistance from the FBI in order to expand his case. The BATF obviously had no jurisdiction to work a drug case. The BATF agent believed the goat man was in a position of trust to buy drugs. The BATF agent could have gone to the DEA Task Force with the case, but he chose to work with the FBI. I agreed to work with him. The goat man first purchased a pound of marijuana for $1,000 from the Jamaicans at a body shop they owned in west Orlando. In order to prosecute a drug case at the federal level, cocaine would need to be purchased.

The plan was to take the case as far it could go in determining the full extent of the Jamaicans' drug trafficking and other criminal activities. My ultimate goal was to exhaust all investigative techniques, possibly leading to a court approved Title III federal wiretap. I was hoping for a major case and to make a huge impact against their drug trafficking. It was not meant to be, though, owing to the goat man's inability to follow instructions. Perhaps it was due to his strong desire to satisfy us, but ultimately the case failed because of the goat man.

Following the successful purchase of the pound of marijuana, the goat man asked the Jamaicans if he could purchase a kilogram of powder cocaine. The Jamaicans said they could sell him the cocaine, but their shipment would not be in for another few weeks. The goat man contacted them two weeks later. They instructed him to come to their body shop three days later with $18,000. I obtained authority to proceed from my supervisor, the USAO, and from FBI Headquarters. I planned and organized the entire operation. About eight agents from my office were recruited to assist, as well as four BATF agents and several Orange County Sheriff's Office (OCSO) deputies. The OCSO's surveillance plane was also used in support of the operation. I wired up the goat man with a transmitter and a Nagra body recorder.

I provided a briefing to all personnel involved and gave specific instructions to the goat man. The goat man was to proceed to the body shop in his pick-up truck with the $18,000. He was instructed to make certain that he saw the cocaine first, prior to showing the Jamaicans the cash. He was to go inside the body shop to view the cocaine and then make the transaction by his truck in the parking lot. He was told in no uncertain terms to end the deal if he saw no cocaine. He was also advised not to leave the premises during any part of the transaction. Unfortunately, his first attempt ended abruptly as the Jamaicans told him they had no cocaine, but they expected a shipment the next week. The goat man departed the body shop and met us at a predetermined location for a debriefing. The entire operation lasted only a few minutes. I dismissed all the participating law enforcement personnel until further notice.

We directed the goat man to call the Jamaicans the following week. They again instructed him to come to the body shop. I made the same preparations as I had done the week before and provided him the same instructions. The result was the same. The Jamaicans again told the goat man that they had expected the cocaine, but it had not been delivered to them. They assured him that they would have it in two days and for him to come back then with the money. We decided to try this scenario one more time in a couple of days. The goat man called them prior to going to the body shop and they advised that they had the cocaine.

I proceeded with the same plan. Fortunately, I gave him instructions in front of other FBI agents, my BATF partner, and numerous OCSO deputies. I was emphatic that he should go inside and make sure he saw the cocaine first before bringing the Jamaicans back out to his truck to show them the money to make the exchange. He was instructed again to only make the deal at his truck as surveillance had this area completely covered should anything go wrong.

The goat man was wired up with a transmitter and a Nagra recorder, not only for safety purposes, but for evidentiary purposes as well. The OCSO airplane was circling the area. FBI agents, BATF agents, and OCSO deputies were all in the immediate area in their vehicles monitoring the meeting. The goat man drove to the body shop, parked in their lot, and went inside. Within two minutes, he returned to his vehicle with two black males. The black males got into two separate vehicles and the goat man proceeded to follow them about two miles down the road. This was in no way part of the plan. I was very anxious about the situation, but I could not stop it.

The surveillance vehicles discreetly moved in the direction of the goat man and the black males to a Jamaican neighborhood in west Orlando. Luckily, the OCSO plane had the eye on them and called out their location. They arrived at a two-story duplex house and parked their vehicles in front. The OCSO surveillance plane called out that all three individuals entered the second story door on the right side of the duplex. The building had garage doors on the ground floor and a wooden staircase and balcony leading to two doors on each end of the duplex. None of the surveillance vehicles could get very close to the building without drawing too much attention to themselves. We had to get somewhat close for safety purposes, but we did not want to burn the surveillance in the all black neighborhood. I drove about a quarter to a half mile past the duplex and parked in an empty church parking lot. The transmitter was a little weak from that distance, but the OCSO plane had a good view and perfect reception.

As I sat in my vehicle with my BATF partner and a female BATF agent, we could hear the goat man counting the money. In the middle of his counting, we heard the goat man scream, "Oh, Lord, no, please no, I'm a good man," followed by what sounded like a gun shot. The reception on the transmitter was not good so I asked the OCSO pilot, "Was that a gun shot?" to which he replied in the affirmative. I then radioed all personnel on the surveillance to proceed to the duplex immediately. I announced that the goat man had possibly been shot, and to apprehend the two black males who fled the scene in their separate vehicles.

The two BATF agents and I were closest to the duplex. We proceeded there immediately, arriving first. I never felt so vulnerable as I raced up the steps to the second floor. I had this horrible feeling as I reached the second floor balcony that someone from inside would open fire through the window and shoot me right off the balcony. I never once hesitated to do my duty, but it was a bad feeling standing there without cover. If the shooters or any other accomplices had still been inside, I could easily have been shot. The door to the house was locked. My misgivings soon subsided when the goat man yelled that he was alone inside and had been shot in the leg. However, he could not open the door. He then broke the window from the inside with a chair. We helped this giant of a man, who was 6 feet 7 inches tall and weighing well over 300 pounds, crawl out the window.

We laid him down on the balcony and pulled his blood-soaked blue jeans off trying to determine the location of his wounds. The female BATF agent called for an ambulance. We found two bleeding bullet wounds in his leg, one above his knee where the bullet entered, and the other on his upper thigh very near his privates, where the bullet exited. We applied pressure to the wounds using his blue jeans. His once white Fruit of the Loom underwear was completely soaked in blood. He had the Nagra recorder and transmitter in his underwear with the wires all wrapped around it. I managed to untangle the wires and remove the recording equipment and transmitter with one hand as I applied pressure to his wound on his upper thigh. The BATF agent applied pressure to the wound above his knee.

Within about five to ten minutes, the ambulance arrived. The front yard was filled with law enforcement vehicles and personnel. OCSO detectives arrived at the scene to conduct forensics in the apartment. They were investigating the matter as an attempted murder, a local crime. As it turned out, the Jamaicans showed the goat man a piece of a two by four inch block of wood wrapped in tape. It was made to look like a "brick" of cocaine, the commonly known term for a kilogram of cocaine. The goat man did not follow instructions and never saw any cocaine other than the phony brick wrapped in tape.

I was full of blood as I walked down the steps of the balcony to the front yard. I will always remember the married ORA agents approaching me. The wife was very worried for me. She had formerly been a medical technician before becoming an agent. She was quite disturbed by the fact that I was covered in the goat man's blood. She immediately told me to wash off with a hose as I might contract AIDS, a major health issue constantly reported in the news at that time. I found a hose by the side of the duplex and sprayed the blood off me.

I then asked what happened to the two Jamaicans. The male married agent explained that the one Jamaican was arrested, but the other one got away. He said that he had followed the second Jamaican's vehicle, but when he saw an OCSO deputy pull over the first car by himself, he let the second car go in order to provide backup to the deputy. He said that he and the deputy arrested the shooter, a thirty-one-year-old black male born in Jamaica. The agent retrieved a .45 caliber pistol from the back seat of the car. He said the pistol had a "stove pipe" jam when he retrieved it.

A stove pipe jam meant that that an expended shell casing from the last bullet fired did not fully eject from the chamber of the pistol. FBI agents were trained from the time they attended the FBI Academy as new agents and throughout their careers at firearms training sessions to "tap, rack and bang" when confronted with this type of jam. Basically, one only needed to pull back on the slide of the pistol to remove the empty shell casing and a live bullet from the magazine went into the chamber upon release of the slide. The "tap" part of this drill referred to tapping the butt of the magazine to ensure it was securely in the gun. The "bang" was shooting the gun. Luckily for the goat man, the Jamaican was not trained to tap, rack and bang to resolve a jam. If he had, the goat man would have never been able to tell me exactly what had happened.

The goat man was taken to the hospital and doctors performed an operation on his leg. He survived the gunshot wounds and was able to tell me that night from his hospital bed the details of the shooting. He was very apologetic for not having followed directions. He knew that he had screwed up. He said he was just anxious to complete the drug deal since the first two attempts had failed in the previous weeks. He said the Jamaicans told him they had the cocaine at their apartment. He followed them there and took the money into the apartment. He sat at the kitchen table and began counting the $18,000. He had seen the wrapped brick of purported cocaine, but never saw any actual cocaine. While he was counting, the one Jamaican pulled out a pistol and shot him. The goat man said he pled for his life, covered his head, and pulled his leg up while seated at the table. He said the bullet apparently entered his leg above his knee and exited his upper thigh. He saw the Jamaican continue to try to pull the trigger to finish him off at point blank range, but the gun was apparently jammed. The two Jamaicans then left the apartment with the money and locked him inside. Then, minutes later, we arrived on the scene and he broke the window to get out.

The goat man repeatedly said how sorry he was and that he knew he had made a huge mistake by going with them to their apartment. The goat man left the hospital about a week later and I paid him $1,500 for his services so he could get out of Orlando and relocate to Tallahassee. He would be safe there, but he walked with a severe limp from that day on.

Upon arriving home that night, my wife was shocked and nauseated to see me covered in blood. Before I explained to her the sensational events of my day, I merely asked her if she could get the bloodstains out of my pants. I was quite upset that my khaki pants which I had been wearing since purchasing them at the FBI Academy during my training in 1987 might be ruined for good. My wife had little or no interest in saving my khaki pants at that moment. Later, after hearing the details of my story, she assured me that she could in fact remove the bloodstains. My khaki pants survived the ordeal.

The next day at the office, I received a call from the Orange County jail advising me that the Jamaican arrested the day before wanted to speak with the FBI. The BATF agent and I immediately went to the jail to see what he wanted. To our surprise, he was angry that he had been arrested for the shooting and that the other Jamaican who was with him had gotten away with the $18,000. The Jamaican inmate was so frustrated with what had happened that he provided us with his accomplice's name and an address in Savannah, Georgia, where he was certain his partner had fled.

I called the AUSA, who I had met with the previous day, to advise that we needed an arrest warrant for the second Jamaican identified. In our conversation in the AUSA's office the day before, he had said that he could not charge drug trafficking in this case because there were no drugs involved. He said there had to be drugs on the table as evidence in a drug case and all we had was a taped piece of wood. The experienced and clever AUSA said he would take the case and prosecute on charges of theft of government property while using a firearm. The firearm charge would add a mandatory five years to their sentences. The government property to which he was referring was the FBI's $18,000 that was supposed to have been used in the drug transaction. The Jamaicans would do more time in prison than they would for being charged locally on attempted murder. An attempted murder conviction would only get them about a seven-year sentence. They would likely only serve one third of that time before getting out on parole. The federal charges would ultimately put them in prison for twelve and thirteen years, respectively, and both would have to serve eighty-five percent of their time before receiving the possibility of parole.

An arrest warrant was issued for the second Jamaican. I sent a lead to the FBI Savannah Division for his arrest and to obtain a search warrant for the address provided in order to locate the $18,000. Agents from Savannah located and arrested the Jamaican without incident, but he did not talk. The search warrant executed at his address did not produce the stolen funds. However, both subjects were later indicted and pled guilty to the charges. Although this case turned out not to be a drug case technically, both subjects received more than twice as much jail time as the subjects in my previous drug cases.

This case was a turning point for me in my career. My goal in drug cases had always been to infiltrate the drug trafficking organizations, either through introducing an undercover agent or through a Title III wire intercept. This case made me think twice about these goals. I knew it was not my fault that the goat man had been shot, but I could not help think how despondent I'd be if an undercover agent got shot on my case. I came to the conclusion that I did not want to be responsible for an agent being shot in a bad deal like the goat man's. The goat man's fate I could live with. I felt bad for him, but ultimately my conscience was clear as I had done nothing wrong. I had taken all necessary precautions. In fact, I was required to submit a detailed report of the entire incident to the Drug Section at FBI Headquarters. The Drug Section reached the conclusion that the informant had not followed directions. However, I still could not shake the idea that if an agent had been shot or killed, I would not have been able to live with such a tragedy. A recording of the radio transmissions involving the surveillance and the aftermath of the shooting was made at the ORA. This tape was later utilized at a training in-service at the FBI Academy in Quantico concerning the use of informants to illustrate what happened when informants did not follow directions.

Spring 1990, still time for fun playing softball with ORA agents and other law enforcement officers. Ethan and I are on the far left.

CHAPTER 10

WHITE COLLAR CRIME

During the next few months, I prepared for the Jamaicans' trial. They pled guilty only days prior to the trial. In March 1991, I had complaint duty in the ORA and interviewed two telemarketers about an alleged telemarketing scam in Orlando. I wrote a summary of the complaint in a memorandum and forwarded it to my SSRA. I was intrigued at the possibility of working a wire and mail fraud case, but I was still assigned to work drugs. A day later, I decided to ask the SSRA if I could work the telemarketing case. I explained to him that I did not want to work drug cases anymore. I saw this as an opportunity to gain experience investigating white collar crime. When I asked him what he had done with the telemarketing complaint, he told me he had put it in an unaddressed work file. He said his white collar agents were too busy with other matters to pursue it. To my surprise, he said I was welcome to open the case and investigate it.

I then spoke with the most experienced white collar crime agent in the office. He said it would be an easy case. He suggested getting subpoenas from the USAO to obtain telephone toll records and then to send out questionnaires to the customers identified from the toll records. His assessment could not have been more wrong. He would have been correct had this been the typical boiler room operation. In most telemarketing scams, the fraudulent business would operate only for a short time before moving to a new location. When the "heat" was on, meaning law enforcement was getting close, the business shut down and moved elsewhere; hence the boiler room term. However, this case proved to be quite the opposite. I tripped upon a scam that was in its infancy, grossing over $12 million in only eight months. The fraud involved approximately 250,000 victims. The principals in this telemarketing operation were doing a brilliant job of convincing everyone they were running a legitimate operation. I was taught at new agent training that although the perpetrators were known in white collar crime cases, the government had to prove their activity was indeed criminal. The AUSA assigned to this case reminded me many times of this fact throughout the investigation. She was a tenacious prosecutor, close to forty years old, divorced, and the mother to a ten-year-old. I never would have been successful in this case without her shrewdness, perseverance, and dedication.

Most crimes involved activities or incidents known to be illegal acts, but the offenders were usually not immediately known. In this case, I had the unique problem of working a long-term investigation wherein neither I, the AUSA, my SSRA, my colleagues in the FBI, nor the Internal Revenue Service (IRS) agent who would become my partner in the case, were one hundred percent certain the activity could be proven in court as fraud. I should clarify, however, that I believed from the outset that this was an out and out scam, as did the AUSA and my IRS colleague. The problem in these types of white collar crime cases was to obtain sufficient evidence to prove to a jury of twelve men and women that the defendants knowingly and intentionally perpetrated a fraud. This task was the great dilemma. During the entirety of the investigation, I never knew if I had a sufficient amount of evidence. This caused me undue stress, which the AUSA exacerbated by constantly telling me, "Gee Bill, I sure hope we have enough evidence to prove this." We both knew full well that it was a scam and we were disgusted by it. We also knew that unless we did something about it, this activity would continue and grow to magnificent proportions.

The fraud itself involved a company called Advanced Interactive Communications, Inc., also known as AICA, headed by a con man who promised customers credit cards or access to banks that would issue them credit cards. The problem was that the potential customers being solicited were individuals who had previously been turned down for a credit card, had either poor credit, or no credit at all. The individuals were told on the telephone that AICI had a "network of banks" or "worked with banks" that specialized in helping people with bad credit. The truth of the matter was that neither AICI nor any of the other telemarketing firms involved had any affiliation with any bank.

In fact, none of the banks listed in the pamphlet issued unsecured credit cards to customers with bad credit. Some banks did offer secured credit cards. This meant that customers with bad credit would be required to make a deposit at the bank in order to obtain a credit card. The idea that customers could obtain a secured credit card from some of the banks on the list became a major part of AICI's defense in this case. The company also claimed a ninety-eight percent acceptance rate and a full money back guarantee. The United States Eleventh Circuit jury instructions described fraud as "any misrepresentation of fact, half-truths, or omissions of fact that otherwise cause an individual to make a decision." It was my job to collect all the evidence possible for the prosecutor to prove the case in court. As stated previously, most criminal cases were easily proven in court, such as a drug case where drugs were seized and recordings were made of the transactions. However, in this white collar crime case, the evidence was not always so black and white to a jury. This case was unpredictable because this type of telemarketing fraud (involving bad credit and the use of 1-900 numbers) was a new scam that had not been previously prosecuted in federal court.

On that fateful day in March 1991, I interviewed three telemarketers who had been previously employed at AICI. They described in great detail the alleged fraud occurring at this company. After obtaining their information and reviewing documents they retrieved from a dumpster at AICI, I determined the nature of the business. AICI was the headquarters in a telemarketing operation that had forty satellite telemarketing rooms located throughout Florida and the United States. They called customers throughout the United States and offered them a credit card. Telemarketers contacted consumers who were recently denied credit. They read from prepared sales scripts and rebuttals. Customers were told that the company was a national financial service company networking with 65 banks nationwide. Customers were further told, "a recent update in our files shows you as now eligible to receive a VISA/MasterCard with interest rates as low as 11.88%." The customer was then told that they would need to get a confirmation and they would get them verified today. Customers were directed to call a 1-900 number to obtain a verification code number and were told that the company's processing department would call them back in seven to ten minutes to obtain the code numbers. The verification codes just happened to be sixteen-digit numbers, the same as on a credit card. The customer incurred a $50 toll charge to their telephone bill as a result of the call. The customer was told when the processing center called back for the code numbers that they would receive their information in the mail in seven to fourteen business days.

The information received by the customer was a six-page pamphlet with instructions on how to get a bank loan and a list of 65 banks where the customer could apply for credit. Investigation determined that the pamphlet was in fact an exact copy ripped off from the Bankcard Holders of America, a non-profit organization in Washington, D.C., which provided the pamphlet to consumers for free. After subpoenas were issued to all 65 banks, it was confirmed that none of the banks had any relationship with AICI or any other telemarketing firm, and that the low interest rate credit cards offered in the pamphlet were for customers with excellent credit ratings only.

Investigation discovered that AICI was the subscriber to all of the 1-900 numbers that its satellite offices were utilizing. AICI received a percentage for each sale its satellite offices made. AICI handled the mailing of the pamphlets and customer service for all its offices. The telephone company service provider for the 1-900 number also got a percentage of each sale. AICI and its offices made over 250,000 sales in just over eight months of operation. The telephone company service provider representative proved to be a good witness at trial, inasmuch as the sales pitch provided by AICI was far different than the misleading sales pitch used by AICI telemarketers with customers. The pitch given to the telephone company indicated clearly from the outset that the customer would receive a pamphlet containing a list of banks. It did not contain the false and fraudulent claims ultimately used in the AICI pitch to customers.

Immediately following the initiation of this case, I made consensually monitored telephone calls to AICI in an attempt to record the sales pitch. However, I was unable to accomplish this since AICI was set up to make outgoing calls by telemarketers reading a sales pitch. My incoming calls were directed to customer service. I did, however, later obtain numerous complaint letters pertaining to AICI and its satellite offices from the Better Business Bureau of Central Florida. All of the complaints from consumers had come from outside the state of

Florida. I personally contacted more than a dozen customers by telephone and interviewed them. I used this information as the central part of my affidavit for a search warrant at AICI and seven satellite locations in Orlando, Florida. I determined that they had seven satellite offices after searching through AICI's trash and finding various documents. I discovered that AICI had forty satellite offices only after executing the search warrants and examining their records.

On May 29, 1991, I obtained eight search warrants and organized the simultaneous execution of the warrants with agents from the ORA and the FBI Tampa offices. I briefed and assigned dozens of agents for the task. I rented a truck, purchased boxes, and retrieved all necessary items including cameras, film, tape, property receipts, and provided a kit to each team of agents executing search warrants at their respective locations.

On May 30, 1991, the day after executing the search warrants at all eight telemarketing locations, I transported a truckload of evidence to a government warehouse located over fifty miles away in Cape Canaveral, Florida, the only place I knew large enough to store the evidence. On that same date, I was paged by the ORA while heading to Cape Canaveral. I telephoned the office and was instructed to return to the USAO in Orlando with the truckload of evidence. A bank officer tipped off the FBI that morning that the President of AICI was attempting to withdraw $2.5 million from the AICI account. I needed to get back to the federal building in Orlando and review the evidence to obtain AICI's financial records for inclusion in an affidavit to support a seizure warrant. I was able to accomplish this task in the parking lot of the USAO after locating AICI's checkbook and financial records from a box in the truck. I turned them over to an IRS agent who had already begun preparing an affidavit with the AUSA alleging that AICI funds were derived from fraudulent activity. The probable cause for fraud was already established in the affidavit for the search warrants. The only additional information required for the seizure warrant affidavit was their financial information. The funds were successfully seized by day's end, however, the government would have to eventually prove its case in court at trial to keep the money.

I returned to Cape Canaveral the following day and unloaded the evidence into a warehouse and began reviewing it under intense heat conditions. The warehouse had no air conditioning and the temperature outside was over 90 degrees

Fahrenheit. One week later, the senior white collar crime agent used his influence at the USAO to secure space within the federal building in Orlando for me to store my evidence and review it under more suitable conditions. I reloaded the truckload of evidence and transported it to the fifth floor of the federal building. Had I not been a very fit twenty-nine-year-old man, I would not have been able to perform this demanding manual labor. This was not what I had imagined myself doing as an FBI agent, but I always did what had to be done. I spent the next several months sifting through a voluminous amount of boxes containing documents. I reviewed every piece of evidence, labeled each item, and organized it in folders in filing cabinets designated for each of the eight locations. I labeled and filed approximately 2,000 pieces of evidence and then implemented a system to have the list of evidence entered into a computer.

The timing of this complex and laborious case could not have occurred at a worse time for me. It interfered significantly with my personal life. At the time of the execution of the search warrants in May 1991, my wife was six and a half months pregnant with our second child. I was not generally available the last months of her pregnancy due to an intense amount of work related with the case. I was only able to take one day of annual leave to be with my wife after my daughter's birth on August 12, 1991. I was unfortunately not available for my family over the next seven months due to the expanding investigation, the execution of more search warrants, interviewing witnesses, organizing evidence for presentation to a FGJ, testifying before the FGJ, and eventually preparing for prosecution at trial. The experienced white collar crime agent, who previously worked at WMFO, told me that if my case was being investigated at WMFO, it would have been assigned to an entire squad.

I conducted over three hundred interviews of witnesses in this matter. I served over two hundred FGJ subpoenas to employees of AICI and its affiliates. On October 22, 1991, I attempted to interview the top former telemarketer from AICI at his business, Frontier Financial Services (FFS). My partner on the case, an IRS Agent, also known as the "Silver Hawk" for his silver head of hair, joined the case with me when he prepared the seizure warrant for AICI's $2.5 million from their checking account. He began assisting me with interviews from that point on, as well as tracking the expenditures at AICI and its affiliated telemarketing rooms. He accompanied me to FFS to interview the telemarketer. Upon entering the business, we observed FFS firsthand conducting the identical business for which AICI was being investigated. It was clear we would have to obtain a search warrant and shut down FFS also.

Neither one of us was happy about what we witnessed at FFS due to the simple fact that we were already overwhelmed with the investigation of AICI. We viewed this expansion of the case as something we did not have time to do. I even said to my IRS agent partner at that moment, "Shit, we're going to have to get a search warrant." After further investigation, I determined that FFS had two telemarketing rooms in Orlando. We were going to have to execute two simultaneous search warrants the following day. Upon conferring with the AUSA later that day, she had the idea that we could prosecute this smaller case at FFS first, and use it as a test case before prosecuting the much larger AICI investigation. FFS would be much more practical and manageable to prosecute and take to trial, she said. She decided that I should prepare affidavits for the search warrants at FFS, as well as for two arrest warrants, one for the owner of FFS, and one for a female manager working at FFS. I had interviewed this female FFS manager previously in connection with the AICI investigation wherein she admitted that she knew this business was a fraud. She had been a manager at Regency Financial Services (RFS), one of the satellites of AICI which was shut down on May 29, 1991. She had also testified before the FGJ and admitted knowing this business was a fraud.

The following was taken from the affidavit used to obtain the search warrants at FFS (subject and witness names have been omitted):

"William A. Larsh, being duly sworn, states as follows:

1. Affiant has been a Special Agent of the FBI since November 2, 1987, and is currently assigned to the FBI office in Orlando, Florida. This affidavit is made in support of an application to search the premises at FFS, located at 5454 Hoffner Avenue, Suite 107, Orlando, Florida, and at FFS, 9521 South Orange Blossom Trail, Cypress Park Plaza, Suite 107, Orlando, Florida, hereinafter collectively referred to as FFS.

2. Affiant believes that there have occurred and are now occurring on these premises violations of federal criminal law, including violations of Title 18, United

States Code, Section 1343 (wire fraud), and Section 371 (conspiracy to commit wire fraud).

3. On July 31, 1991, (NAME DELETED), formerly a manager at RFS, a company being investigated by your affiant for wire fraud, was interviewed by affiant. During the interview, (NAME DELETED) revealed that she currently worked at FFS, which did exactly the same thing that RFS had done. A search warrant had been executed by the FBI at RFS on May 29, 1991. (NAME DELETED) said that FFS was located on South Orange Blossom Trail in an office across the street from Sam's Wholesale Club. She said they had two 1-900 numbers with MCI, but were going with a 1-900 number with AT&T in about a week. She said that (NAME DELETED) was the owner at FFS. She said the script read to customers at FFS said that they network with 65 banks and that a recent update in the credit files had made them eligible to receive a VISA/MasterCard. She said the script also read that it was an unsecured card and there was no deposit required. She said she had not seen FFS's package that was mailed to customers.

4. The FFS female manager (NAME DELETED) described the sales pitch being used at FFS as substantially identical to the sales pitch that was used at RFS. She stated that the pitch at RFS was deceiving and led customers to believe that they would get a VISA/MasterCard. She further said that the pitch was deceiving in that it said there was a recent update in computer files, but there was no computer. She said that regarding the phrase 'network with 65 banks,' the company had no affiliation with banks. Nonetheless, she has continued to participate in this activity having acknowledged its criminality.

5. On October 13, 1991, (WITNESS NAME DELETD) contacted the FBI office in Tampa, Florida, and advised that she worked at FFS on South Orange Blossom Trail, Orlando, Florida, as a telemarketer for credit cards. She contacted prospective clients under the guise of providing clients with a promise of providing a VISA/MasterCard, when in fact all that

was done was to refer clients to a 1-900 number which cost the client $50.

6. On October 22, 1991, affiant and IRS Agent (NAME DELETED) visited FFS, located at 5454 Hoffner Avenue, Orlando, Florida, to interview (OWNER NAME DELETED). OWNER's mother, (NAME DELETED), advised that her son was not there and she paged him. Affiant and IRS Agent observed the premises and noted a woman in the front room near the front door apparently speaking to customers and reading from a script and rebuttals propped up on a table. IRS Agent advised he heard this woman tell a customer they 'tied in with the banks.' Affiant read the script and rebuttals that were propped up on the table. Affiant observed ten to fifteen telemarketers in the back room with the same script and rebuttals in plastic folders reading them to customers. OWNER'S mother later spoke with her son on the telephone and advised him that affiant and IRS Agent were on the premises waiting to see him. OWNER'S mother asked what the matter was in reference to and she was advised it was regarding his employment at AICI. She advised that her son would arrive in forty-five minutes. Affiant advised he could not wait and asked the mother to have her son call affiant. Affiant then asked the female FFS manager, who was working on the premises, for a copy of the script and rebuttals. She advised affiant he would have to ask the OWNER'S mother. Affiant asked the mother for copies of their script, rebuttals, and fulfillment package which she supplied. The script and rebuttals provided were identical to those being utilized by the telemarketers (see Exhibits 1, 2, and 3). She provided the booklet mailed to customers, attached as Exhibit 4. She had also said they got their 1-900 number through AT&T. She also said they had purchased bad leads that week at a cost of $10,000.

7. On the same date, OWNER contacted affiant by telephone and an interview was set up for 8:45 a.m., October 23, 1991. He asked if the interview was in regard to his employment at AICI.

8. On the same date, affiant interviewed a former employee. She said she worked at FFS over a month ago. She said she worked there for two days and made six sales. She responded to an ad in the newspaper for a secretary, but when she arrived at FFS, she was offered a job as a telemarketer. The former employee was provided with a script and rebuttals and was told to follow them word for word. She was not shown the package being sold. She was told to sit behind a petite girl who was the top salesperson for training. She was referred to as the "head trainer." The former employee sat behind the petite girl and listened to her. The head trainer had also told her that customers will love it and can't refuse. She said the head trainer said they were doing a wonderful thing. She said the head trainer, as well as (NAME DELETED), a manager, specifically said to hang up on anybody that's negative and go to the next call.

9. The former employee said that on her second day, she asked (NAME DELETED) what happened after customers get their package and he told her they'd have to select the bank and call the "900" number for the bank. She said (NAME DELETED) then said that "what he gets is an application, but don't tell him that." She said she was on the phone with a customer when (NAME DELETED) said this. She said the script and rebuttals give the impression that the customer is getting a card. She said she had the impression that customers got cards until (NAME DELETED) said the above to her. She said she thought the customer picked the bank and got a card.

10. She said the head trainer had told her, in essence, that the 65 banks have less stringent requirements to get a card and Citibank requires higher standards to get a card. She said the script also said that these cards were unsecured cards. She said the petite girl said banks required secured accounts, but theirs are unsecured. She was told that the computer lists of the people called came from larger banks. She said that was said vaguely in the script.

11. She said the script read that a recent update in our computer shows you are now eligible to receive a

VISA/ MasterCard through our network of banks that deals with 65 banks. She said the customer was told that they've recently been denied credit and now they're eligible. She said the script was vague. She said the script went on to say that there would be a processing charge of $50 through an AT&T number and got them to call a 1-900 number.

12. She said the rebuttals said they were members of the Better Business Bureau and said something to the effect that the 65 banks are smaller and less stringent. She said the cards are unsecured and you don't have to make a deposit.

13. She said the whole focus was to call the 1-900 number. She said the telemarketers filled out an index card of the sale and gave it to the manager who called the customer back in ten minutes to get their verification code number. She said this was also explained in the script.

14. She said she called the 1-900 number once and the recording was computerized and said "your verification code number is," and she said she then hung up.

15. She said she quit after her second day and the head trainer told her to pick up her check at their office on Hoffner Avenue.

16. On October 23, 1991, affiant was told by OWNER'S mother that her son was the owner of FFS. She further said FFS had no affiliation with the banks listed in their book.

17. On October 23, 1991, the IRS agent observed in Suite 107, Cypress Park Plaza, 9521 South Orange Blossom Trail, Orlando, Florida, telemarketers on the phone in four banks of telephone booths, six people each. The IRS Agent spoke with a male who identified himself as the manager who said that they were operating a telemarketing business that sells information packages for VISA/MasterCard credit cards.

18. The scripts being used by the telemarketers are fraudulent in that they:

    a. Claim that FFS networks with 65 banks nation-wide, which is not true;

    b. Claim that FFS has an update in its file, whereas FFS maintains no files on its customers;

    c. Claim that the customer is eligible for an unsecured VISA or MasterCard, whereas FFS has no knowledge as to his or her eligibility; and

    d. Fail to advise the customer that he or she will be receiving a booklet on rehabilitating credit, and instead advises the customer he or she will be receiving a credit card.

19. On October 23, 1991, a representative from the Better Business Bureau, Maitland, Florida, advised that FFS, (OWNER'S NAME), President, joined the BBB on July 23, 1991.

20. On the same date, Orlando Utilities advised that National Telegroup, Inc., dba FFS, telephone number 826-9410, 5454 Hoffner Avenue, Suite 107, Orlando, Florida, has had power since August 23, 1991.

21. On the same date, Southern Bell Telephone said that 407-826-9410 was subscribed to National Telegroup, Inc., 9521 South Orange Blossom Trail, Suite 107, Orlando, Florida, as of June 13, 1991.

Further your affiant sayeth not."

This affidavit was sworn before the United States Magistrate on October 25, 1991, to obtain two search warrants. I used a variation of this affidavit to obtain two arrest warrants, one for the owner, and another for the female manager.

THE FBI – THEY EAT THEIR YOUNG

The following were the attached exhibits to the affidavit:

Exhibit C   copy

PITCH

HELLO MAY I SPEAK WITH____PLEASE? MY NAME IS____AND I'M CALLING FROM
FRONTIER FINANCIAL SERVICES. WE ARE A NATIONAL FINANCIAL SERVICE
COMPANY AND WE NETWORK 65 BANKS NATION WIDE. THE REASON I'AM CALLING
YOU TODAY IS THAT A REASON UPDATE IN OUR COMPUTER FILES SHOWS THAT
YOU HAD APPLIED FOR A VISA AND MASTERCARD, AND AT THIS TIME, WE SHOW
YOU AS ELIGIBLE FOR AN UNSECURED LINE OF CREDIT ON BOTH CARDS. ARE
YOU STILL INTERESTED IN RECEIVING A VISA OR MASTERCARD?

O.K., LET ME GET A CONFIRMATION ON YOU. WOULD YOU SPELL YOUR LAST
NAME PLEASE? AND YOUR MIDDLE INITIAL IS____. YOU STILL LIVE AT
(STREET ADDRESS) AND THATS (CITY, STATE, ZIP). IS ALL THAT CORRECT?

GREAT, I'LL GO AHEAD AND NOTIFY THE PROCESSING CENTER THAT I DID GET
A CONFIRMATION ON YOU. THEY WILL BE CALLING YOU BACK IN 5 TO 7
MINUTES TO GET YOUR VERIFICATION CODE NUMBER. NOW THE TELEPHONE
NUMBER I'M GOING TO GIVE YOU IS TO GET YOUR VERIFICATION CODE. NOW
(MR.OR MRS.)____THERE IS A ONE TIME PROCESSING FEE OF $50.00 THAT
COVERS BOTH CARDS. HOWEVER, THE GOOD NEWS IS THAT IT IS A ONE TIME
FEE AND NOT, I REPEAT, NOT AN ANNUAL FEE. IT IS ALSO GUARANTEED.
YOU'LL RECEIVE EVERYTHING IN 7-14 BUSINESS DAYS. AT THAT TIME YOU'LL
CHOOSE WHICH BANK IN OUR NETWORK THAT WILL ISSUE THE CARDS TO YOU.

DO YOU HAVE A PEN AND PAPER HANDY?

TAKE THIS NUMBER DOWN 1-900 AND I'LL EXPLAIN THAT IN A MOMENT
420-3838.

NOW, (MR.OR MRS.)____AS YOU CAN SEE THIS IS A 900 NUMBER AND IT IS
ASSOCIATED WITH TOLL CHARGES. HOWEVER, WHEN YOU CALL THIS NUMBER,
THE TOLL CHARGES HAVE ALREADY BEEN INCLUDED AND ACTUALLY MAKE UP THE
ONE TIME PROCESSING FEE. THERE ARE NO ADDITIONAL CHARGES.

WHEN YOU CALL THE NUMBER, YOU WILL BE ISSUED FROM A COMPUTER AN 8
DIGIT VERIFICATION CODE NUMBER AND YOU MUST WRITE IT DOWN CORRECTLY.
WHEN THE PROCESSING CENTER CALLS YOU BACK IN 5-7 MINUTES THEY WILL
ASK YOU FOR YOUR CODE NUMBER AND THEN ISSUE YOU OUT. DO YOU
UNDERSTAND?

O.K. GREAT, GO AHEAD AND CALL RIGHT NOW, REMEMBER TO WRITE YOUR CODE
NUMBER DOWN CORRECTLY, AND ENJOY YOUR NEW CREDIT CARDS.

Exhibit 2   copy

REBUTTALS

1) **AM I APPROVED?**
YOU ARE NOW ELIGIBLE TO RECEIVE BOTH CARDS.

2) **WHERE DID YOU GET MY NAME AND MY NUMBER?**
WHEN YOU APPLIED FOR A CREDIT CARD YOUR NAME GOES INTO THE
COMPUTER, AND WHEN YOU ARE ELIGIBLE WE CALL TO INFORM YOU.

3) **WHEN WILL`I RECEIVE MY CARDS?**
YOU WILL RECEIVE EVERYTHING FROM OUR OFFICE IN 7-14 BUSINESS
DAYS. THE CREDIT-CARDS SHOULD FOLLOW IN ABOUT 3 WEEKS FROM
THE BANK.

4) **IS THIS A SCAM?**
NO! WE HAVE A 98% ACCEPTANCE RATE, A FULL MONEY-BACK
GUARANTEE AND WE ARE A MEMBER OF THE BETTER BUSINESS BUREAU.

5) **AM I GUARANTEED A CREDIT-CARD?**
YOU WILL BE ISSUED A CARD THROUGH OUR SERVICE OR YOUR MONEY
BACK AND IT'S ALL GUARANTEED.

6) **WHAT IS THE INTEREST RATE?**
10.5%-16.5% THROUGH THE VARIOUS BANKS IN THE NETWORK OF 65.

7) **WHAT IS MY CREDIT LINE?**
THEY VARY FROM APPLICANT TO APPLICANT BETWEEN $500 AND $10,000.
I AM NOT PRIVILEGED TO KNOW THAT INFORMATION, THE BANK WILL
HAVE THAT FOR YOU.

8) **WILL THIS BE ON MY TELEPHONE BILL?**
YES, IT WILL BE BILLED THROUGH THE AT&T NETWORK WITHIN 6
WEEKS AS AN INCERT TO YOUR PHONE BILL. IS THIS BILLING
PROCESS A PROBLEM FOR YOU?

9) **I DON'T THINK I WANT THIS.**
SO YOU JUST DON'T WANT A VISA OR MASTERCARD. YOUR GONNA LET
$50 HOLD YOU BACK FROM GETTING THE CREDIT YOU NEED.

10) **WHY DO I HAVE TO CALL A 900 NUMBER?**
WE HAVE YOU CALL A 900 NUMBER SO THAT WE CAN DELAY THE BILLING
WITHIN 6 WEEKS.

11) **I HAVE A 900 BLOCK.**
IS THERE A FRIEND, NEIGHBOR OR RELATIVE YOU CAN MAKE THE CALL
FROM? IF YOU CANNOT, YOU CAN SEND IN YOUR PROCESSING FEE. IT
IS SLIGHTLY LESS. IT IS $40 IN THE FORM OF A CASHIER'S CHECK
OR MONEY ORDER. THE ADDRESS IS: **FRONTIER FINANCIAL SERVICES**
ATTN: (OPER #)
P.O.BOX 720245
ORLANDO, FL 32872-0245

WE CAN HOLD THE FILE OPEN FOR 10 BUSINESS DAYS - NO - MORE, SO
YOU NEED TO SEND THE PROCESSING FEE IMEDIATELY.

Exhibit 3   copy

VERIFIER

Hello, may I speak with   please? My name is
    and I'm calling you back from the Data Processing
Center here at Frontier Financial. I'm ready to issue you out.
Can you read me your code number please.

               #

    And your address is (street, city, state, zip). Is there an
apartment number?

    O.K. - Great! Go ahead and look forward to receiving
everything in 7-14 business days. At that time, simply choose
which bank in the network of 65 that you desire the cards issued
through. You are now eligible through all 65. Contact the bank
over their 800 line. All the information will be there for you.
And, the bank will have your approval and credit line for you.
And enjoy your new credit cards.

Exhibit 4 copy

FRONTIER
FINANCIAL SERVICES

The credit source of the 90's
Helping people help themselves

P.O. BOX 720245 • ORLANDO, FLORIDA 32872-0245 • CUSTOMER SERVICE CALL 407-826-9410

HOW TO GET A BANK LOAN

The first step is to acquire at least two bank loans. This method involves arranging secured loans at two different banking institutions. The process starts by depositing money into a secured savings account at a local bank (passbook savings account only). Shortly thereafter, a loan is secured from this bank using the passbook savings as collateral. The bank will gladly do this since a loan of this nature has no risk.

Simply take the money from this loan and then deposit it into the second bank the same as the first bank.

Wait two days before going back each time to apply for the loan. On your first trip to the bank go to the desk for "new accounts" and indicate that you want to open a simple passbook savings account, (do not put money into any other type of account even if it does pay a higher interest rate.) Take your passbook home and wait two days.

THE FIRST LOAN

Make sure you have your passbook with you along with all your information since you will be required to fill out an application. When you get to the bank ask to see a loan officer, greet warmly, and you might say you have a small business opportunity that has come up and that since you don't want to take money out of your savings, in addition to developing a borrowing relationship with the bank, you would like to borrow against your savings.

Actually, the bank could care less what the loan is for since it is 100% secured. Next you will be asked to fill out a credit application, this is standard. Again the loan is 100% secured and because of this fact, in many cases, you may be funded the same day. You may, however, be asked to come back the next day. But, in any case, the decision will be favorable.

Repeat this process for the second bank.

HOW TO LOCATE PARTICIPATING BANKS

Start by grabbing the local Yellow Pages and calling about 7-10 different banks. Ask for the loan department and ask the following questions: What is the minimum amount the bank will loan on a passbook savings account? Do you report credit activity to a credit reporting agency? What is the percent you can borrow?

Listed below are four examples of banks who will open a secured account along with their requirement. Minimums range from as little as $250 to $3,000. Most will have a $500 minimum and will let you borrow 100% of the amount on deposit. Try the local banks first before going out of town. Loans should be repaid in 4-16 weeks, remember banks are NUMBER ONE. Now you should have two bank loans and still have $250 to $500 cash in HAND! Next, go to "HOW TO GET MAJOR BANK CARDS."

Banks that Offer Savings Secured Loans

	RATE & PASS.	MIN. BORROWED	TRW?	% CAN BORROW	OUT OF STATE?		RATE & PASS.	MIN. BORROWED	TRW?	% CAN BORROW	OUT OF STATE?
California Federal 160 W. Foothill Upland, CA 91786 981-2821	12% 5%	$ 500	Y	90%	Y	Citicorp Savings Finance 1487 Foothill La Verne, CA 91750 593-7991	11%	$ 500	N	90%	Y
Chino Valley 818 N. Mountain Upland, CA 91786 946-6921	11% 5%	$1000	Y	100%	N	Empire Bank 7746 Haven Ave. Cucamonga, CA 91730 944-5200	18% 13%	$ 500	Y	100%	Y

Again your first effort should be to locate and call 7-10 local banks. These banks require $500 to $1,000 to get started, you will find many local banks that will require only $250 to open an account. However, the examples are real banks and their current requirements.

On November 13, 1991, National Telegroup, Inc., doing business as FFS, the owner, his mother, his father, the male manager, and the female manager were all indicted on 114 counts of wire and mail fraud. Prior to the indictment, I worked twelve to fourteen hours per day, including many weekends, conducting more than 150 interviews of FFS telemarketers, customers, and other witnesses, and sifting through the mountain of evidence seized from the search warrants at FFS. I worked well into the evenings calling customers from all over the country to determine potential witnesses for inclusion in the indictment as victims. I worked very closely with the AUSA and helped her prepare the indictment.

I prepared a questionnaire to be mailed to customers from both FFS and AICI. FFS had 29,000 customers of which I sampled 1,000 to be polled. AICI listed 234,000 customers in their computers that were seized, 6,000 of whom I sampled for the questionnaire. I personally had to complete this task of mailing out these questionnaires, which required applying labels to envelopes; stamping the FBI ORA address to 7,000 franked return envelopes; copying 7,000 three-page questionnaires; and stuffing the questionnaires and return envelopes into larger envelopes to be mailed to customers.

I spent a week working on this task and took items home in the evenings so the questionnaires were mailed out in a timely fashion. Within days, the responses began coming into the office. I had to review hundreds of responses to determine which customers would make the best witnesses in the case. I narrowed it down to about fifty or so customers and telephoned them. I advised the AUSA which victims were appropriate for inclusion in a superseding indictment, raising the number of counts to 171 against the five subjects. The superseding indictment was returned December 11, 1991.

I contacted appropriate representatives from all of the 65 banks and determined that none of the banks had any relationship at all with either FFS or AICI. I conducted interviews with representatives from VISA and MasterCard. I further interviewed the owners and management of two telephone service companies leasing 1-900 numbers to FFS and AICI. These two telephone companies acted as middlemen between the telemarketing companies and AT&T. I also interviewed representatives and attorneys with AT&T. Representatives from the Bankcard Holders of America, a non-profit organization in Washington, D.C., confirmed that the pamphlet provided to customers by FFS and AICI was identical to their pamphlet provided free to consumers.

I interviewed individuals across the country from companies that sold lead sheets to FFS and AICI. These computer printouts consisted of lists of names, addresses and telephone numbers of people who had previously been turned down for credit. This aspect of the investigation led me to speak with Citibank internal investigators who advised that a leak at Citibank in New York was enabling companies such as AICI and FFS to contact people with bad credit. They advised that their investigation determined that Citibank employees were illegally selling computer magnetic tapes containing 700,000 names per month of individuals being denied credit from Citibank. Two lead brokers in New Jersey and New York were reportedly selling the lists to lead companies throughout the country.

I spent hours on end dictating hundreds of FD-302s. The FD-302 was the form used by FBI agents to document evidentiary interviews or to document any evidence seized. I prepared countless leads to other field offices to conduct interviews and to serve subpoenas. I personally served more than thirty trial subpoenas locally in and around Orlando. I arrested four more subjects following the December FFS superseding indictment: the owner's father and mother, a male manager, and another female manager at FFS named Autumn, who had also previously worked at AICI. Autumn pled guilty and agreed to testify against all subjects from FFS and AICI.

I also found an outstanding witness against the owner of FFS. A telemarketer named Rhonda provided direct evidence to help prove his intent to defraud customers. The owner told Rhonda that their claim to customers of a ninety-eight percent acceptance rate was correct because he only made five or ten refunds per month. He told Rhonda that "people just figured they were screwed again." Rhonda said that the owner later refused to give refunds to any customers. She told him she could not keep lying to people and finally quit FFS.

In November 1991, at the height of my investigative activity, FGJ testimony, and trial preparation, I received my FBI transfer orders to WMFO. Normally, an agent had ninety days in which to report to his/her new office. However, in my case, the USAO requested that my transfer be delayed until the conclusion of the FFS trial, scheduled to begin January 21, 1992. I received new orders changing my reporting date to WMFO to May 1, 1992.

I was quite pleased that I would be returning to Maryland. I had called the SAC in Tampa the year before to request a rotational transfer to Baltimore or Washington. My mother had been battling leukemia since 1978 and then suffered a heart attack in December 1990. At that time, new agents were receiving Top-12 rotational transfers to major cities after serving three or four years in a smaller office. I explained my personal need to get back home to be near my mother. The SAC was most understanding and called the Transfer Unit at FBI Headquarters on my behalf. He told me that an immediate transfer to the Newark office was available. The SAC suggested that if I waited a year, I would most likely get a transfer to WMFO. One year later, after receiving my orders to WMFO, I immediately called the SAC to thank him. The SAC, in typical FBI management style, told me he was just glad that the needs of the Bureau coincided with my personal needs. He was not going to admit that his influence had any effect. I would nevertheless be eternally grateful to him. I was still at the point in my career when I believed in the FBI family.

The FFS trial started on my eighth wedding anniversary, January 21, 1992. Needless to say, my wife and I were not able to celebrate. During the three weeks prior to trial, I worked late into every evening and on weekends, including the entire Martin Luther King holiday on Monday, January 20, 1992. The AUSA and I prepared for the trial that long weekend, fourteen to sixteen hours each day.

In early January, the AUSA and I traveled to several states to prepare witnesses for trial. These were customers at FFS who could best articulate exactly how they were victimized. I assisted the USAO in arranging travel and lodging arrangements for many of the witnesses for trial. I was also responsible for organizing the sequence of all witnesses appearing at the trial, which totaled approximately eighty people. I organized trial exhibits for every witness each day. Throughout the trial, she and I worked late every evening preparing trial exhibits and witnesses for the next day's proceedings. The trial lasted thirteen days before going to the jury on Thursday, February 6, 1992.

The trial was very stressful. I began by testifying about my investigation and introducing more than one hundred trial exhibits, largely the evidence I had seized at FFS during the search warrants. This testimony was routine in nature, but took an entire day. The evidence consisted of the sales pitches, rebuttal sheets, verifier's pitches, the bank pamphlet, application files, job descriptions, refund files, complaint letters, leasing records, incorporation records, payroll records, FFS check stubs and cancelled checks, lead sheets, telephone bills, sales files, and a variety of other documents from FFS. I was also able to introduce evidence against the subjects whom I had interviewed, including the father, the mother, the male manager, and the female manager. I never interviewed the owner, so I could say nothing about him. I was allowed to refer to my FD-302 for each person I interviewed during my testimony.

The father, mother, and the male manager really said nothing incriminating during their interviews. The evidence against them derived mainly from customers testifying about their conversations over the telephone with them. The evidence I had on the female manager was that she admitted to me in an interview during the summer, and then again before the FGJ, that she knew AICI was a fraud. Yet she went to work at FFS in what she knew was an identical operation. The most unusual incident of the trial occurred when I tried to introduce evidence against her detailing her admissions.

The United States District Court Judge presiding at the trial would not allow me to testify against her and would not let me submit the transcript of her FGJ testimony as evidence for the jury. The judge's ruling for not allowing it to be entered as evidence was, he said, "It was exclusionary as to the jury." This was actually mumbo jumbo that had no legal meaning or precedent. No one at the USAO knew what it meant, except that the judge apparently did not want the female manager convicted, which she absolutely would have been had the jury been able to hear my testimony and read her FGJ transcript. We surmised that the judge did not want this pretty, but rather naïve and stupid, twenty-five-year-old girl, to go to prison.

He apparently did not want the mother to go to prison either. At the conclusion of the prosecution's case, prior to the defense presenting their case, the judge dismissed charges against the female manager and the mother. The case against the female manager was non-existent without my testimony against her or the FGJ transcripts, so that was understandable. However, the case against the mother was proven beyond a reasonable doubt. Customers with whom she spoke testified against her personally. The judge obviously felt that putting both the owner's mother and father in prison, as well as his best friend, was overkill. The judge spared the mother and the young girl, clearly out of sympathy. The evidence against all of the defendants in the case was rock solid.

On my second day of testimony, I was cross-examined for hours by the defense attorneys. The owner's attorney was the most brutal. I was accused of intimidating witnesses because of an incident that occurred on Monday morning, October 28, 1991. I went to an apartment where four employees at FFS resided. The Silver Hawk did not accompany me that day. I interviewed them alone. None of these four employees from FFS were particularly cooperative. In fact, two of them, brothers, were downright rude and belligerent. I spoke to each of them separately for over two hours. I interviewed one of the brothers last. He was the most disrespectful and very defensive of both the owner and the company. Upon leaving their apartment and listening to him and the others defend the fraud they committed, I lost my patience and told them that they were "full of shit" and that "I really hope you fucking guys testify for FFS because the prosecutor will rip you a new asshole on the stand." It was very unprofessional of me and clearly not the smartest thing I ever said during an investigation, but they were just pissing me off.

This incident was used against me at the trial to portray me as unprofessional and intimidating. Fortunately for me, this was the only time I lost my temper at anyone during the hundreds of interviews I conducted throughout the entire investigation. However, this fact did not prevent the defense attorney from asking every last witness if I cursed or pressured them for their testimony.

During my cross-examination, the defense attorney asked me about the October incident swearing at the FFS employees in their apartment. He first asked me if I was aware that the two brothers were youth ministers at their Christian church. Of course, I said no. He then asked me to state the exact words I said to them upon leaving their apartment at the conclusion of their interview. I was very uncomfortable talking about it and I did not want to repeat verbatim in court what I had said to them. He was hammering away at me and asking me every different kind of way he knew how to get me to repeat exactly what I said. All I would admit was that "I got frustrated with them and used some profane language." Finally, after he and I went back and forth several times, the judge interrupted and said, "I think what Agent Larsh is trying to say is that they were bullshit." The entire courtroom broke out in laughter. I could have kissed the judge. He saved me from embarrassment and we moved on.

On a break later, the Silver Hawk reassured me that nobody on the jury would have ever believed I intimidated witnesses. He just laughed at the thought of it, indicating that I was way too nice to ever be perceived as intimidating. The Silver Hawk was such a great guy.

The defense attorney then started asking me about the execution of the search warrants, shutting down FFS, and how I was responsible for putting all these poor telemarketers out of work. He then made the mistake of asking me about seizing the FFS bank account and preventing the employees from getting paid. I reminded him that although we did identify $730,000 in forfeitable assets, we were only able to seize $5,000, in view of the fact that the owner had diverted $162,000 to the defense attorney himself and his law firm as a retainer for services to defend him in this case. At the next break in the lobby, the defense attorney said to me, "Agent Larsh, I have to congratulate you for sticking it up my ass in there about my retainer." I felt great about receiving that compliment. If he only knew how truly uncomfortable I was.

My biggest fear testifying was breaking out in a sweat in front of everyone. I was so relieved that it was not hot in the courtroom. If I had been just a little warm and started sweating, I never would have stopped. I always perspired out my forehead and upper lip. I never perspired from my underarms for some reason. I kept thinking that the jury would never have believed anything I had to say if I was sitting there like Richard Nixon with sweat on my upper lip, or even worse, with sweat dripping from my forehead. Thankfully, this never occurred during my testimony.

The trial ended with a mountain of evidence against the three remaining defendants. The defense attorneys were hammering away that their clients were running a legitimate business selling pamphlets on how to improve credit, and were not trying to sell credit cards. The jury deliberated for two and a half days. On Tuesday, February 11, 1992, the jury returned its verdict. The FFS corporation was found guilty on 49 counts of conspiracy, wire fraud, mail fraud, and money laundering. The owner was convicted on 52 counts of the same. The father was convicted on 38 counts of conspiracy, wire fraud, and mail fraud. The male manager was convicted on 39 counts of the same. They were convicted on every count listed in the indictment against them.

Following the announcement of the guilty verdicts, the prosecutor reacted with jubilation. I did not show any emotion after the verdict, inasmuch as I did not want to appear to be gloating. In fact, I left the courtroom immediately to call my wife with the good news. As I entered the elevator to go down to the USAO, the owner's two brothers followed me in. The younger brother was full of emotion and angst. He looked at me with a great deal of contempt. I sensed that he was going to take a swing at me. I looked at him and said, "Don't do it. You don't want to assault a federal officer." I then glanced at his older brother who looked a bit more level-headed. The elevator then opened on the third floor and I walked out. I had come in contact with the brothers two months previously when I seized two new Cadillacs at their home in St. Cloud. The younger brother was particularly irate at that time too.

These convictions had the effect that the AUSA had hoped for. Following the trial, the AICI subjects, including the mastermind of the entire fraud, the President of AICI, began negotiations for plea agreements with the USAO. Two days after the convictions of the FFS subjects, the FFS owner's attorneys advised the AUSA that their client would be willing to provide assistance to the government's case against AICI and testify against them. This was quite common in federal cases in all crimes. A federal defendant could receive a reduction in sentencing with substantial cooperation. The FFS owner was obviously willing to do all that he could to lessen his sentence. Defendants in the federal system generally had to serve approximately eighty-five percent of their sentences.

FFS and the defendants in the case were convicted on money laundering charges totaling $730,000. The FFS owner's 1991 and 1992 Cadillac El Dorados, worth $33,000 and $37,000, respectively, purchased with FFS funds, were seized and forfeited by the government. Unfortunately, we only found $5,000 left in their bank account. We also seized about $10,000 worth of computers during the search warrants. The real money was seized from AICI. Approximately $100,000 worth of computer equipment was seized from AICI and its affiliates during the execution of the eight search warrants on May 29, 1991. Subsequent to the AICI search warrants, more than $2.5 million was seized from AICI's bank accounts, and two vehicles registered to AICI, a 1991 BMW worth $72,000, and a 1991 Porsche worth $60,000, were seized.

On February 19, 1992, the female manager co-conspirator, Autumn, who testified against the FFS defendants at trial was sentenced to 16 months by the presiding judge at the trial. On April 15, 1992, the judge sentenced the owner, his father, and the male manager to 70, 30, and 27 months imprisonment, respectively.

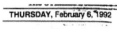

THURSDAY, February 6, 1992

Bank card deal called a swindle

☐ The victims will tell an Orange County jury that instead of getting a credit card they got a booklet that cost $50.

By Jim Leusner
OF THE SENTINEL STAFF

Dolores Kinsey was sick in bed Sept. 28 when the phone rang in her Beverly, N.J., home. It was a representative from Frontier Financial Services in Orlando, who said she was pre-approved for a low-interest Mastercard.

The timing of the call couldn't have been better. Kinsey, 56, had two other credit cards charged to the limit, and Christmas was fast approaching. She accepted.

A month later, Kinsey found she was one of 29,000 people nationwide who prosecutors say were scammed by slick-talking Orlando telemarketers promising low-interest credit cards from a network of 65 banks.

All Kinsey said she got for her $50 processing fee — charged to her phone bill for calling a 900 phone number to verify the deal — was a "stupid booklet" explaining how to rehabilitate her credit and where to apply for bank credit cards.

"I was furious," said Kinsey, a McDonald's shift manager. "I have five children, and you're out $50 you could spend on your kids."

Please see **CREDIT, B-5**

Witnesses to tell jury that a credit card deal was a scam

CREDIT from B-1

Kinsey complained to her telephone company, AT&T, and later received a credit because it was the first time she had called a 900 number. But most of the 29,000 customers weren't so lucky.

Over the past 2½ weeks, two dozen customers and former employees testified about the inner workings of Frontier Financial Services Inc., which operated from May to October 1991. The company, its owner and two top employees are on trial in U.S. District Court in Orlando, charged with 55 counts of mail fraud, wire fraud and money laundering. The jury will begin deliberations this morning.

In closing arguments Wednesday, Assistant U.S. Attorney ▮ charged that Frontier and its owner, ▮, preyed on working-class people desperate for credit.

The case centers around ▮, a 23-year-old salesman who left another telemarketing company, Advanced Interactive Communications Inc. of Altamonte Springs in March. He formed his own company and grossed $1.4 million over four months. Internal Revenue Service agent ▮ testified.

Eight AICI offices and subsidiaries were raided in May by federal agents armed with search warrants, who are investigating sales practices at those firms. FBI agent Bill Larsh testified. That investigation led FBI and IRS agents to ▮'s company offices at 5454 Hoffner Ave. and 9521 S. Orange Blossom Trail.

While there to interview former AICI employees in October, agents overheard what they believed were fraudulent sales pitches and arrested ▮ and another employee. No charges have been filed against AICI or its subsidiaries.

On trial are Frontier: ▮; his father, ▮, 48, both of St. Cloud; and ▮, 23, of Orlando. Judge ▮ threw out charges against ▮'s mother, 42, of St. Cloud. A fourth employee pleaded guilty to a conspiracy charge and three others were placed in a program similar to probation that will clear their names if they stay out of trouble.

Defense attorneys ▮ and ▮, who represent Frontier and ▮, respectively, argued that ▮ was an inexperienced businessman who worked in telemarketing only since January 1991.

They argued his intentions were good and planned to refund money to dissatisfied customers but was thwarted by agents who shut down his business.

They said the company only was selling the credit information booklet, not credit cards.

FBI agent Larsh testified that lists of customers who were denied credit were purchased by Frontier officials and used to seek out business.

Many of those recently were rejected from Citibank in New York, which had an employee arrested last fall for selling confidential credit-denial lists to customer list brokers, he testified.

Orlando Sentinel, dated 2/6/1992, regarding telemarketing case.

My Rio Pinar Country Club friends in Orlando in April 1992, giving me a fun
send-off.

A fake newspaper article given to me by an ORA co-worker
at my going away luncheon. Big joke!

CHAPTER 11

MOM

After the trial, my wife and I took our children on a ten-day house hunting trip, paid in full by the FBI in connection with my transfer to WMFO. We decided to move to Crofton, Maryland, due to its proximity to Washington and Baltimore. The commute to Washington, D.C. from Crofton was an hour's drive, twenty-five miles away. My parents' home in Perry Hall was about forty miles north. Cindy's mother's and grandmother's house in Lisbon was about forty miles to the west. We found a very nice home on Crofton Parkway, two doors down from the police station and next to the Crofton Elementary School and playground, conveniently located out the back gate of our fenced-in yard. My parents came to see the house on the house hunting trip. I asked my father to inspect it for me. He gave it the thumbs up.

I returned to Orlando to finish up my cases and to prepare to transfer. I was still busy at work my last six weeks in Orlando. I testified before the FGJ on the AICI case in March 1992. I reassigned the AICI case and my other cases before I departed. My last month in the ORA was largely spent helping other agents on their cases with interviews and arrests.

I looked forward to my transfer to be closer to my mother. She had not been well in the last few months. She developed a horrible fever blister over Christmas that was still there in March when we saw her on the house hunting trip. Her leukemia had apparently gotten so bad that her immune system could not even fight off a fever blister. She was, however, in very good spirits during our visit in March. She seemed extremely happy that we would be moving closer to home. She loved her grandchildren and constantly told me that I had the two most beautiful children. However, I called her in April and she sounded really depressed. She was not herself and was apparently losing her zest for life. I did not know it at the time, but I learned later that she had been telling my father how she wanted a funeral mass when she died. She had mentioned this to Cindy at Christmas because she said nobody would listen to her. My father was always very optimistic and I knew he did not want to hear anything like that. However, by the time we got to Maryland in May, I learned that my mother had spent two weeks in the hospital with pneumonia. She was released and sent home, but was still receiving drugs intravenously (IV). My father said he did not want to tell me about her worsening condition since I had too much to worry about with my transfer.

After transferring to WMFO and moving to Crofton, we visited my parents' house over the weekend the first week of May 1992. My mother was in her nightgown pulling around her IV stand and was very thin. One of her lifelong friends, Ruth "Toodles" Clark, came for a visit. We sat in the living room talking. Toodles was her normal self, very outgoing and full of life. My mother was usually the same. However, on this day, my mother did not smile once. She was obviously not well. She said very little and was visibly depressed. Her friend tried very hard to be upbeat, but my poor mother was not up to being even mildly sociable due to her deteriorating condition.

Unfortunately, I had to go to work Monday through Friday. Cindy visited my mother during the week and tried to help her in any way she could, but there was not much anybody could do. The cancerous white blood cells had taken over her body. She did not have long to live and she knew it. She reiterated her desire to Cindy for a full funeral mass. Cindy told her she would get better, which only made my mother more persistent with her request. She told Cindy that this was what my father would say to her. Cindy finally did promise that she would remember her wishes for a funeral mass. None of us wanted to believe she would die.

Over the previous fourteen years, my mother battled her leukemia valiantly, beating numerous bouts with pneumonia. We all thought this time would be no different. At the end of May, she was admitted to St. Joseph's Hospital in Towson, Maryland. We went to visit her on the weekend and she seemed better and more vibrant. Her older brother came to visit her, which picked up her spirits considerably. The two of them were laughing and having a good time. When I was talking to her, she was being a mom. I was telling her that I had more time to run and work out at my new job at WMFO. She told me that running was not good for my joints and knees. When we were leaving, Cindy was holding our nine-month-old daughter. I was holding my two and a half-year-old son's hand. My mother didn't scold me exactly, but asked me sternly why I didn't want to hold the baby. I merely said, "Cindy's got her." Little did I know that these would be the last words we would say to one another.

When we returned to the hospital the next Sunday, she had slipped into a coma. I remember wanting so badly to tell her that I had won my flight the day before in the Crofton Country Club Golf Championship. My mother had for years told me to quit golf because she hated seeing me disappointed after not playing well. I was astonished to find her unconscious in her hospital bed. My father had said nothing to me of her worsening condition. The nurse came in and laid a ventilator on the bed next to her. My father told Cindy and me that she had been sleeping the previous two days. My father still seemed optimistic, which gave me some hope. I had seen her in bad shape with pneumonia in the past so I believed that she would recover.

The next day at work at about 4 p.m., I received a telephone call from my wife. She said my father had called her and advised that we should come to the hospital right away. I told my new SSA at WMFO that I had to leave. She lost her husband about two years previously, the former Assistant Director in Charge of WMFO, who had died suddenly of a heart attack. She was obviously very understanding. I drove my Bureau car, a 1984 Oldsmobile Delta 88 with about 130,000 miles on it, as fast as I could north on the Baltimore-Washington Expressway to the hospital.

On Monday evening, June 8, 1992 at 7:20 p.m., my mother died with her five children, her husband, and Cindy by her bedside. I don't remember if anybody else was there. Everyone became very excited when she opened her eyes shortly before she passed. I was holding her right hand when she opened her eyes a second time. I then saw her take her last breath. My father stood at the other side of the bed. I told him that she stopped breathing. Her eyes remained open so I shut them. My sisters began crying hysterically. I remember looking up and feeling her presence above us. I knew that she had opened her eyes one last time to say goodbye.

Her death was difficult to accept for all of us because of the fact that we had seen her battle back from pneumonia many times before to continue a normal life. However, this time she succumbed to the leukemia. The doctor said that cancerous white blood cells had multiplied to such a degree in her liver, enlarging it way beyond normal size, that nothing could have been done to save her.

I went into the hall and immediately called my uncle. He said he would call his siblings to let them know of her passing. Mom passed away at the age of sixty-six, far too soon. I felt cheated that I would never see my mother again. I was only thirty years old. I was saddened to think that she would never see my children grow up. She loved them so much and seemed to take such joy being around them. I went home with my father that night and spent the night in my boyhood bedroom. After we had walked through the front door to a house we knew would never be quite the same without my mother in it, we both broke down in tears and embraced one another in the living room for several minutes. It was heart wrenching to lose the sweetest woman we ever knew. She was a loving and devoted wife and the most wonderful mother to all of her children. All of our lives centered around her and now nothing would ever be the same.

Two things happened that night that remained with me forever. While my father and I hugged and cried together in the living room, he told me that I could take comfort in knowing that Cindy and I had the same love for each other that he and Mom had. Then after I went to sleep, I had the most vivid dream of my mother moving across the sky on a cloud, like an angel, but without wings. She was at peace and told me that everything was going to be all right.

The next morning was even more surreal. I went with my father to the Schimnuek Funeral Home in Perry Hall to pick out a casket. I called my SSA and told her my mother had died. She told me to take as much time off from work as I needed. She was very sympathetic and asked me to call her with the funeral arrangements, which I did later that day. The viewings at the funeral home were scheduled for Tuesday, Wednesday, and Thursday evening. A funeral mass was planned for Friday morning at 9 a.m. at St. Joseph's Catholic Church in Fullerton, three miles south of my parents' home. Our family had attended St. Joseph's Parish since 1961 when the family moved to Perry Hall from Baltimore City.

The priest conducting the funeral mass was one of only a handful of Catholic priests in the world who was actually married with children. He had previously been a priest in the Episcopalian Church, but had converted to Catholicism. The Catholic Church allowed him to become a Catholic priest. I had attended Mass many times when he was leading Mass. He was a great speaker. He seemed more insightful and much more down to earth than most other priests. His homilies were always more poignant, maybe because he was more like everybody else in the congregation. He was also more impressive than the other priests because he never used notes. He would step out from behind the lectern and speak to the congregation at the front of the altar. He spoke beautifully at my mother's funeral mass. The music made me cry like a baby, especially when the choir sang *How Great Thou Art* and *Amazing Grace*.

I was quite touched when several of my new co-workers from my squad at WMFO came to pay their respects. My SSA came to the funeral home in Perry Hall, northeast of Baltimore, all the way from her home in northern Virginia. Two other agents from the squad also came to the funeral home. On Friday morning at the gravesite in St. Joseph's Church Cemetery, I noticed that the entire squad had shown up for the funeral. I was moved by their thoughtfulness. I had only known them and been working with them for a little over a month.

When I got back to work, I thanked each person on the squad individually. Everyone was very gracious and said they were sorry for my loss, except for one agent. This ignorant agent responded, "Well, it was a free day off." I would never forget his callous remark.

This was not the only inappropriate thing said to me following my mother's death. At the wake at my parents' house, the laughing and the party atmosphere bothered me. I was at the lowest point of my life and I was uncomfortable with people having a good time less than an hour after my mother was buried. Then my aunt came up the steps from the basement and asked me, "Where is Granddad Fowler's framed portrait that was hanging in the basement?" I took that to mean that she wanted it now that my mother had died. I could have been wrong, but that's the way it sounded.

I was told that my mother was her father's favorite. I don't know how, but she ended up with the earliest known picture taken of her father, a large professionally made photograph in an approximately two-foot long oval-shaped frame. The picture appeared to have been taken when he was about twenty years old. He was born in 1893 and died on March 29, 1962. My mother missed his funeral on April 2nd because she was still in the hospital after giving birth to me the day before. I told my aunt at the wake that my mother had given it to my other aunt a year or two ago. I remember being disappointed that my mother gave this picture away. I loved family history and genealogy. She gave it away because my mother was the sweetest, most generous person I ever knew. She truly never wanted anyone to be unhappy.

I couldn't bear any more of the atmosphere at the wake and went outside. I sat on a set of steps in our front yard leading down to the sidewalk by the street. I was sitting there in my own thoughts, trying not to cry when my boyhood friend came up the street. I had not seen him at the funeral, but I figured it was nice of him to have at least come up to see me and give his condolences. However, his idea of condolences was not the same as mine. His only remark concerning my mother's death was that, "We're all just organisms, and all organisms die." I have not seen him in almost twenty-five years. I am glad I never saw him again, because this unfeeling and insensitive remark stuck with me forever.

I went back to work one week to the day after my mother's passing. It had been one hellacious week, the worst of my life, but I was not one to wallow in self-pity. I also felt it was my duty to get back to work.

CHAPTER 12

AICI

I was requested by the USAO to return to Orlando several times following my transfer to WMFO. Only two weeks after arriving, I had to return for a week in May 1992 to testify before the FGJ. At the end of June 1992, I returned again to assist the AUSA in a proffer (an offer of cooperation by a defendant prior to a formal plea agreement with the USAO) by the President of AICI and his attorney. During the summer of 1992, I went back to testify before the FGJ two more times before finally indicting the corporation in August. Then, a year later in July 1993, I returned to testify at trial. The dates of my testimony at trial fell right in the middle of a previously planned vacation in Ocean City, Maryland. We stayed Saturday to Saturday, but I had to leave for Orlando that Monday through Wednesday.

The trial went well and was not nearly as contentious as the first trial had been with the FFS attorney. The AICI attorney was a former AUSA turned defense attorney. I had previously worked with him and liked him. He was a genuinely nice fellow and not as aggressive or abrasive as the FFS attorney. My AUSA and the IRS Agent told me not to be as combative as I had been in the first trial. The AUSA told me to just answer the questions and she would object or handle any problems on cross-examination. The trial was against the corporation, AICI, to criminally forfeit AICI's assets. The President of AICI pled guilty in March 1993, but the Vice-President at AICI was not cooperating and did not want to forfeit the $2.5 million in AICI assets already seized.

My only uncomfortable moment in the trial came when the AICI attorney asked me if I knew what a "Forthwith" FGJ subpoena was. I had never served or even heard of a Forthwith FGJ subpoena. All of the FGJ subpoenas I ever served had a date and time on them for the person being served to appear. I was not familiar with it, but I figured out quickly what he meant and where he was going with his questioning. He was attempting to present a defense that AICI did not intentionally defraud customers and were refunding thousands of customers at the time the FBI raided the eight offices on May 29, 1991. His contention was that the execution of the search warrants and the subsequent seizures of all AICI's identifiable assets prevented AICI, a legally registered and above-board company, from fulfilling its obligations to all its dissatisfied customers.

The attorney asked me if I could have gotten all the records and documents from AICI and its subsidiaries through the issuance of a Forthwith FGJ subpoena, instead of executing search warrants and shutting down the business. I answered that I could have, but we opted to do the search warrants. I never liked the way I answered his question, but the AUSA had instructed me not to be combative. It really made no difference at all and the AUSA did not even follow up with any questions about it. I think the jury realized the search warrants were appropriate in order to obtain all the evidence.

On July 22, 1993, AICI was convicted in federal court of bilking over 250,000 customers nationwide out of $12.5 million in a bogus credit card scheme. The jury needed only two and a half hours of deliberation to find the corporation guilty on 3 counts of wire fraud and 17 counts of money laundering, resulting in the criminal forfeiture by the government of the previously seized AICI's assets, consisting of more than $2.5 million in cash, cars, computers and telephone equipment.

This concluded my participation in what turned out to be my single greatest accomplishment in a criminal investigation for my career. The remainder of the defendants in the case, the Vice-President of AICI, and several other owners of the AICI subsidiaries that were raided on May 29, 1991, all pled guilty to wire fraud following the AICI conviction. I was always extremely proud of my efforts in this case, particularly since I initiated the case myself, convinced the SSRA to remove it from the unaddressed work file, and virtually investigated the case on my own, notwithstanding the invaluable assistance from the IRS agent. If it had not been for my initiative, this telemarketing fraud might never have been stopped as quickly as it was.

My efforts in ending this fraud had a resounding effect on what was becoming a pervasive problem in telemarketing fraud in the Central Florida area at that time. As a direct result of my investigations and the subsequent convictions of the subjects, the 1-900 number credit card scams virtually disappeared. Prior to my investigations, there were hundreds of these telemarketing rooms nationwide offering credit cards through the use of 1-900 numbers. The execution of my search warrants on May 29, 1991 had the direct effect of simultaneously closing forty of these rooms nationwide since AICI was the subscriber to all of the 1-900 numbers for its forty subsidiaries. AICI also handled customer service and the mailing of the pamphlets from its Altamonte Springs location. In addition, as a direct result of my investigation, AT&T decided to discontinue all of their 1-900 numbers related to credit cards and credit information, effective January 31, 1992. Sprint Telephone discontinued the use of their 1-900 numbers in these types of businesses in August 1991.

The FBI had never before investigated this type of telemarketing fraud. The industry offering credit through the use of 1-900 numbers was in its infancy and was an entirely new type of boiler room operation in which the perpetrators of the fraud tried very hard to convince law enforcement that these were legitimate operations. My persistence in gathering overwhelming evidence in this matter proved beyond any reasonable doubt that this activity was in fact a crime, and for this I was truly proud.

At the conclusion of the FFS trial, the SSRA asked me to prepare a summary of the case for a recommendation to receive a cash incentive award. I subsequently received $1,200. He later told me right before my transfer he had planned to put me in for a Quality Step Increase (QSI), but couldn't because an agent couldn't receive both a cash award and a QSI in the same year. A QSI was better than a cash award. A QSI would have increased my pay every year until my next grade increase. In other words, I was a GS-12, step 1 at that time. My promotion to a GS-13 would not have occurred for another three years. The QSI would have been the equivalent of a $2,400 incentive award every year for the next three years. The SSRA apologized to me and said he didn't realize an agent could not receive a QSI if they had received an incentive award in the same year. The irony of my misfortune was that the forfeitures to the government in these two telemarketing cases far exceeded my total FBI salary for my entire twenty-seven and a half year career. This episode would not be the last time that receiving an incentive award for my work would leave a sour taste in my mouth.

U.S. Department of Justice

Federal Bureau of Investigation

Office of the Director   Washington, D.C. 20535

April 2, 1992

PERSONAL

Mr. William A. Larsh
Federal Bureau of Investigation
Tampa, Florida

Dear Mr. Larsh:

    I have learned of your outstanding efforts in connection with the Fraud by Wire investigation involving Bruce Grossman and others, and I am pleased to commend you. The enclosed check is representative of an award you have merited.

    Throughout this complex operation, you effectively utilized a myriad of investigative and interviewing techniques to achieve success. You displayed great initiative by reviewing voluminous financial transactions under the most difficult conditions, and you implemented a system to have the list of evidence entered into the computer. In order to determine the best possible witnesses for this case, you prepared and mailed detailed questionnaires to numerous customers of the companies involved. You quickly processed the results and contacted the prime subjects to be used as witnesses. During the trial, you devoted a tremendous amount of time and effort creating court exhibits and assisting the Assistant U.S. Attorney with all facets of witness preparation. Because of your invaluable contributions, the results of this project were truly positive, and I wish to personally thank you for a job well done.

Sincerely yours,

William S. Sessions
Director

Enclosure

FBI/DOJ

Letter of Commendation and Incentive Award, dated 4/2/1992, from Director William S. Sessions.

U.S. Department of Justice

United States Attorney
Middle District of Florida

Orlando Division
201 Federal Building
80 North Hughey Avenue
Orlando, Florida 32801-2280

407/648-6700

November 19, 1993

Louis J. Freeh, Director
Federal Bureau of Investigation
9th and Pennsylvania Avenues
Washington, D.C. 20535

Dear Mr. Freeh:

    Re: Commendation for Special Agent William Larsh
           Federal Bureau of Investigation, Washington Metro Field Office
           Washington, D.C.

    I would like to commend Special Agent William Larsh, of the Washington Metro Field Office, for his assistance to this office in the investigation and prosecution related to a nationwide telemarketing scheme which resulted in a fraud perpetrated on over 250,000 individuals.

    It has been brought to my attention that it is largely due to Special Agent Larsh's diligent efforts that we achieved success in stopping this fraudulent activity and obtaining convictions on various fraud and money laundering charges as to seven individuals. In addition, this office was successful in forfeiting approximately $3,000,000 in cash and other assets.

    This investigation involved a network of telemarketing rooms that spanned the United States, but was controlled and organized in Orlando, Florida. The case involved a tremendous amount of investigative work, including the execution of nine separate search warrants, the review of literally rooms of documents, and the coordination of almost 100 grand jury witnesses. The entire investigation spanned approximately two and one half years. Special Agent Larsh worked on the investigation throughout this entire period of time, marshalling evidence, locating and interviewing witnesses, and assisting at two trials related to this scheme, each trial lasting between two to three weeks. Special Agent Larsh was an integral part of the trial team on each of the trials.

Letter of Commendation (p. 1), dated 11/19/1993, to Director Louis J. Freeh from United States Attorney, Middle District of Florida, Orlando, Florida.

This telemarketing scheme was executed as follows: telemarketers were employed to telephone individuals who had recently been denied a Visa or Mastercard credit card, and instructed to use a fraudulent sales pitch to convince those customers that they had now been approved for a credit card and that they needed to call a 1-900 telephone number to obtain their confirmation numbers. This resulted in over 250,000 people calling the 1-900 numbers controlled by the targets of the investigation, each victim incurring a $50 charge. The total loss to the consuming public was over $12,000,000. As a result of this investigation, both AT&T and MCI now refuse to allow individuals selling "credit information" to obtain 1-900 telephone numbers. Accordingly, the investigation not only had an impact on stopping the individuals who were currently perpetrating this fraud, but essentially eliminated the ability of any person to accomplish this particular fraud in the future.

Special Agent Larsh exhibited the highest level of professionalism and diligence. In many instances, the successful completion of the investigation, as well as preparation for the criminal trials, required extremely long work days, and dedication of weekend time. Special Agent Larsh unfailingly put forth whatever efforts were necessary into achieving the successful result described above.

Please accept my congratulations and extend my thanks to Special Agent William Larsh for a job well done. Through his efforts, we ended a fraudulent scheme of nationwide scope, which was directed at a group in our population that could ill afford to be the victims of crime.

Very truly yours,

DOUGLAS N. FRAZIER
United States Attorney

Letter of Commendation (p. 2), dated 11/19/1993, to Director Louis J. Freeh from United States Attorney, Middle District of Florida, Orlando, Florida.

CHAPTER 13

WMFO

Working at WMFO was at a much slower pace than I had been accustomed to in the ORA. I worked many evenings and weekends during my time assigned in the ORA. I didn't mind working the extra hours and days because it was very satisfying, worthwhile, and often fun. I worked with other dedicated agents like myself who would help me at any time and I would always reciprocate when they needed assistance. Not every agent in the ORA had this attitude, but most did. A few of the older agents did not want to work nights or weekends and would only do so if directed by the SSRA. The rest of us did whatever needed to be done and we would stay out all night if circumstances required it. Some of the agents working FCI in the ORA never wanted to help. They were supervised by an SSA in Tampa. The SSRA could not force them to assist in criminal matters, however, some of them always volunteered.

At WMFO, I was assigned to work FCI. WMFO was one of the larger FBI offices. The majority of agents worked at Buzzard's Point in an old building overlooking the Anacostia River, the second most polluted river in the country at that time, I was told. Agents also worked at the Northern Virginia Resident Agency (NVRA) located in Tysons Corner, Virginia. NVRA agents mainly worked white collar crime and public corruption matters. I was assigned to an FCI squad, CI-10, based on the manpower needs of WMFO. It had nothing to do with my background, as I had no FCI experience, nor did it have anything to do with my own personal preference. I had no say in the matter and was never asked. However, the location at Buzzard's Point was a far better one for commuting from Crofton, Maryland, than the NVRA. It took me less than an hour to get to Buzzard's Point. Tysons Corner was on the other end of the I-495 Washington Beltway and would have added at least another forty minutes to my commute, depending on traffic.

My squad at Buzzard's Point was an open area with four rows of wooden desks lined up four across. It was referred to as the "bullpen." The main goal on the squad was to recruit foreign nationals to spy for the United States. I thought that I would never be able to accomplish anything like that since I did not speak a foreign language. The reigning star on the squad spoke a foreign language fluently and had recruited individuals in the past. This agent seemed impressed with my criminal background and was very interested in my telemarketing case, which was still being prosecuted in Orlando. He told me that it was good to have someone on the squad with a perspective in working criminal cases since everyone else on the squad had only worked counterintelligence matters during their careers.

I attended two FCI training in-services at Quantico after being assigned to Squad CI-10. The first was an introduction to FCI and the second was an FCI Undercover Seminar. At one of these conferences, an FCI street agent from San Francisco gave a two-hour, pointless, boring, rambling presentation regarding his case targeting an official at a foreign consulate. At the conclusion of the in-service, students were asked to anonymously evaluate each speaker. These evaluations were used by FBI Headquarters personnel to improve training, but were not seen by the guest speakers. I wrote positive comments for all of the speakers, except the San Francisco agent. For his assessment, I wrote a rather sarcastic and scathing response. A few weeks later, the star agent, seated next to me on the squad, hung up the telephone after speaking with an SSA at FBI Headquarters. He turned to me, chuckling, and said the SSA told him that some agent who attended the recent FCI training in-service wrote an evaluation regarding a San Francisco agent's presentation, stating, "I'd rather be hit in the head with a ball-peen hammer than listen to him for two hours." I burst out laughing and told him, "That was me!"

The agents on the squad were strictly nine to five agents. I really did not mind this after all the time I had put in at the ORA. It was nice to get home at dinner time. I usually got to work by 7:30 a.m. and left at 5 or 5:30 p.m. It was a relatively easy day. The first half-hour was spent reading the newspaper.

At lunch time, I worked out at the gym at Ft. McNair, which was no more than a mile away. I lifted weights and ran three to four miles around the base. The star agent on the squad generally went there to work out too. The other agents either went to Ft. Myers in Arlington or to a private gym. Although work was at a far slower pace than the ORA, I still wanted to succeed and make a difference.

When I arrived on the squad, one agent had a recruitment at a foreign embassy. The official wanted to stay in the United States so he made a deal with the FBI to provide information in return for being able to remain in the United States. The star agent told me that the recruitment was of no value, insofar as he had no access to any secret intelligence information. He further told me that since the official was scheduled to go back to his home country, and therefore was leaving the embassy, he would not be able to report on anything current from the embassy. The FBI was really getting little, if nothing, in return for helping this diplomat remain in the United States.

Many of the foreign diplomats coming to the United States realized immediately that the standard of living was far above that of their own country. Yet, not many were willing to make the giant leap of staying in the United States, mainly due to their loyalty and devotion to their job, career, government, country, friends and family. The official recruited by this agent possibly decided to stay for a better life in this country. Whatever his motivation, the bottom line was that he had nothing to provide our government in terms of any vital intelligence. He could only offer general information regarding the organization at his embassy, which was already known. His only other value as a recruitment would have been his assessment of personalities of individuals at the embassy he knew or believed were intelligence officers, however, he had no knowledge of any intelligence officers.

A couple of months later, the agent received a $2,500 incentive award for this so-called recruitment. I could not help but think of the countless evening and weekend hours, the hundreds of interviews, the ten search warrants, the numerous arrests, indictments, convictions, trial preparation, and the seizure and forfeiture of almost $3 million in assets in my landmark telemarketing cases, and all I got was a lousy $1,200. I know this agent did not put in the effort I did. All he did was talk to this one person who revealed that he did not want to return home.

CHAPTER 14

RECRUITMENTS-IN-PLACE

I spent the next year and a half on the squad working diligently to the best of my abilities and trying to develop sources. I had done nothing extraordinary, but my SSA was happy with my efforts and could see I was an aggressive investigator. After about a year and a half, my chance for a big case came. It was nothing I did that led to this point other than my assigned responsibilities targeting a hostile foreign embassy. The press section at the embassy was one of many sections assigned to me.

One of the agents on the squad, a congenial, middle-aged agent who often fell asleep at his desk at around three in the afternoon, had one of the best sources on the squad, a retired CIA employee whose code name was Sam Spade. Sam Spade was an expert on the foreign government we monitored. He befriended many officials at their embassy and was invited to many functions there. He befriended a diplomat, a press spokesman for his government's embassy, who conveyed to him that he despised espousing the party line for a government whose policies and ideology he did not believe in. This information was passed on by Sam Spade to the FBI agent on my squad.

I finally had something drop right into my lap, a chance for a recruitment-in-place. It seemed easy, but I was terrified I would blow it. The agent arranged it for Sam Spade to introduce me to the diplomat at his house. I would make the pitch for recruitment. It was fairly simple and straightforward. I would have to listen to what the diplomat had to say and then convince him to work for the United States government. He was ripe for recruitment, but all eyes were on me to pull it off. It was decided by my SSA, with input from the veteran agents on the squad, that I should not present myself as the FBI. The veteran agent who was most helpful to me regarding my approach was an agent I will call Bob. I had the most respect and admiration for Bob.

Bob was the most interesting agent on the squad. He was a veteran agent looking forward to transferring and then retiring to his wife's hometown. He was number one on the OP list where his wife was from, due to his seniority. He had a peculiarity of arriving late to work every Monday morning. My closest friend on the squad told me why. He advised that Bob's greatest achievement in the FBI was an espionage case against a hostile foreign national. Bob had been debriefing the spy in prison after he pled guilty and was awaiting sentencing. During this time, however, the individual hanged himself in his cell one night. This event apparently affected Bob psychologically in a profound and lasting manner. Bob arrived late to work every Monday morning for the rest of his career. He apparently could not sleep Sunday nights in anticipation of starting the workweek. He was always two to three hours late, calling in sick every Monday morning.

The other fascinating story was one in which Bob told me himself. It turned out Bob had been shot on the job. However, it was not what I had imagined, being shot in the line of duty. He was accidently shot by another agent on the squad who sat at the desk next to him. The agent was no longer on the squad when I arrived, having received his OP transfer years previous to my arrival. Bob described the shooter as a little high strung with slight obsessive-compulsive tendencies, but that he was generally a good guy and a good agent. The agent evidently organized his desk in a very orderly manner with nothing ever out of place.

One morning, while Bob was reading the *Washington Times* newspaper at his desk, this agent arrived to find a telephone book on his desk which he had not placed there the night before when he departed. He was visibly annoyed, and after picking up the telephone book, he slammed it on the empty desk to his right. Still agitated, the agent then grabbed at his holster with his loaded revolver to remove it from his waistline and place it inside his desk. The holster was the type in which a clasp on the back of the holster held it to his pants.

The manner and force in which the agent pulled at his holster to remove it caused him to accidently pull the trigger. The revolver went off and the .357 magnum caliber bullet from the gun was shot into the floor, ricocheting to the left and up toward the ceiling, grazing Bob's lower back before resting in the white tile of the hanging ceiling. Bob instinctively jumped forward over the front of his desk. He then felt a terrible burning sensation on his back where he knew he had been shot. He was so relieved shortly thereafter to learn that it was only a skin abrasion and nothing serious. He said, however, that he was naturally quite shaken from the event. The bullet was only inches from possibly causing him serious bodily harm or even death.

Bob said that during the subsequent shooting investigation by the FBI, he never divulged that the agent had been clearly agitated and forcibly and carelessly yanked his holster from his waist causing the gun to fire. Bob said the agent was wracked with guilt over what had happened and actually tried to give Bob one of his two Purple Hearts received during combat in Vietnam. Bob said he did not accept the medal. Bob said he would never rat out a fellow agent, not even in front of a FGJ. When I told Bob I would never lie under oath, he gave me a look in what I could only describe as one of disbelief and suspicion. However, I always liked and respected Bob. His advice to me regarding my approach to the diplomat for recruitment proved to be indispensable.

The foreign nationals being targeted by the FBI reportedly had a history of being very intimidated by the FBI. They viewed the FBI as sort of leather-booted thugs, similar to the Nazi Gestapo or Storm Troopers. Their perception could not have been further from the truth, but it was decided that I would use my undercover identification. I had used it a couple of times in the past to present myself to foreign nationals. My undercover identity was William J. Kelly. My father used an alias, Ed Kelly, largely for making dinner reservations and the like. He became irritated having to repeat or spell Larsh to people, so he said Kelly instead. Somebody bought him a t-shirt once with the name, Ed Kelly, printed on the back. I got a kick out of showing him my undercover identity. He loved it. My credentials showed that I worked for a fictitious government entity. I made up my own cover story that I worked for this group which was affiliated with the National Security Council. I also pretended to work in the Old Executive Office Building, although I had never set foot there.

THE FBI – THEY EAT THEIR YOUNG

William J. Kelly
Special Assistant

**Interagency Committee
For Asian Affairs**

Washington, D.C.   (202) 554-4986

My business card with my undercover identity.

One nice perk was that I got to drive an undercover vehicle, a 1986 Mercedes-Benz 450SL convertible. I never felt so delighted behind the wheel of a car in my entire life. That car drove like a charm. I would highly recommend getting one. My personal cars at the time were a 1984 Nissan Sentra hatchback and a 1987 Nissan Sentra four-door sedan without air conditioning, not even close to the quality of a Mercedes-Benz.

The meeting was set for Tuesday afternoon during the first week of March 1994. Sam Spade introduced me to the foreign national, a middle-aged man with a slight build and a kindness in his face. Sam Spade had us sit at his dining room table and then he excused himself to the basement. Sam Spade was told not to tell him I was with the FBI. I introduced myself as Bill Kelly and only divulged that I worked for the United States government. The foreign national did not question my credentials or even ask to see them. I guess he believed his friend had the connections to put him in touch with the right people. He proceeded to tell me exactly what was previously reported by Sam Spade to the agent on my squad.

The foreign national was very unhappy working at the embassy and did not believe in his government's policies. He told me of his associate, a younger female, who he said also did not believe in the policies of their country's government. He was of the opinion that his government would never change. He told me of the hardships he endured since he was a young man.

The foreign national made it clear that he did not want to go back to his home country at the end of his tour. He said that his associate had no desire to return either. I never specifically asked if they were in a romantic relationship, but I assumed they were. I told him that I could probably make that happen, but the two of them would have to work for me until their tours at the embassy ended. I told him I would have to speak to her as well.

He said that would not be a problem and that she felt the same way he did.

I asked him if he had access to secret information. He told me that he had full access and could pass on all of the information he obtained. He said, however, that his associate did not have access. I told him that I could only help him if he helped me. I could not make any promises as I would have to wait to determine if the information he provided was truly worthwhile.

He agreed that my terms were acceptable, but he said that he did not want our relationship to be strictly a business one. He could only proceed if we became friends. I responded that I believed we would indeed become friends. I was not really one hundred percent sure of this at the time, but I wanted to put him at ease and have him believe in me. However, I am a man of my word, so when I said I would be his friend, I fully intended to fulfill this promise. He would in fact become a very good friend to me. He has been truly one of the nicest people I have ever known. I promised him that if he helped me, I would do everything in my power to help him and that I would be his friend for life. I am glad I kept that promise. In the years to come, I did help him on several occasions long after our professional relationship had ended.

During my operation with these two recruitments-in-place, he and I met secretly every week in the evening in a room at the Embassy Suites Hotel in Washington, D.C. to discuss the information he gleaned from his embassy. His girlfriend was not a participant in the transfer of information. Nevertheless, I had fun with the entire operation and codenamed him, Miles Archer, and her, Brigid O'Shaughnessy, after the characters from the movie, *The Maltese Falcon*. Sam Spade was Miles Archer's private eye partner in the movie. However, the FBI did not approve my code names. They said they no longer allowed names of people as code names, but I continued to refer to them unofficially as these characters. I did spend one night at the hotel after a meeting with the recruitment feeling absolutely awful. After the recruitment departed, I turned on the television to watch the news. The top story of the day was the killing of two FBI agents, Martha Dixon-Martinez and Michael John Milner, and a Washington Metro Police Department Officer, Sergeant Henry "Hank" Joseph Daly.

A suspect in a triple homicide arrived at the Metro Police Department for questioning by members of the cold case homicide squad. The suspect opened fire, killing the two agents and the sergeant, and wounding another FBI agent and a fifteen-year-old boy. As I watched the news program, I not only felt bad about the killings, but I experienced the worst feelings of guilt. My job meeting the diplomat every week at the hotel seemed too easy. I was never in any danger.

About seven months later, another agent at WMFO, Bill Christian, was killed. Bill was the only slain agent I ever knew personally. I didn't know him well, nor did I ever work with him, but I saw him in the office on a daily basis and we exchanged pleasantries. He was forty-eight years old and a twenty-year veteran with only fourteen months remaining before being eligible for retirement. He was assigned to SOG at the time of his death. SOG was called out to assist in locating a fugitive whose approximate location was determined through pings on cellular telephone towers from the fugitive's cellphone. Bill had been scheduled to leave for Germany with his wife on a vacation the following morning. He could have been excused from going on the surveillance, but being the conscientious agent that he was, he participated. He parked his vehicle in a school parking lot. The fugitive, who was wanted for shooting and injuring two police officers, and was suspected in the murder of a third officer, spotted Christian in the parking lot. The fugitive approached the vehicle from the rear and executed him through the car window. Bill never saw it coming.

Despite these tragic incidents, my case continued. After the second meeting with the recruitment, he advised that he would try to surreptitiously take notes from secret communications he read at his embassy, inasmuch as the information was too voluminous to remember. By the third week, he arrived at our meeting with copious notes written in his native language. He explained that it was very risky, but that this was the only way to capture all of the details.

After a couple of months of the meetings at the hotel, he expressed an interest in meeting my family. Although I was in an undercover role and not revealing that I was in the FBI, I relayed the details of my actual personal life. It would be easy for him to meet my family. My children were only three and four years old and had no idea I worked for the FBI. My wife would have to remember two things: one, she was Cindy Kelly, and two, don't mention the FBI. Everything else could be the truth. In our first social meeting with them, my wife and I met them for dinner without the children.

The Larsh Family

The first order of business was getting permission from my SSA to take my wife in the Bureau undercover vehicle, my beloved 1986 Mercedes-Benz 450SL convertible. The FBI's most common misconduct issue was the misuse of a Bureau car. The Bureau car was strictly for business use. Any agents found misusing their vehicle were given an automatic 30-day suspension. If unauthorized passengers were found to be in the car, an additional seven days was put on the suspension. I obtained permission from my SSA to take my wife with me in the undercover Mercedes-Benz. My wife felt as though she was committing a felony by being in that car. I had conditioned her for years that she was not allowed anywhere near the Bureau car.

We met the diplomatic couple at an ethnic restaurant in Washington, D.C. on a Saturday night. Ironically, we were only about six or so blocks from FBI Headquarters. I had made a reservation for the four of us under the name of Kelly. The first thing my wife said when we arrived, right in front of the foreign couple, was that we had a reservation under Larsh. I quickly told the hostess it was under Kelly. My wife was mortified and thought she ruined my undercover identity. I don't think either of them even heard it. We sat down and ordered dinner. My wife loved the ethnic food and was thrilled to be eating in one of the nicest restaurants in Washington. She said it was the best dinner of that ethnic food she ever had. Being the picky eater I was, I hated it. With the exception of Italian food, I had never taken my wife to dinner to eat any kind of ethnic food before or since. I washed everything down with big gulps of orange juice, refilling my glass three times before finishing my meal. From then on, they believed I loved orange juice and would always offer me a glass at a restaurant or wherever we were. They thoroughly enjoyed meeting my wife. I would continue to socialize with them, even inviting them to my home for birthday parties, cookouts, etc. We truly became good friends.

After recruiting the foreign national, he immediately began providing current information on a weekly basis derived from his access to information from his embassy. At that time, the Central Intelligence Agency (CIA) and the United States Department of State (USDS) advised their counterparts at FBI Headquarters that this was the best information being provided regarding this country's government. The Secretary of State at that time, Warren Christopher, was briefed on two occasions regarding top secret intelligence being provided. Most of the information concerned diplomatic relations and trade talks between the United States and his government. He was getting the negotiation strategies prior to the talks, giving the United States the upper hand in the negotiations. He put his life in extreme danger in collecting this information and had he been caught, he would have been imprisoned and then executed. When he later walked away from his embassy rather than return to the foreign affairs office in his home country, I arranged with the USINS for him to obtain political asylum. He did not "defect" to the United States as most people might expect. By simply walking away from the embassy, his country's government had no idea what happened to him and never knew he had spied against them. After a year, he obtained his green card and believed he was on his way to soon becoming a United States citizen.

In 2002, he applied for his citizenship, but ran into trouble with the Assistant Director of the USINS Washington District Office. He told me that he thought the Assistant Director wanted a bribe, but he could provide no evidence to support his claim. He merely stated that government officials routinely took bribes in his government and he had a feeling that the Assistant Director wanted a bribe, too. I advised him that I could not make such an allegation to the FBI without some type of substantiation to this claim. The USINS Assistant Director told my recruitment he would have to wait ten years from the time he left before applying for citizenship because of a technicality.

I contacted an SSA in the Counterintelligence Division at FBI Headquarters and requested that a letter be sent to the USINS on my recruitment's behalf to expedite his citizenship. The SSA, however, did some research and advised that the USINS Assistant Director was correct regarding the technicality. In a letter to the Director at the USINS Washington District Office from the Assistant Director of the FBI Counterintelligence Division, dated April 3, 2002, it was requested that the technicality be waived and my recruitment's application for citizenship be approved. The USINS Assistant Director maintained that the technicality not be waived and would not approve his citizenship.

My recruitment applied again for citizenship in 2004 after the timetable for the technicality expired, but the same USINS Assistant Director remained an obstacle and still would not approve his application. The SSA in the FBI Counterintelligence Division who helped me in 2002 was no longer there. By 2004, I was assigned to FBI Headquarters. My former colleague from my WMFO squad and the former star of the squad was now a Section Chief at FBI Headquarters in 2004 with FCI responsibility over my recruitment's country of origin. I thought this was fortuitous. Surely, my former CI-10 squad coworker would understand the recruitment's predicament and the need to assist this man who had risked his life stealing secrets for our government. I believed that if anyone could facilitate my recruitment's citizenship, it would be this guy. I met him in his office to advise him of the trouble my recruitment was having. His response to my request was, "Bill, you have to let these sources go." I was appalled. He had personal knowledge of the recruitment's contributions, having worked on the squad with me during the entire time I handled the case. I responded, "I made this man a promise and I intend to keep it. He risked his life for our country." I couldn't believe this arrogant ass would not help this recruitment who had done so much for our country.

In early 2006, the USINS Assistant Director told my recruitment that his citizenship was being held up due to a delay with an FBI name check. I called the Section Chief in charge of the Name Check Unit at FBI Headquarters and explained the situation to him. He advised that his name had been sitting at FBI Headquarters for sixteen months, but he said he would expedite it. In July 2006, my recruitment telephoned me to tell me that the USINS Assistant Director was indicted and arrested on federal bribery charges. I almost fell out of my chair. I felt terrible that he had suspected this back in 2002 and now after four years, his allegation, albeit based on no more than a hunch, proved to be entirely true. I immediately looked up the case on the FBI computer system and determined the name of the case agent at WMFO. The female case agent was very interested in speaking with my recruitment and subsequently scheduled an interview with him.

I then contacted an SSA in the FBI Counterintelligence Division regarding the situation and asked if he could intercede on behalf of his application for citizenship. In mid-July, the case supervisor at immigration, now part of Department of Homeland Security (DHS), told my recruitment that his application was being denied because he had applied at the wrong time, missing a deadline. The immigration case supervisor then proceeded to tell my recruitment that he would have to reapply. The FBI was working jointly with the Office of Inspector General of DHS in its investigation of the USINS Assistant Director. The SSA in the FBI Counterintelligence Division was able to intercede on my recruitment's behalf wherein he not only did not have to reapply for citizenship, but he was granted citizenship a few weeks later.

My recruitment was thrilled and extremely grateful to me. He had been working for the USDS as a foreign language instructor in a part-time capacity for several years with no benefits. However, with his citizenship, he was able to gain full-time employment with full health and retirement benefits. He worked several more years at the USDS before retiring. He received a Meritorious Honor Reward for his steadfast commitment and dedication to the mission of providing outstanding language and culture instruction at the USDS.

My experience with the recruitment and my prestige in the FBI was never higher than in 1995. I felt a great sense of accomplishment and self-satisfaction. The press spokesman's associate did very little in the way of providing intelligence. She was really just part of the package so the two of them would not have to go back to their home country. The deal was that when both of their tours ended, they would walk away from the embassy. She left the embassy first and moved into an apartment paid for with cash I had provided to her as payment from the FBI for all of the secret information her boss had been providing. I assisted her with getting her political asylum and after a year, she received her green card. She left her northern Virginia apartment to attend an Ivy League university. She received her Master's degree in Business Administration and went to work on Wall Street. She became a United States citizen with none of the difficulties her former boss experienced. My recruitment had to stay at the embassy for another four months after his associate left. He was under great suspicion since she was his only subordinate. He had to play stupid and claim he knew nothing of her intentions. Fortunately, no one knew of their personal relationship. He continued to gather information and pass it on to me until his tour ended. They both legally changed their names after leaving the embassy and lived the American dream as United States citizens.

THE FBI – THEY EAT THEIR YOUNG

U.S. Department of Justice

Federal Bureau of Investigation

Office of the Director

Washington, D.C. 20535

July 21, 1994

PERSONAL

Mr. William A. Larsh
Federal Bureau of Investigation
Washington, D. C.

Dear Mr. Larsh:

It is truly a pleasure for me to commend you for your superb efforts in connection with two highly sensitive intelligence operations. To further recognize you, I have approved a cash award for you which the enclosed check represents.

Although you were responsible for other priority investigations, you committed extra time and effort to these matters. You ensured that all details were adequately coordinated and properly handled, thereby ensuring the successes realized. Your innovative and resourceful efforts resulted in the development of intelligence information for the Bureau as well as for the intelligence community. You performed the time-consuming yet vitally important responsibilities of these matters with a high degree of competence and skill, and I thank you.

Sincerely yours,

Louis J. Freeh
Director

Enclosure

FBI/DOJ

Letter of Commendation and Incentive Award, dated 7/21/1994,
from Director Louis J. Freeh for Recruitments-in-Place.

Director Louis Freeh with members of Squad CI-10 after receiving a Meritorious Unit Citation for Exceptional Service in 1994 (Director Freeh is third from the right. I am second from the right.)

Meritorious Unit Citation for Squad CI-10, dated 6/2/1994.

CHAPTER 15

DISILLUSIONMENT

After my greatest success in the FBI, the FBI management reared its ugly head. I remembered what the ORA veteran agent had said back in Orlando regarding being known to management. He said basically that it was better if they did not know you. He was specifically speaking of the ASAC in Tampa not knowing you in Orlando, but this was the same idea. My troubles in the FBI really began following this case. First, I was suspected of foul play by the SAC at WMFO regarding my approved payment of $100,000 to my recruitment for his assistance to the FBI at the end of the case. I had been paying him $5,000 a week from April through December 1994 for his services. Then, after he left the embassy, I requested a final payment of $100,000, which FBI Headquarters approved. I received an FBI check which I took to a bank converting it to a cashier's check in my undercover name. I then deposited this check into the recruitment's bank account at a different bank. These steps were taken to hide the fact that the money was from the FBI. It was all according to FBI procedure.

The only flaw in this system was that my recruitment was too anxious to get his money. I advised him that the money had been deposited, but he apparently grew impatient with regard to the check clearing at the bank. In an effort to expedite getting his money, he told the bank that the check was from the FBI. After he left the embassy, I had finally told him I was an FBI agent. I explained that I kept my identity a secret during the operation for security reasons. He accepted my explanation and had no reaction. Someone at the bank apparently thought something was amiss and called WMFO. The SAC at WMFO called my SSA and demanded to know why this individual was calling the bank. After I was summoned to explain to the SAC personally what happened, he told me to detail all my actions in a memorandum. My SSA indicated that the SAC was of the suspicion that I might have been trying to steal a part of my recruitment's payment. Needless to say, this was all very insulting and demeaning.

Then there was the issue of my undercover vehicle, the 1986 Mercedes-Benz 450SL convertible. I had acquired this vehicle at the start of my undercover role with the recruitment. Following the case, I continued utilizing the vehicle in my role as Bill Kelly. I was meeting with other embassy officials and sources in attempts to recruit these individuals. The SSA suddenly decided to transfer the vehicle to another squad. The word was that the star agent on the squad complained about my having the car. My friends advised me that this agent was jealous that I was getting all the attention with my recruitment. They said it was he who complained to the SSA that I no longer needed the Mercedes-Benz. She had always been strongly influenced by the star agent.

Bob did not like the SSA at all and gladly complained to her on my behalf, since I was not making an issue of it. He said she was completely unreasonable. When he told her it was wrong to take the car away from me, her response was that I should not be allowed to drive a Mercedes-Benz. When Bob argued that I was using the vehicle operationally in a case, she said, "I don't think any agent should be allowed to drive a Mercedes-Benz." It didn't matter anyway, because I was soon assigned to CIA Headquarters in Langley, Virginia, for ninety days to work on a high priority espionage case.

Initially, I thought being assigned to CIA on a spy case would be a great opportunity. After all, the FBI had caught another CIA spy, Aldrich Ames, a few years previously in one of the most famous and prestigious cases the FBI ever investigated. However, when I arrived at CIA and was briefed on the case, it did not sound very exciting. A full FBI squad consisting of about twelve agents was already permanently assigned to the case. Another dozen agents were brought in to help on a temporary basis.

The case at this point consisted of allegations from a very reliable source that a CIA employee who had been stationed in Southeast Asia in the past five years was working for the Russians. Basically they knew it was a male in his 30s or 40s, and some other characteristics of which I no longer remember. A matrix had been created with these characteristics in an attempt to match CIA employees who had been assigned to the various stations in Southeast Asia over the past several years. My job and the job of the other agents temporarily assigned was to review CIA employee files to determine who matched the characteristics on the matrix. This was one of the most tedious tasks I had ever been given, but I worked on it diligently for three months. In fact, I reviewed more CIA employee files than anyone else during those three months.

The case agent realized what a hard worker I was and asked me to transfer to the squad permanently. I politely declined and explained to him that I did not enjoy working cases that might go on for years. The cases I had always worked had a resolution. I told him that I did not want to work on a case that might never be resolved or even one that got resolved years down the road. He understood, but when he came back into work the next morning, he told me I had depressed him and that I was right, this case might never be resolved. I told him not to listen to me and that I was always wrong. "I am sure it will get resolved," I said. "It's just not for me." What I did not tell him was that I did not want to be the low man on the totem pole on a squad and be relegated to reviewing files for months on end or assigned other menial tasks.

It turned out I was entirely wrong about the case. The CIA employee was later identified as Harold Nicholson and a successful espionage case was made against him. The case agent and all the members of the squad received the Director's Award for their investigation, the most prestigious award given for an investigation by the FBI. I ran into the case agent a few years later at FBI Headquarters, where we both had been promoted. We had a good laugh about me depressing him that day. I said, "I told you I was always wrong." I regretted that I had not accepted his invitation to be on the squad. I would have been so proud to have received the Director's Award.

The award I received for my recruitment turned out to be a huge insult. I thought maybe I would receive a QSI for my efforts, but the SSA gave the QSI award to a part-time female agent. The FBI had a program for female agents wherein after having a baby, the agent could come back to work part-time. I had nothing against this policy, as it probably kept many women from resigning from the FBI; however, nobody on the squad thought she deserved the QSI. I received a $1,200 incentive award for my recruitment efforts. More salt was poured into the wound when I learned that another female agent on the squad received an $800 incentive award for my case.

The SSA had initially assigned her to do translation on my case. I was meeting with my recruitment every week at the Embassy Suites. He provided his notes to me written in his foreign language. This female agent translated his notes for me, but never in a timely fashion. She would take a week or more to complete the translation and only after I nagged her. She would always have an excuse and tell me she was too busy working her own cases.

I was getting very frustrated after a few weeks of her nonsense. The intelligence being provided was time-sensitive. I was very anxious to get his information into teletype form and forwarded to FBI Headquarters for appropriate dissemination. On my third visit with the recruitment, I asked him if he was capable of translating his notes into English. He said he would gladly do that. The next day I told the female agent that I would no longer need her services. I did not tell her I thought she was unreliable, nor did I tell the SSA. All I wanted to do was to get the job done and to get his information disseminated as quickly as possible.

When the female agent received her $800 award for my case, the principal relief supervisor on the squad at the time was so incensed that she herself complained to the SSA, advising her that this female agent had only done translation work on the case for two weeks. I was told that the SSA's response was that she liked to spread around the incentive award money. Even my wife was annoyed. Cindy believed that she had contributed far more to the case than this agent, and Cindy didn't even get a "thank you" from the Bureau.

After the assignment at CIA, word around the office was that WMFO management would be creating several espionage squads with agents from existing counterintelligence squads. I was beginning to see the writing on the wall. I believed that I would be assigned to one of these new squads, particularly since two agents from my squad were already slated for one. I had it in my mind that being on one of these new squads would be another tedious affair. I wanted to control my own destiny, so I applied for supervisory jobs at FBI Headquarters. The only job at FBI Headquarters that interested me was in OPR. The reason was because it appeared to be the only job available at headquarters in which one could remain an investigator. All of the other positions seemed to be desk jobs with oversight responsibilities to field offices.

In September 1995, an ASAC at WMFO called me to his office and asked if I would like to transfer to a newly formed WMFO espionage squad. He told me he wanted aggressive agents on the squad to work a top secret case with a very interesting target. I asked him if I had a choice in the matter, and if so, I would prefer to stay where I was. He said that if I knew who the target was, I would want to be transferred, but it was my choice. I said, "No, thank you." Two days later, I was again called to the ASAC's office. He told me that he wanted me to sign a non-disclosure agreement so he could tell me all of the details about the espionage case. I signed the form, which basically said that I could be convicted of a felony if I disclosed any information about the case.

The ASAC proceeded to tell me that the new espionage squad being formed was targeting a current FBI agent, Earl Pitts, who was presently assigned at the FBI Academy in Quantico, Virginia. Pitts had previously been assigned to the FBI New York Division in the 1980s working counterintelligence against the Russians. A Russian defector from the KGB had recently named Pitts as a mole in the FBI who sold top secret intelligence information to the KGB. I still had it in my mind that I would end up being assigned the most tedious tasks, as I had been just a month or two before in the Nicholson investigation at the CIA, so I politely said, "If I have a choice in the matter, I would prefer to stay where I am." I told him that I was working on some other potential recruitments on my squad and that I was completely happy with my work. He was somewhat surprised at my response, but seemed very understanding about it.

The next day on Saturday morning at home, I received a telephone call from the ASAC. He told me that the SAC wanted to see me at 7:30 a.m. in his office on Tuesday morning (Monday was a federal holiday, Columbus Day). The ASAC said to me, "Bill, we really want you on this new squad." In hindsight, I am sure I would have done things differently, but in my head I felt I had a choice in the matter. I was always a bit hardheaded and liked to do things my own way. I enjoyed my FBI career because I basically worked my own cases and only received help from others when needed. I enjoyed this autonomy and did not want to change. I really had a fear of being just a flunky on another squad.

Part of my refusal to want to work on a team-type squad derived from a performance rating I received from the SSA of the Nicholson case after my ninety days at CIA. My SSA on Squad CI-10, in spite of her faults, had given me the highest rating, "Exceptional," for my work with the recruitments. After my assignment at CIA, where I reviewed more personnel files for their matrix than any other agent, the SSA of that squad gave me a performance rating of "Fully Acceptable," which was an average rating. I told my SSA on CI-10 that I did not believe this was fair due to my file review output. She said that the SSA told her I never said anything or contributed anything at the weekly squad meetings, which was why he gave me the average rating. This insulted me since I had performed so diligently on my task. My SSA said not to worry about it since she would not count his input toward my annual performance appraisal anyway. At any rate, my thinking on the issue of transferring to another squad had to do with controlling my own destiny and not getting stuck with an SSA who did not appreciate my efforts.

On Tuesday morning at 7:30 a.m. promptly, I met with the SAC. I sat in a chair in front of his desk. He got up from behind his desk and sat in the chair right next to me. He leaned in close to me, uncomfortably invading my space, but acting as if we were good friends. He explained how important the Pitt case was and how he'd like me to transfer to the squad working on this case. I then explained that the ASAC had presented this to me and made it clear it was my choice. I said to the SAC, "If I have a choice in the matter, I'd prefer to stay and continue my work on my squad." The SAC immediately jumped up from his seat next to me, his demeanor completely changed. He was clearly agitated and returned to behind his desk. He became very animated and said, "Well, this just tells me what kind of agent you are that doesn't want to work on an important case like this!" He was fuming. He said nothing more so I slowly rose from my chair and left the room. I went back to my desk on my squad. A few agents on the squad had arrived and were drinking coffee and reading the newspaper. I told them what had just happened. One of the older agents looked at me and said, "You're the walking dead."

He could not have been more correct. The next morning I received a call from the SAC secretary. She said that the SAC had designated me the CFC Coordinator for the division. CFC stood for Combined Federal Campaign. CFC was much like United Way, a giant charitable organization consisting of hundreds of charities. Contributing to CFC in the FBI was supposed to be on a volunteer basis, but pressure had always been exerted by management to achieve one hundred percent participation. If an employee chose not to make a charitable deduction from their paycheck, then cash donations of as little as one dollar were welcomed in order to achieve the goal of full participation. I knew immediately that this was a punishment from the SAC for not capitulating to his request. I decided that I would go all out in the division in promoting CFC. I had a small budget that allowed me to purchase poster boards.

I asked my wife to help me draw up graphs depicting all of the WMFO squads and their percentage participation in CFC. I placed the graphs on each floor at the elevators, filling them in daily to show the increased participation during the two weeks of the CFC campaign. I wanted the SAC to see my efforts, which I am sure he could not have missed. After about a week and half into the CFC campaign, I was on the first floor filling in the percentages when two agents I did not know came out of the elevator. They stopped and looked at the chart. The one agent said, "This is bullshit pitting squads against each other. I wonder whose idea this was." I turned toward them as I was filling out the chart, smiling as I said, "It was mine." The agents gave me disgusted looks and walked away. FBI Headquarters evidently thought I had done a fantastic job as CFC Coordinator and gave me a "Time Off" award of eight hours of annual leave.

In the beginning of November, a few weeks after my horrible meeting with the SAC, I was sitting at my desk in the back corner of the squad area at lunch time by myself eating my peanut butter and jelly sandwich, when I saw the SAC approaching me. As he walked down the aisle passing three rows of desks to get to me, I could not help but think that he was going to tell me, "Hey asshole, you're being transferred to the espionage squad." I never could understand why he just didn't transfer me to the squad to begin with. I was sorry the ASAC ever gave me a choice. I was waiting for the bomb to drop. Instead, the SAC smiled at me, shook my hand and said, "Congratulations, you got the job at OPR." I said thank you, but I was thinking how he had berated me only a couple of weeks ago. His deriding comment, "This just tells me what kind of agent you are that doesn't want to work on an important case like this" was imprinted on my brain, not to mention that this was the same SAC who evidently suspected me of stealing my recruitment's money. The hypocrisy was mind boggling. Now I was going to be in management. I was determined to be a different kind of manager in the FBI. Never would I be like this phony.

CHAPTER 16

OPR

At the time, I was very happy leaving WMFO. I did not want others dictating where I should go. I made the choice myself to go to OPR. It seemed like it would be interesting work and it turned out to be everything I thought it would be and more. My promotion from a street agent to a Supervisory Special Agent (SSA) included the added benefit of a significant pay increase from a GS-13 to a GS-14. I started the day before Thanksgiving. I was assigned a multitude of cases immediately. The range of allegations of misconduct made against FBI employees was beyond comprehension. One of the most common misconduct issues was misusing a Bureau vehicle. At one time or another, I imagined, every agent misused his/her vehicle by being somewhere they were not supposed to be. The agents that got caught were usually in accidents, revealing they were not on official business. However, one case involved an ex-wife reporting to the FBI that her ex-husband drove his Bureau car every weekend to pick up their children in Frederick, Maryland, and then drove them back to his home in northern Virginia. These cases were straightforward and simple. By law, under Title 31, United States Code, Section 1349, employees misusing government vehicles received an automatic 30-day suspension without pay. If the misuse involved an unauthorized passenger in the vehicle, then another seven days was added to the suspension.

One of the most interesting cases during my two years working in OPR involved a new agent at the FBI Academy. The agent was only a week shy of graduating when an allegation surfaced involving her reported drug use. She had previously worked as an actress in Hollywood. Her name and picture had appeared in a recent nationally published article detailing diversity among newly-hired FBI agents.

She had applied to a local police department prior to getting hired by the FBI. On her application to the police department, she indicated that she had tried cocaine twenty-five times. On her FBI application, she indicated that she tried cocaine three times over ten years ago. The FBI drug policy, in order to get hired as an agent, was that an applicant could have tried cocaine no more than three times ten years prior to their application. The FBI hired her before receiving and reviewing her police application. This was obviously due to an administrative oversight during her background investigation. Unfortunately for her, the police department finally sent a copy of her application to the FBI revealing the discrepancy shortly before her graduation from the FBI Academy.

I was assigned the case. The former actress was immediately pulled out of training and reported to OPR to give a signed, sworn statement. I asked my favorite co-worker in OPR to assist me with the interview. He arrived in OPR shortly after I did. We hit it off immediately. He had a great sense of humor. After I answered him once in my Jim Carrey via Ace Ventura impersonation of "aaaallllrighty then," he laughed heartily and said how much he loved that movie. We became fast friends and worked many cases together over the next two years.

The interview of the woman and her defense were laughable. First, she said that she was not accurate on her police application. She explained that she only used cocaine on three occasions. She said she first tried cocaine by rubbing it on her gums when she arrived in Hollywood, but she didn't count this incident as "using" cocaine since she did not ingest it through her nose. She then described using cocaine on three occasions during 1985. She was obviously cognizant of the ten-year rule with regard to the FBI's policy. Her FBI application was dated September 15, 1995, so she was making sure not to admit to any use within ten years of that date. She was also trying very hard to stay within the policy of only using it three times, except her defense was to the point of being ludicrous.

Rubbing it on her gums did not count as using cocaine, according to her. She described two incidents when she used cocaine in early 1985, but her definition of incidents differed from any logical person. She described two separate occasions when she spent the evening using cocaine numerous times throughout the night, but insisted that each night was only one incident of cocaine use. She admitted that she and her friends would typically snort a line of cocaine at their apartment prior to departing for the evening, then do a line in the limousine, a couple more while at the night club, and maybe a line in the limousine on their return home. She admitted to snorting a total of five or six lines of cocaine during each evening, but insisted that each night counted as only one incident of use.

She admitted that she last did a line of cocaine at a Hollywood party on Labor Day in 1985. She said she remembered it distinctly because Len Bias, the college basketball player who had been picked in the first round draft to play in the NBA, died suddenly after using cocaine in celebration of his selection. She said his death had a profound effect on her. She said the host of the party brought out a pile of cocaine and put it on the coffee table. She said she snorted one line of cocaine along with many of the other guests, but decided then and there that she would never do it again because she did not want to die like Len Bias. In summary, she insisted that she only took cocaine on three occasions which occurred more than ten years prior to the date on her FBI application. My partner and I both knew this was nonsense, but she signed her statement as the truth.

I never really thought that the FBI would accept her version of the number of times she used cocaine. However, I believed she had a made a mistake regarding Len Bias' death. She stated it was 1985, but I recalled it as being in 1986, which would put her admitted cocaine use within ten years of her application. My partner and I both knew that this woman used cocaine many more times, incidents, occasions, nights, or whatever she wanted to call it, than she was willing to admit. I told my partner I believed Len Bias died in 1986 and would confirm it at home that evening after reviewing my 1986 World Book Encyclopedia Yearbook. Sure enough, Bias was in the 1986 Yearbook indicating he died in June. I came back to work the next day with the 1986 Yearbook, made a Xerox copy of the Len Bias article, attached it to my report, and sent it to my Unit Chief. She was summarily dismissed from the FBI for violating the FBI drug policy and falsifying her FBI application.

I enjoyed working in OPR for two years. I did not have to worry about generating cases because new ones were assigned to me daily. I worked with near complete autonomy. I checked in with my superiors on important cases to keep them up-to-date, but they generally left me alone. I traveled approximately one week out of every month around the country to conduct my investigations, collecting signed, sworn statements from witnesses and subjects. One week while I was traveling, the OPR Unit Chief called a meeting of the eleven remaining OPR SSAs and took a vote from them on who they thought deserved the QSI incentive award for the year. The Unit Chief announced that everyone else would receive cash incentive awards, but that one agent would receive the QSI, a much more profitable award, as explained previously.

When I returned from my trip and went into the office the following Monday, my partner told me about the vote and that it was unanimous that I should receive the QSI. He said that everyone knew I worked the hardest and resolved more cases than anyone else. However, he immediately added, "But you're not getting the QSI." My shoulders slumped and my happy expression turned into disbelief. He said that two OPR SSAs complained and convinced the Unit Chief that he should choose the QSI recipient. The Unit Chief then picked one of the complainants. My partner told me that the SSA chosen for the QSI was very friendly with the Unit Chief and the two of them frequented auto shows together on the weekends. This disappointment was right up there with the injustice done to me at WMFO. Although I did receive another $1,200 cash award, this otherwise rewarding chapter in my career left another bad taste in my mouth.

The next chapter in my career was leaving FBI Headquarters. The normal management progression in the FBI was to work two years as an SSA at FBI Headquarters and then work as an SSA in the field. I was quite happy to pursue this avenue and move on to something new. I was no longer happy living in Crofton, Maryland, with the tedious hour to an hour and a half commute to work every day in my own car. Agents at FBI Headquarters were not given vehicles, with the exception of Assistant Directors. I lived across the street from the Crofton Country Club and had enjoyed playing golf with friends every weekend. However, in the summer of 1996, former Vice-President Spiro Agnew died. Agnew had been rumored to be the owner of the golf club. A former Secret Service agent who protected him when he was Vice-President was apparently the straw owner of the club. Immediately following Agnew's death, the club was sold to the Arnold Palmer Corporation. Dues at the club tripled, so I quit. My golfing partner down the street, a CIA employee who worked at the United States Navy Yard in D.C., also quit the club. We began playing at the Fort Meade golf course about fifteen miles away. It was a bit annoying to live across the street from a country club and then have to drive a half hour to play somewhere else. I was ready for a change.

I got some bad advice from several agents at FBI Headquarters with regard to transfers. The general consensus was that an SSA needed to put in for numerous jobs at once in order to get picked for an SSA job in the field. Everyone told me I needed to glut the market with applications. It made sense, but only if you were not very marketable. I misjudged how marketable I was. I had been on so many trips to different field offices working OPR cases that I was known and liked by many of the field divisions' front offices.

For instance, I had worked a media leak case in Atlanta concerning Richard Jewell, the hero turned suspect in the 1996 Olympics Centennial Park Bombing. Richard Jewell was working as a security guard at the Olympics and discovered the backpack of explosives in Centennial Park. Jewell saved many lives by moving people away from the backpack, which eventually exploded. He was initially treated as a hero until it was leaked to the press that he was considered a suspect by FBI profilers. The media reported at great length how Jewell may have planted the bomb, discovered it, and made himself out to be the hero. Eric Rudolph was later identified as the perpetrator and convicted of several bombings around the country, including the 1996 Olympics Centennial Park Bombing.

An OPR case was initiated at Director Freeh's insistence. The investigation was virtually impossible to resolve due to the large universe of people from countless federal, state, and local law enforcement agencies who were involved. Director Freeh was responding merely for public relations purposes. I conducted numerous interviews, but to no avail. My recommendation to the Department of Justice was that the universe of individuals was too immense and no viable leads existed as to the origination of the leak. My only real accomplishment in the case was making an impression on the FBI Atlanta Division front office, particularly their ASAC. They appreciated my professionalism, candidness, and relentless hard work.

I did such a good job on that media leak case that my Unit Chief assigned nearly every subsequent media leak case to me. In 1997, Director Freeh ordered another media leak case to be initiated following an article appearing in the *Washington Post*. It was reported that Freeh told Attorney General Janet Reno in private in a hallway after a meeting at DOJ that she should appoint an independent counsel to investigate the current Democratic Party fundraising scandal. I was a bit nervous about this case because the first thing I had to do was question Janet Reno about her conversation with Freeh, and then ask her who she told at DOJ about the conversation. I also had to interview Freeh regarding who he told.

I had previously met Janet Reno while assigned to her protection detail in 1995. Following the Oklahoma City bombing of the Murrah Federal Building in 1995, it was decided that Reno's security detail should be increased. FBI agents permanently assigned to the security detail protected her, but more agents were brought in from WMFO. I volunteered for two weekends. It proved to be a memorable experience for me. The first Saturday night, Reno attended a dinner with the United States Supreme Court Justices, which was held in the large open area in the United States Supreme Court building in front of the courtroom. I had never been inside this building and enjoyed the experience. Of course, I did not get to have dinner with any Supreme Court Justices. I waited in the basement of the building in a security office watching the World Series while Reno attended the dinner.

The next weekend, I was assigned with another WMFO agent to a Democratic Party fundraiser at the Washington Convention Center. One of the agents on Reno's regular security detail told us that Reno hated party fundraising events, but she was obliged to attend. President Bill Clinton spoke at the fundraiser. My partner and I could have gone inside to watch, but we both could not stand Clinton and opted to stay outside. At the end of the night, I realized what a genuinely nice person Janet Reno truly was. Prior to entering her apartment building located only two blocks away from DOJ, she made a point to thank each and every agent, both on her regular detail, and to those like myself, who had volunteered. She told everyone how much she appreciated the sacrifice made on her behalf.

I then got to meet her again two years later while investigating the media leak case. Prior to my asking any questions at all, she told me how much she appreciated the work we did at OPR and how difficult it was. She was again very genuine and gracious. I could not help but feel guilty about how I had immediately disliked her upon her appointment as Attorney General. Her first declaration to the press was to announce that her number one priority was to go after deadbeat dads. I thought, "Really? Not drug traffickers, organized crime members, espionage subjects, or even violent crime offenders, but child support violators?" I was not impressed and did not think she should have been appointed as chief law enforcement officer of the country. Her politics and mine were probably miles apart, but after having met her, I really liked her as a person. With regard to my questions to her about the media leak case, she said she relayed Director Freeh's recommendation to many of her subordinates at a subsequent meeting, to include several Assistant Attorney Generals.

I had an appointment the following day to speak with Director Freeh, but I came down with the flu. As much as I did not want to miss the opportunity to interview the Director of the FBI, I could not reschedule with him so I asked another OPR agent to interview him. Freeh provided a list of several FBI Assistant Directors with whom he told of the conversation with Reno. This was a typical media leak case. The more people that were interviewed, the larger the universe became of people who knew about it.

I did have an interesting interview with the Deputy Director, my old Drug Section Chief from 1986 who mistakenly thought I had two college degrees. He laughed the entire time I interviewed him. He was amused by the fact that he knew me as a support employee over ten years ago and that now I was an OPR investigator asking him questions. I should have been the giddy one; a Deputy Director was the highest promotion any FBI agent could achieve. Following FBI Director J. Edgar Hoover's death in 1972, no FBI agent had been promoted to Director of the FBI. Clarence M. Kelley was appointed FBI Director in 1973. He was a former agent who retired in 1961. He retired as FBI Director in 1978. Since then, no former agent from the FBI has served as its Director. Every Director has come from outside the FBI, Judge William H. Webster, Judge William S. Sessions, former United States Attorney (USA) Louis J. Freeh, former USA Robert S. Mueller, former USA James B. Comey, and former Assistant Attorney General Christopher Wray.

In the media leak case concerning the conversation between Freeh and Reno, I interviewed numerous Assistant Attorney Generals, Assistant Directors, and other FBI and DOJ executive management, only to determine that too many people knew about Freeh's conversation with Reno in the hallway at DOJ. Outside of an admission or giving polygraph examinations to half the DOJ and FBI executive management staffs, the source of this leak would never be known. It didn't help that the Associated Press and Reuter's Wire Services had offices on the first floor at DOJ. I was surprised that anything in that building ever remained a secret.

Some FBI front offices in the field would never have hired me as an SSA, not due to the quality of my work in OPR investigations, but because of whom I investigated. One prime example was an investigation regarding the son of an SAC. The SAC had previously been assigned to the FBI Academy. The son applied as an FBI agent and began new agents training at the FBI Academy while his father was in charge there. On the first day of his training, the SAC's son developed stress fractures in his shins following the two-mile run, preventing him from any further participation running. Within a few weeks into training, a nurse at the FBI Academy determined that he was using an asthma inhaler. Asthma was a medical condition at that time that precluded an agent from being hired. He was recycled twice during his training, meaning that he was held back from graduating with his original class in order to give his shin fractures time to heal. The SAC's son eventually graduated from the FBI Academy, despite having never passed the necessary physical requirements, such as running the two-mile course or the 120-yard shuttle course within the minimum time requirements. He was assigned as an agent to a field division.

An anonymous letter was later sent to OPR with allegations against the father, signed "A concerned FBI employee." The charges against the SAC included unprofessionalism and misusing his position. These were relatively minor infractions. A more serious allegation was that the SAC used his influence to graduate his son from the FBI Academy as an agent, although he failed to meet the running requirements and had asthma. A review of the son's FBI agent application revealed no medical problems in his history, except for allergies. Investigation at the FBI Academy confirmed the information regarding his asthma. A nurse at the FBI Academy indicated in a signed, sworn statement that he used an asthma inhaler.

In sworn interviews to OPR, the son admitted having allergy problems his entire life, but refused to acknowledge that he was ever diagnosed with asthma. He knew that disclosing this condition on his application would have precluded him from becoming an agent. Agents who developed asthma after being hired, however, did not lose their jobs. He did not disclose until a subsequent interview that the reason he developed shin fractures was because he was born with a clubbed foot. He only made this admission after being confronted with medical records indicating he had been operated on at the age of nine to repair it. He then wore leg braces for a year following the operation. He had signed release forms in the first interview in order that all his medical records could be obtained and reviewed by the FBI. He was adamant, though, that his childhood medical problems never precluded him from playing sports or anything else growing up. He acknowledged that he did not reveal this information on his application or in his previous signed, sworn statements.

He advised further that his father had nothing to do with his graduating, in spite of the fact that he did not meet the running requirements. The son said he kept in shape at Quantico riding a stationary bike. Investigation at the FBI Academy determined that he not only did not pass any running requirements, but that he was given special compensation in passing the firearms courses. Part of the pistol qualification course required the student to run from the 50-yard line to the 25-yard line and fire the weapon in a certain amount of time. He could not complete this part of the course in the required time, inasmuch as he had to limp to get to the 25-yard line, according to a signed, sworn statement from a firearms instructor. He fired his pistol with accuracy, but not within the time limit, yet he passed.

Investigation determined that executive management in the Personnel Division made the final decision to pass him, notwithstanding his obvious physical limitations. The head of the Personnel Division admitted that the boy's father was a friend of his. He further admitted that the father had telephoned him periodically during his son's training period, but that he in no way tried to influence him or had any bearing on his son being able to graduate. He said he made the decision to graduate him after consulting with the FBI Office of General Counsel (OGC), formerly known as the Legal Division. He said he was advised by OGC that it was not deemed legally defensible in court to fail a new agent who had passed every other aspect of training except for the running requirements. He said the SAC's son did try to run, but could not run within the time limits set for passing. I asked if a case with this issue had ever gone to court, to which he replied it had not. The attorneys in OGC were not FBI agents, but attorneys hired from outside the FBI. When I first started working for the FBI, all of the attorneys in the Legal Division were FBI agents. I doubted that FBI agent attorneys would have come to this same conclusion.

It was clear to me that he graduated because his father used his influence. The case against the father could never be proven, since his friend in the Personnel Division was never going to admit any influence was exerted. The Personnel Division set a terrible precedent that could have had a profound effect on physical requirements for new agents. In my opinion, he clearly made an exception for the SAC's son as a favor to a colleague and friend.

A few years previously, with the passage of the Americans with Disabilities Act of 1990 (ADA), agent applicants with disabilities were no longer denied the opportunity to try to pass the physical requirements at the FBI Academy. For instance, the physical requirements to get hired were reduced and the weight requirements were eliminated. In other words, prior to the ADA being passed by Congress, FBI agent applicants had to pass physical tests consisting of sit-ups, push-ups, pull-ups, running, and even a trigger-pull test before attending the FBI Academy to ensure that applicants would be able to meet the minimum physical requirements. Following the passage of the ADA, the pre-FBI Academy tests were eliminated. This change in the law resulted in overweight, out of shape, and handicapped individuals being allowed the opportunity to attend the FBI Academy. However, they all failed to pass the physical requirements while at the FBI Academy and were sent home. It only proved to be a huge waste of time and money, while at the same time hampering the FBI's ability to hire qualified agents.

The FBI later reinstituted the pre-physical requirements. I did not know if this was a result of a court ruling or if common sense won out. The fact of the matter was that new agents had to possess the physical capability to apprehend criminals or lives could be put in jeopardy. The SAC's son had limited physical ability to carry out the arrest powers that are part and parcel in performing one's duties as an FBI agent. When it was all said and done, however, the reason for his dismissal from the FBI was not his inability to pass these physical tests, but for his lack of candor in his signed, sworn statements during the OPR investigation, and for falsifying the medical portion of his FBI application by not disclosing his complete health record.

One very amusing incident that occurred during my two years in OPR involved a female colleague in OPR. She had completed an interview of an agent under an administrative inquiry. The agent was flown into FBI Headquarters to give his signed, sworn statement. I don't recall what the allegations against the agent were or anything about his case. In fact, I had no involvement at all and never even laid eyes on him. Nevertheless, I witnessed the female investigator preparing his written statement following his interview while she ran back and forth from our office to the interview room across the hall where the subject was waiting. She was making corrections and modifications to his statement, then taking them to him for his review before he agreed to sign it.

After several trips back and forth, she returned to our office and said (paraphrased), "That guy is such an asshole. I was being so nice and patient accommodating him. I told him I was sorry for all the trouble, and then he said to me, 'Don't apologize, it's a sign of weakness.' I think he's being sexist." I laughed and told her I didn't know about that, but the guy was quoting John Wayne from an old movie. I asked her if she had ever seen the movie, *She Wore A Yellow Ribbon,* to which she replied no. I explained that John Wayne played a Captain in the United States Calvary in the movie and repeated that line to his subordinate officers throughout the movie, except John Wayne actually said, "Don't apologize, <u>Mister</u>, it's a sign of weakness."

"The guy's not even being original," I said to her, laughing. She got a big kick out of it. She laughed, too, and was apparently no longer annoyed. She just thought the guy was an idiot.

During February 1996, a major blizzard hit the northeast causing the federal government to close down in Washington, D.C. for an entire week. On a Monday, after the first day back at work, my personal vehicle, a 1984 Nissan Sentra hatchback, broke down on my commute home that night. The clutch went out before I reached the city limits. Luckily, I was able to drift into a self-service gas station and convenience store parking lot. I telephoned for a tow truck. The tow truck driver advised he would do his best to get to my location, but it would be hours before he could get there. The traffic all over the city was practically at a standstill due to the approximately five feet of snow piled up on the edge of every roadway.

I stood outside the convenience store for four and a half hours waiting for the tow truck. I was wearing a very expensive, full-length, pure wool, winter overcoat over my suit. It was a very bad neighborhood with a homeless shelter around the corner. Many seedy-looking characters were loitering in the area. I was sticking out like a sore thumb. I was worried I might not be able to retrieve my Sig Sauer P226 9mm pistol from my holster under my coat in a timely manner, if necessary. I therefore removed my pistol from the holster and placed it in the right-hand pocket of my overcoat for protection. I had my hand on the gun in my pocket with my finger on the trigger, fully prepared to shoot a hole in my $250 coat to protect myself. Within a very brief time, a crazed-looking black man dressed in a ratty winter coat approached me from a short distance away. He was holding a hammer above his head, waving it like a hatchet, and making unintelligible utterances. I believed he was attacking me with a hammer until I finally understood him asking me, "You wanna buy a hamma?" I raised my left arm in a defensive posture and told him "No, now get away from me." He had no idea I was pointing a gun at him with my finger on the trigger, within a second of shooting him.

Commuters were stopping continuously to get gas. I watched another black man approaching every customer, offering to pump their gas. Each person he asked said no and most appeared apprehensive as he approached them, some recoiling. After witnessing the black man try this unsuccessfully for more than an hour, I asked him, "Why are you asking these people to pump their gas for them? You're only scaring them. They think you're going to rob them." He responded unashamedly, "I'm trying to get some money." I said, "You look like a normal guy. You're dressed well and make a good appearance. Why not get a job?" He said matter of factly, "I need $10 for heroin." I knew heroin users could do little else with their lives until they got their daily dose. I asked him, "Aren't you afraid of getting AIDS with a dirty needle?" He said his mother was a diabetic and he used her new needles.

He was an extremely affable fellow and quite normal. At one point, he drew my attention to a man pumping gas. He said to me, "That guy's a cop. I can spot a cop anywhere." I said, "Is that so?" I almost pulled out my badge and credentials to show him he hadn't spotted the FBI agent standing next to him, who had also been pointing a gun at him the entire evening. It was tempting, but I refrained from doing so. I did, however, enjoy talking to him that night, passing the time until the tow truck finally arrived at about 10:30 p.m. The poor guy never did get anybody to allow him to pump their gas for them. I don't know how he ever got his $10.

U.S. Department of Justice

Federal Bureau of Investigation

Office of the Director   Washington, D.C. 20535

August 28, 1997

PERSONAL

Mr. William A. Larsh
Federal Bureau of Investigation
Washington, D. C.

Dear Mr. Larsh:

    I am greatly pleased to have this opportunity to recognize you for your sustained exceptional performance during the past several months. To demonstrate my appreciation, I have approved a cash award for you which will be forwarded separately.

    In your approach to each of your assignments, you have repeatedly displayed professionalism and exceptional expertise, and your unparalleled talents have earned you the utmost respect. Your hard work and persistence have yielded numerous statistical accomplishments, and your fine work reflects positively on you and the Bureau as well. Thank you for your devoted support to our many missions.

Sincerely yours,

Louis J. Freeh
Director

Letter of Commendation and Incentive Award, dated 8/28/1997, from Director Louis J. Freeh for my work in OPR (Consolation for not getting the QSI that the majority of my co-workers voted for me to receive).

CHAPTER 17

LOUISIANA

After a year and a half in OPR, I began to apply for supervisory positions in the field. I had it in my mind that I wanted to be an SSRA. I believed being in charge of an RA away from the field division front office would be the ideal job. I thought I would have more independence as an SSRA.

For me, though, the old adage of Murphy's Law applied, "Anything that can go wrong, will go wrong." The idea of flooding the market with applications proved to be a mistake, as well as thinking that an SSRA position would provide me more autonomy.

As stated previously, I would never get selected in certain offices. The SAC whose clubbed-footed, asthmatic son got fired, would never have selected me in a million years. I put in for jobs where they liked me, such as SSRA Macon in the Atlanta Division; SSRA Tyler in the Dallas Division; and SSRA Shreveport/Monroe in the New Orleans Division. In all three of these divisions, the front office management met me during OPR investigations and were pleased with my work and the outcome of the cases.

These offices all ranked me number one, but it was the New Orleans Division that was the first office to pick me. The SAC in New Orleans selected me for the job in Shreveport, but then he took a promotion a couple weeks later to be the Assistant Director in Charge at the Criminal Justice Information Systems (CJIS) Division in Clarksburg, West Virginia. The New Orleans Division selected me before I finished my required two-year assignment at FBI Headquarters before being transferred. I did not arrive in Shreveport until almost five months later. In the meantime, a new SAC was assigned in New Orleans. This new SAC had a bad reputation in the FBI. The Inspector-in-Charge of OPR warned me before I left to be very careful what this SAC told me to do.

A scandal in the FBI had taken place a few years earlier involving numerous executive management personnel. An Assistant Director from the FBI Academy was about to retire and one of his colleagues wanted to have a huge retirement party for him. Most of his friends were SACs in offices all over the country, so a party was arranged in conjunction with a bogus conference planned for FBI executive management. The SACs flew into Washington on the government's dime under the guise of attending a conference at Quantico. A conference was held, but was later determined to have been organized for the sole purpose of hosting a retirement party.

My new SAC had been assigned to a special internal affairs investigation of this matter following the scandal. The case was not worked under the normal channels in OPR, in view of the fact that it involved some of the highest-ranking members of the FBI. My new SAC was widely seen as whitewashing the entire investigation. None of the FBI executive management personnel involved received any kind of punishment. Years later following my tenure in Shreveport, a review of this investigation by DOJ took place. The final DOJ report indicated officially that my new SAC had indeed whitewashed the entire investigation. The Inspector-in-Charge knew it years before the DOJ report and warned me about him.

Upon my arrival at the Shreveport Resident Agency (SRA), I was immediately told by one of my subordinates that the new SAC had it in for me. I was flabbergasted. "What? Why did he have it in for me?" I asked incredulously. The agent said that he heard that I had gotten a friend of the SAC fired. I then realized exactly what the agent was talking about, but it was all wrong. The agent said that the SAC hated OPR, which I had already heard from the OPR Inspector-in-Charge and others. He also said that the new SAC was furious that the outgoing SAC had selected me. My new SAC was also widely known for being extremely vindictive.

I had met my new SAC when he was an ASAC in San Francisco. I had spent two weeks there on another media leak case. This case concerned a leak to CBS News that the FBI was about to arrest Ted Kaczynski, the Unabomber. I spent two weeks taking signed, sworn statements from a dozen or so FBI agents/management assigned to the Unabomber Task Force. It was a typical, perfunctory media leak investigation. The universe of people with knowledge of Kaczynski's impending arrest was astronomical. The ASAC had been friendly during my visit, but I determined later in Shreveport that he had me confused with my old partner in OPR.

My old partner had been assigned an OPR case regarding a missing MP5 automatic weapon in San Francisco. The then-ASAC was furious with OPR for having opened an OPR case in the first place. He wanted the case to be handled strictly within his division. The agent to whom the MP5 was assigned claimed that a retired agent had stolen it. The ASAC opened a criminal investigation against the retired agent for theft of government property. OPR management insisted that an OPR case be opened against the agent to whom the gun was assigned. This agent was evidently a very good friend of the ASAC. The ASAC not only argued vehemently with OPR executive management against opening an OPR case, but also with my old partner who was assigned the case.

After the OPR case was opened, the agent to whom the gun was assigned failed a polygraph examination. Following his failure of the polygraph, he admitted that it was not the retired agent who had stolen the gun. He confessed that he had stolen the MP5 and it was hidden in his attic. The agent was ultimately fired from the FBI for stealing and lying under oath, but this did not deter my new SAC's fury against OPR. To make matters worse, he had me confused with my old partner. I thought I could clear this up by simply reminding him we met when I worked on the media leak case. I did just that in our first meeting and even told him that I thought he had me mixed up with my old partner. However, this did not help. He either did not get it or it just did not matter to him. As far as he was concerned, I was from OPR and I got his friend fired. Never mind that his friend was a liar and a thief, OPR and I were to blame.

He made my life miserable during my tenure as SSRA Shreveport. My predecessor told me he rarely ever had to travel to New Orleans. Supervisor meetings were held monthly in New

Orleans, but my predecessor normally participated on speakerphone from his office in Shreveport. The new SAC increased the frequency of these meetings to be held every two weeks. He further insisted I attend in person. I had to drive 325 miles each way every other week. It was really quite an inconvenience. I drove down the night before in order to make the 9 a.m. meetings. The meetings generally consisted of going around the table one by one as each SSA discussed his/her squad's most important cases, even if they were not that much to brag about. I spoke daily on the telephone with the ASAC regarding all of the major cases in Shreveport and Monroe anyway. I always had plenty to talk about because I had two squads of agents, one in Shreveport, and the other in Monroe.

It was a great job being SSRA Shreveport, in spite of the executive management. I was in charge of the FBI for all of northern Louisiana. Many people in the division said I was like a mini-SAC, a term I am sure my SAC would have detested if he ever heard it. He was known to be vindictive, as well as possessing a massive ego. The Administrative Officer (AO) in the New Orleans Division, the highest ranking support employee, told me he had a desk two inches longer than the SAC's desk. Upon discovering the slightly larger desk, the SAC directed the AO to order him a larger one.

The ASACs never treated me well from the day I arrived. I knew it was because of the SAC's influence. Everything I did was not good enough. An ASAC once chewed me out for not calling him immediately regarding civil rights allegations against a Shreveport police officer. I advised the ASAC of the case the next day during my usual morning call to him, but he was mad because he had already read about it in the morning newspaper. It was deemed by the ASAC as a failure on my part for calling him a day late. I explained that the case had been opened and was already being investigated. The ASAC said he needed to know about these things before reading them in the newspaper. I responded somewhat indignantly, "We just opened the case yesterday afternoon and it's being handled!" My defense and arguments only seemed to make them more annoyed with me.

FBI to review brutality charge

■ Shreveport chief seeks help to clear his department's name.

By NITA BIRMINGHAM
The Times

FBI agents will review the arrest of Melvin Lewis, who was injured during a confrontation with Shreveport police, to determine if they should investigate officers' actions.

The federal involvement comes at the request of Shreveport Police Chief Steve Prator, who sent a letter Tuesday to Bill Larsh, supervisory senior resident agent of the FBI Shreveport office.

"At this point, we're just trying to gather some preliminary facts," Larsh said. "If the facts merit an investigation, we will investigate."

Police scuffled with Lewis on

April 16 after a traffic stop. A family member said Lewis was hospitalized with neck injuries the next day. Complaints of civil rights violations were alleged by Lewis' family and a City Council member.

The FBI has jurisdiction to investigate civil rights complaints against federal, state or local law enforcement officials.

It is a crime for a person acting under his or her authority as a law enforcement official to deprive or cause someone to be deprived of their civil rights. Punishment varies from a fine to imprisonment or death, depending on the circumstances and injury, if any, sustained by

Prator

■ See INTERNAL 2A

FBI forwards Lewis probe to Justice Department

By NITA BIRMINGHAM
The Times

The FBI has finished its investigation into the Melvin Lewis case and forwarded its report to the U.S. Department of Justice civil rights division.

Bill Larsh, supervisory senior resident agent of the FBI Shreveport office, said he couldn't comment on the results of the investigation, the number of people interviewed or if agents interviewed Lewis.

Larsh said it's standard for the division to review the FBI's report to determine if a civil rights violation occurred. The Shreveport Police Department will not receive a copy of the report.

Justice spokesman John Russell said members of the civil rights division will study the bureau's report to determine if a grand jury investigation should be done or the matter should be dropped. That determination could take months, he said.

Allegations of excessive police force were made by Lewis' family after a physical confrontation April 16 between Shreveport police officers and Lewis. Police said Lewis was stopped for traffic violations. His family said he had to be hospitalized the next day because of neck injuries.

The federal investigation began in early May after Shreveport Police Chief Steve Prator invited

the bureau to review the case. Lewis, 46, is in a room at LSU Medical Center. A relative said he has two broken bones and one chipped and one dislocated bone in his neck and is paralyzed from the neck down.

Lewis was moved July 1 from the hospital to a local nursing home, but was there only one night and had to return to LSUMC, said his mother, Ruby Kirksey. She said Lewis requires round-the-clock care and can't feed himself.

Lewis was stopped by police for not wearing a seat belt and not using a turn signal. A police department release stated Lewis was uncooperative and became progressively erratic and violent.

Two officers fell to the ground with Lewis after he tried to flee, which may be when he injured his neck, Prator said in late April. The fall is believed to have been the only physical contact between Lewis and the officers, the department has stated. But a sister of Lewis' said he told her two days after his arrest that officers beat him.

Lewis was arrested for several traffic violations, simple battery and resisting an officer; booking information on the department's computer stated Lewis kicked officers.

The police department's internal investigation found no wrongdoing by the officers who had contact with Lewis.

Shreveport Times, dated 7/22/1998, regarding civil rights case.

The FBI routinely investigated these types of cases, usually at the behest of the Shreveport Chief of Police to offset bad public relations. The problem with Shreveport was that it was a segregated city in the late 1990s. The west side of Shreveport was populated by blacks and was rife with black gangs, the Bloods and Crips, and others. It was a violent and scary part of town. To the east of downtown Shreveport was the Red River. Across the river was Bossier City, a town consisting of a mainly white population, considered more or less to be a nice, middle-class suburb of Shreveport.

The newspapers and the NAACP accused the Shreveport Police Department of discrimination and racism whenever a black individual was hurt or killed in an arrest, no matter what the circumstances, sort of like today. This was not to say that Louisiana was not the most racist place I had ever seen, it was. I am merely saying that the majority of civil rights investigations in which I was personally involved concluded that the police officers used necessary force. However, Louisiana was the first place I had ever heard the n-word used so frequently. I had heard this term used numerous times throughout my life, but normally by people I thought were low class, uneducated, or just ignorant.

In Louisiana, I heard my neighbor using the term in everyday conversation without blinking an eye. She was otherwise a very nice lady with young children, apparently well-bred and educated, but possessing deep prejudices that I surmised were ingrained in her upbringing. My parents were not bigots and I never heard them utter the n-word. The closest they came to being prejudiced was in describing their childhood homes, row houses in the middle of Baltimore City. When they were kids in the 1920s, 1930s, and 1940s, my parents said the residents were proud of their homes and would even scrub their marble doorsteps. By the 1970s, these neighborhoods were all black. When talking about the condition of their childhood homes, my parents said, "Now, they just don't care."

I went to a bar in the evening following work with some of the agents after first arriving in Shreveport. I overheard a conversation between an agent, who I would describe as a good old boy from the South, and a former USA in the Northern District of Louisiana. They both used the n-word in conversation at the bar that sounded as if they had been talking like that their entire lives. I was really quite appalled to hear these two using such language, but I was after all in the deep South. The worst case of racism occurred about a year and a half later in Monroe. An agent investigated a civil rights case involving the sheriff of the parish who allegedly beat a black prisoner with a sap (a leather-covered hand weapon similar to a blackjack or billy club) as he was admitted into the local jail after being arrested on drug charges. Two witnesses, a male guard and a female employee at the prison intake, testified at a federal trial that the sheriff beat the man with a sap, telling him words to the effect, "I don't want no drug dealing nigger son of a bitch in my parish ever again." The all white jury found the sheriff not guilty. They apparently appreciated his sentiments.

The ASACs in New Orleans never got off my back or gave me a break. When I first arrived, an agent in Monroe had an undercover operation proposal regarding police corruption that he had been having trouble getting approved prior to my arrival. I helped the agent re-write his proposal after consulting with the Public Corruption Unit at FBI Headquarters. They advised that a local undercover review committee at the field office level had to approve the proposal. After the field division approved it, the proposal had to be sent to FBI Headquarters for approval by the undercover review committee there.

After the agent in Monroe informed me of the delay in getting his undercover operation approved, I called my ASAC to advise him of the urgency to approve the proposal. I explained to the ASAC what my agent had told me. The agent had an informant who had advised that a sergeant in the Tallulah Police Department took bribes to protect drug traffickers. The city of Tallulah, Louisiana, was very close to the Mississippi state line just north of I-20. The grounds for a fictitious scenario to form the basis for an undercover operation targeting the sergeant had already been set in motion. The informant had a discussion with the sergeant regarding the need for the protection of a drug shipment expected to come through Tallulah soon. The sergeant indicated he would be more than willing to protect the drug shipment for a price.

The problem now was getting this scenario approved by the FBI New Orleans Division, and then by FBI Headquarters, in order to proceed. The longer the wait to begin the undercover operation, the worse the informant's credibility would become. This dilemma was explained to the ASAC, who was most uncooperative. As I was telling him about this potentially successful and important case for the FBI to pursue, the ASAC's response was, "Bill, we do things at our own pace in this division." I was astounded at his response and said, "But the informant's credibility diminishes over time and a delay in implementing this scenario might lessen its chances for success." The ASAC became irritated with me and just said we'd have to wait. The only reason I could surmise for his uncooperative response was because of the SAC's influence. This incident was as illogical as being reprimanded for waiting to call him the following morning regarding the civil rights allegation against the Shreveport officer. I knew this was all just personal. I could not believe the FBI management was this stupid. This was obviously being done out of spite.

The undercover scenario did not get under way for another three months. We had to wait for the New Orleans Division to finally meet and approve it, then for FBI Headquarters to approve it, and finally for an undercover agent to be selected and for funding to be received for the case. After all these steps were accomplished, a house was rented in Tallulah for the undercover agent to use. The house was wired for video and audio to record meetings with the sergeant. The scenario was set for the informant to introduce the undercover agent to the sergeant as his cousin. The undercover agent would then set up a drug shipment to come to Tallulah requiring the sergeant's protection. The first meeting was set at a local bar in Tallulah where the informant would introduce the undercover agent. This first meeting would merely be a social one and no drug shipment would be discussed yet.

On the Friday night when this was to occur, I called the ASAC at 5:30 p.m. to inform him of the meeting that was scheduled to take place in Tallulah 9 p.m. that evening. The ASAC told me very abruptly to get out there and be on the scene. I told him the meeting was being adequately covered with a surveillance team. I further advised him that the meeting was simply an introduction and nothing of substance would be discussed. The ASAC said, "I don't care, I want you out there." I responded, "You do know that Tallulah is two and a half hours away, don't you?" He said, "I want you there at every meeting." I said okay and proceeded to Tallulah. The meeting took place with the undercover agent being introduced, but nothing eventful occurred.

The following week, the informant asked the sergeant to come to his house and discuss business with his cousin. The sergeant said he would be able to come next week. I received a telephone call from the ASAC who told me I had to attend civil rights training at Quantico that same week. I explained to him that the sergeant, the informant, and the undercover agent were to meet that week at the rented residence. "You said you wanted me to be present at every meeting," I said. The ASAC responded, "Send your relief supervisor to the meeting, you are going to training." I said, "Okay, you're the boss." I was getting fed up with the bullshit from the front office. It was clear to me that they were just fucking with me.

Following my return from Quantico, I participated in every surveillance involving the undercover agent. I am sure no other SSRA in the FBI was so deeply involved in their agent's case. I really did not mind it too much, as I enjoyed being on the street in the middle of the action. The case was a huge success. The meetings at the house captured the sergeant on tape agreeing to protect a drug shipment in Tallulah for the sum of $500. A bogus drug deal and a phony shipment of drugs were planned at a motel. The sergeant had accepted his $500 bribe, memorialized on audio and video tape, and was later observed by the surveillance team (to include myself and the Tallulah Police Chief) at the motel in his cruiser providing police protection to the drug deal he believed was transpiring inside.

U.S. Department of Justice

Federal Bureau of Investigation

Office of the Director

Washington, D.C. 20535

September 25, 1998

PERSONAL

Mr. William A. Larsh
Federal Bureau of Investigation
New Orleans, Louisiana

Dear Mr. Larsh:

    I am genuinely pleased to have this moment to commend you for your special efforts in connection with a Corruption of State and Local Public Officials investigation. Moreover, I have approved a cash award for you which will be forwarded at a later date.

    Your professional competence, initiative, and commitment to duty enabled you to make material contributions to the successful outcome attained. While supporting the Bureau, you executed your duties with the utmost professionalism and tenacity to help achieve the overall mission. I want to express my gratitude for your services during this undertaking. Thank you for a job well done.

Sincerely yours,

Louis J. Freeh
Director

Letter of Commendation and Incentive Award, dated 9/25/1998, from Director Louis J. Freeh for my work on the police corruption case in Tallulah, Louisiana.

Despite my supervision over some of the biggest cases in the division, I received only average performance appraisals. I had another agent who worked on two Title III wiretap investigations targeting major drug trafficking organizations in northern Louisiana. Undercover operations and wiretaps were the most prestigious types of cases in the FBI. They involved the most sophisticated investigative techniques used in cases. When I recommended both my case agents for QSIs for these cases, the ASAC said only one agent could receive the QSI because only one was given per squad. I reminded him that I actually had two squads, Shreveport and Monroe, which no other SSA had. He just stared at me with contempt and said, "You only get one QSI, pick one agent." So only the one agent ended up getting the QSI, but at least I was able to get the other agent a cash incentive award. It was a painful reminder of how I never received my QSIs. I had been treated unfairly in the past and now I felt like I was treating an agent unfairly, although through no fault of my own.

A first-office agent was assigned to Shreveport who had been a former officer with the Hillsborough County Sheriff's Office in Tampa, Florida. His background was investigating drugs so I immediately assigned him to the FBI Gang Task Force. This first-office agent hit the ground running producing more federal indictments in his first nine months in the FBI than any other agent I had ever seen. He led the task force with his aggressive investigative techniques and his instant camaraderie with the local law enforcement assigned to the task force. His performance and output exceeded every agent in the office. On his first performance appraisal, I gave him the highest rating attainable, "Exceptional." The ASAC in New Orleans called me immediately after seeing his rating and said, "You can't give a first year agent an exceptional rating." I responded, "Yes, I can, since he's the hardest working agent in Shreveport and produced more stats by far than any other agent in the office." He had no argument. For once, I got my way.

✣FEBRUARY 27, 1999

Mooretown drug raid nets Crips arrests

■ Latest sting should make area safer, officials say.

Gang activity decreases

By Don Walker
The Times

From Staff Reports

Eight prominent members of the Rolling 60s Crips gang are in federal custody and a ninth is being sought in connection with cocaine trafficking in Shreveport's Mooretown neighborhood.

The FBI's Gang Task Force made five of the arrests Friday during an early morning sweep through west Shreveport. A sixth suspect was arrested Friday afternoon.

Two other gang members already were in custody on other drug-related charges. And a ninth suspect, 27-year-old Titus Rogers, remains a fugitive, authorities said.

The arrests stem from federal grand jury indictments issued **Rogers**

Thursday, following a year-long investigation by city, state and parish police agencies into cocaine and crack cocaine distribution sales in Mooretown.

Friday's raid will jam the drug trade and make Mooretown safer from other crimes as well, said police Lt. Alan Hall, who heads Shreveport's street-level interdiction unit. Robberies are common, and often drug-related.

Charged with Rogers in the indictments on distribution and conspiracy to distribute cocaine are John E. Williams Jr., 39, of Bossier Parish and Shreveporters Thomas "T.J." Kanavari, 31, Luke Samuels, 29, Darren Cannon, 32, Brad Gaston, 23, James "Jay" Smith, 23, Eddie "Little E" Johnson, 25, and Bryan Moran, 19.

"These are considered major drug distributors in the city," said Bill Larsh, head of the FBI in Shreveport. The amount of the cocaine involved was referred to only as "significant."

"There was a lot of cocaine going through that area," said as-

Reports of area gang-related crime aren't nearly as prevalent today as they were in the drive-by shooting-plagued 1980s.

Most problems now stem from young gang wannabes, say area law enforcers.

The youths wear gang colors, spray gang graffiti at parks and on buildings and act like gangs, but they're not recognized by actual gang members, said Lt. Alan Hall, who heads Shreveport police's Street Level Interdiction Unit.

But some neighborhoods are plagued by real gangs of older males, especially those in their late 20s and early 30s, who commit mostly drug-related crimes.

The Rolling 60s Crips in Mooretown would be one such gang. A gang by the same name operates in the Martin Luther King Jr. Drive area. In Queensborough, Bloods have staked turf.

In Webster Parish, the firebombing of a car three weeks ago in Springhill allegedly was gang-related. In nearby Cullen, young men are wearing red Bloods' and blue Crips' colors, a trend that has increased in the past eight to six months, according to Police Chief Dexter Turner.

■

Times reporters Don Walker and Melody Brumble contributed to this report.

sistant U.S. Attorney Jim Cowles.

Mooretown was the target of a crime crackdown by police in August 1996. Annie Bell, a 39-year resident of Mooretown, was pleased to hear about the arrests but said more needs to be done.

"It seems like every time they get somebody out, more people come in to cause problems."

The suspects face life in prison if convicted.

"They are a danger to the community and likely will be detained without bond" before trial, Cowles said.

Shreveport Times, dated 2/27/1999, regarding FBI Gang Task Force arrests.

By November 1998, I'd had it working for what I perceived as a bunch of petty, spiteful jerks. My father died on November 2, 1998. I was devastated upon learning the news of his death. I immediately flew home with the family for a week. I was touched when I saw flowers at the funeral home from the FBI personnel in Shreveport, as well as flowers from the Tallulah Police Chief. Upon returning to Shreveport after the funeral, my relief supervisor told me that the SAC had called her the day I left for home, questioning her about whether or not I called New Orleans regarding my departure. She said he asked nothing about my father's death and seemed to have little concern about it. He was mad because of my immediate departure, which made me furious.

Several weeks later, my new ASAC called me with more idiotic criticism regarding yet another non-issue, missing another supervisor conference. In the conversation, I defended myself by telling the ASAC how busy I had been recently. As I detailed my busy schedule, I mentioned that I had been out of the office for a week to attend my father's funeral the previous month, causing me to miss the supervisor conference. He surprisingly said, "I don't want to hear about your father dying again." I could not believe his insensitivity. I became incensed. I unloaded on him and told him I was fed up with him, the SAC, and all their pettiness. My emotions were running high. "I am tired of all this Goddamn nonsense," I said. He finally hung up on me and called back a few minutes later, sheepishly saying, "You can't curse at me, I'm your supervisor." My blow-up at him did not help my situation. This new ASAC continued to nit-pick everything I did. On my next visit to New Orleans for the supervisor conference, the ASAC criticized me for never staying in New Orleans long enough to go to lunch with him and the other SSAs. I explained to him that I drove 325 miles the night before to get to the meeting. I left for Shreveport at 11 a.m. at the conclusion of the supervisor meeting because I had a five-hour drive back to Shreveport. I told him I had work to do. I further told him that I did not want to be away from my wife and two small children any longer than necessary.

On one occasion, I did have one extraordinary trip to New Orleans. A senior agent in the SRA had a meeting at the FBI New Orleans office on the same day as one of my supervisor conferences. This senior agent was good friends with the owner of Davison Trucking in Ruston, Louisiana. I never met the owner, but I knew he was a very rich man. He told my senior agent that if his boss ever wanted to play golf or stay on his yacht while in New Orleans, he should let him know. The senior agent did let him know and we stayed the night on his $3 million yacht, the *Dixie Gem*, on Lake Pontchartrain. The yacht was huge with a captain and full crew on board. The trucking company owner was not there. The senior agent and I were the only guests.

Upon our arrival in the late afternoon, the captain gave us a private tour around Lake Pontchartrain. He later provided us with *Dixie Gem* hats and t-shirts as souvenirs. For dinner, a chef from a renowned French Quarter restaurant took our requests and prepared our meals. I asked for a filet mignon. It was the fanciest meal I had ever eaten. The problem was that I was born the pickiest eater in the world. I figured that a steak would not be too complicated. I told the chef I didn't want mushrooms or any sauce on it. I'm sure he wasn't impressed. He brought us a bowl of soup I had never seen before. It was a thick orange broth with black swirls on top. It looked like something out of a magazine, more like an artistic presentation of soup. I had no idea what it was, but I had to eat it. I didn't like it very much, but I forced it down. When the salads came, I pleaded with the senior agent to eat some of mine since it was covered with a million things I didn't like. Luckily, he did. I was so embarrassed and didn't want the chef to know I didn't like anything. However, the filet mignon and the potatoes were to die for, probably the best steak I'd ever eaten.

When we got up in the morning, the same chef was there to take our orders for breakfast. The senior agent ordered a full breakfast. I ordered scrambled eggs, toast, orange juice and milk. I told him to fix the eggs plain, no cheese and no pepper, nothing on them at all. The chef gave me the same look as the night before when I ordered my plain filet mignon. It was all very uncomfortable. This renowned chef was being wasted on me. The senior agent, however, ate everything. The chef brought out two plates of sliced melons and cantaloupes, more items I did not like. The presentation on the plate of these melons was like everything else, almost like a work of art. I again pleaded to the senior agent to eat some of mine. He gladly did as he was enjoying everything much more than I was. The eggs and toast were good, but I'm not sure the chef had ever experienced the likes of me before.

After the supervisor meeting that same morning, I met up with the senior agent who was through with his meeting as well. Our next leg of the trip before heading to Shreveport was to play golf at the English Turn Golf and Country Club, located southeast of New Orleans, compliments of the trucking company owner. This exclusive golf club was home to the PGA tournament, the Zurich Classic. The owner arranged for us to play, but again he was not there. We played with an older gentleman whose name I have forgotten. The senior agent told me that this gentleman was only worth $800 million, while his friend was worth more than a billion dollars. At any rate, we had the best time playing golf on the most well maintained course I had ever played. If the chef from the French Quarter was wasted on me, playing golf at this course was wasted on the senior agent. He was not a golfer. Although he never finished a hole, he appeared to be having a good time.

I was in heaven on this course. I played well due to the fact that I had a caddy who knew every break on every green. He would point to a spot on the green when I putted, and the ball invariably broke toward the hole after hitting his spot. This method was more effective on the short putts. I made every short putt based on where he said to putt it. Only once all day was he wrong when he pointed to an inch outside the cup and my ball stayed an inch outside the cup. I shot an 82. I was thrilled with my score and the opportunity to have played at such a great golfing venue.

The experience on the yacht and playing at the golf club was the highlight of an otherwise troubling time for me while in Louisiana. It was a shame really. I loved being in charge of the two offices. I liked all of the agents working for me and enjoyed working with them. I believed they liked me and my management style too. I relished being involved in the cases, working with the other law enforcement agencies, appearing on television and in the newspaper speaking on behalf of the FBI, and making friends in and around Shreveport. However, I just could not stand the FBI management in New Orleans.

In January 1998, a horrendous crime occurred in Shreveport. Two white males, Timothy D. Taylor and Michael A. Taylor (not related), aged eighteen and twenty, teamed up on a crime spree, beginning with the murder of a Shreveport car salesman, Chester Howell, a black male. The Taylors requested Howell to take them out for a test drive. They drove to a remote wooded area and murdered him in cold blood, leaving his body on the road and fleeing in the stolen new car.

I attended Chester Howell's funeral on Saturday morning in west Shreveport. I was the only law enforcement officer there. I not only wanted to give my sincere condolences, but I wanted to ensure the family that the FBI was doing everything in its power to apprehend these murderers and bring them to justice. I also understood what it meant to loved ones of the deceased to know that people cared, having buried my father less than two months earlier.

The first lead in the case came in from Arkansas the day after Howell's murder, where the Taylors reportedly held up a gas station and then acquired an Arkansas license tag for their stolen vehicle. A few days later, they robbed a bank in Lamoni, Iowa, shooting and wounding the Police Chief there during their escape. A week went by with no word on the whereabouts of the fugitives. The FBI assisted the Shreveport police with efforts to locate and apprehend the two alleged murderers. One of my agents immediately obtained a UFAP federal arrest warrant. The police and the FBI interviewed their family members and friends as part of the investigation.

A search warrant was conducted at their residence in Blanchard, a town northwest of Shreveport, which proved to be the most disgusting search warrant in which I was ever involved. The house was owned by one of the boy's mothers. Based on the condition of the inside of the house, the inhabitants had to have been the worst white trash I had ever encountered. The house was pure filth. The bathroom had a pile of dirty clothes, many of which were stained with feces. They apparently had no toilet paper and were using clothing to wipe. The best evidence we uncovered was from a family member who told us that the two boys had repeatedly watched the Woody Harrelson movie, *Natural Born Killers*, in the days leading up to the car salesman's murder. They may have been motivated by the extremely violent movie. I had never seen it, but I was told that the characters in the movie went on a murderous crime spree.

The FBI Shreveport office was consumed for nine days with the investigation of these murders and the apprehension of the fugitives. We had a tip from one of their friends that they were coming back to Shreveport on a bus. The entire office set up surveillance for the night at the Greyhound bus station down the street from the office. The fugitives, however, did not return to Shreveport. The next evening, FBI San Antonio Division notified me that the fugitives were stopped by Mexican authorities on a bus twenty miles inside Mexico.

The fugitives were able to travel across the border into Mexico since the Mexicans did not have a checkpoint on the border. They conducted their customs checks twenty miles inside their borders. When the fugitives could not produce passports, the Mexican authorities sent them back to Laredo, Texas. The United States Customs ran identification checks and discovered the two were fugitives. They were arrested without incident. I had been speaking to the press daily during the nine-day manhunt and it continued to be the top story in the Shreveport media when they were caught.

Front page story regarding the fugitives in the *Shreveport Times*, dated 1/16/1999.

This was the last big case in which I was involved in Shreveport or Monroe. I had written a proposal six months previously justifying an SSRA position for Monroe, which FBI Headquarters approved at the end of the year. The new SSRA was someone I thought was a nice guy, but our paths crossed later in my career, proving he was anything but nice, decent, or even honest. I spent the month of February 1999 in constant contact with the Transfer Unit at FBI Headquarters. I put my name on the Philadelphia Division OP List for Harrisburg. I was first on the list. I figured this was the closest I could get to home. Harrisburg was about sixty miles north of Baltimore.

My father had died tragically in November, and Cindy's sister, Betsy, was having her third heart operation at the age of thirty-seven to make further repairs on her weak arteries. Between my grief for my father and my wife's worries for her sister, not to mention the shabby treatment I had received from the FBI New Orleans management, I was ready to get out of there.

I had purchased a home next to the ninth tee at the Palmetto Country Club after transferring to Shreveport. After one year, however, the membership decided to close the course for a year to rebuild their sand traps. They voted to continue collecting dues, despite not being able to play. I immediately quit. I was in the same situation as I had been in Crofton. I lived on the golf course, but had to play somewhere else. This predicament was yet another reason I wanted to leave.

In March 1999, I got the call from the Transfer Unit. They did not offer me Harrisburg, but instead offered me the State College Resident Agency (SCRA), located about eighty-five miles northwest of Harrisburg. It was explained that the Philadelphia Division was not going to transfer anybody to Harrisburg in the near future and had decided they wanted an agent with an FCI background to fill a spot in State College. This seemed my only chance to leave. I had previously been on the Baltimore OP List where I was ranked twentieth, which was why I changed my OP to the Philadelphia Division. If I wanted to leave Shreveport, this was my opportunity.

My wife hated Shreveport from the start. The public schools were substandard to what she was accustomed to and she detested their corporal punishment policy. She had to provide a signed letter to the school stating that we did not wish the school to utilize corporal punishment on our children. Their elementary school had barbed wire around its perimeter. The curriculum had no science, social studies, music, art, or physical education. She was anxious to get the children away from Louisiana and also to get back close to Baltimore, even if it was as far away as State College. The following year, the *USA Today* newspaper reported that convicts on a work crew on the road next to the very school where our children attended were caught participating in lewd acts while school children were on the playground.

Prior to leaving Louisiana, I witnessed a tornado right outside my window and I didn't even know it. It was on Holy Saturday in April 1999. I played golf at the Barksdale Air Force Base in Bossier City at 11 a.m. At about 3 p.m., I was on my way home to Benton, about eight miles north. I noticed the skies were darkening and believed a thunderstorm was coming. By the time I got home, it was pouring down rain with thunder, lightening, and heavy winds. The electricity was out due to the storm when I arrived at the house. No one was home. I remembered Cindy had told me that she and the children would be visiting a friend's house a few neighborhoods away.

Since everyone was gone, I thought it would be a good opportunity to finally read a batch of love letters my father had written to my mother during World War II before they were married. I had retrieved them the previous winter from my father's house after he died. Since no lights would go on, I sat on a couch by a large bay window in the garden room at the rear of the house overlooking our patio. As I began reading my father's letters, I became fascinated with the information being revealed about my parents' courtship. My father's letters clearly indicated his love and devotion to my mother, but he was full of uncertainty as to her feelings toward him.

I became so engrossed in his letters that I did not notice the deadly storm right outside my window. I didn't comprehend that the winds had picked up and the rain was more horizontal than vertical. The American flag on the railing of the patio appeared to almost be getting blown out of its mount. Visibility had become very poor. Our house was located on the golf course, but I could barely see anything beyond my back yard. I simply believed a severe thunderstorm was taking place.

I continued to enjoy my father's letters, which were reading like a novel. My parents' story had a happy ending, despite some bumps along the way with hurt feelings, jealousy, and all the usual relationship problems. The letters revealed that my mother finally declared her love for my father while he was away at war. It was also fascinating to learn of my father's experiences during his military duty. He seemed to be mostly bored and homesick. While on his ship, he said that while most of the guys craved a beer, all he wanted was a chocolate ice cream soda. The storm passed and Cindy and the children arrived home. The phone and electricity were still out.

Cindy came into the garden room and asked what I was doing. I told her I had been reading my father's letters. She looked a bit rattled and asked if had taken cover from the tornado. I said, "What? A tornado?" Cindy said that her friend had a battery-operated radio on after the electricity and phones went down. The radio warned that a grade four tornado with 150-175 mph winds was heading toward Benton. Cindy said that she, our son, Ethan, our daughter, Mary, the neighbor and her two children, all took cover under mattresses in the hallway in the middle of the neighbor's house.

When I told Cindy I had been sitting right there reading the entire time, she shook her head in disbelief. The houses on the other end of the golf course, maybe 600-800 yards away from our house, were completely demolished. When I saw them the following day, the area reminded me of the bombings I had seen on television in Beirut, Lebanon, in the early 1980s. Some of the homes were swept completely off their concrete foundations. Surprisingly, no one in these neighborhoods was killed. However, the news reports indicated that several people were killed in nearby trailer parks. An hour later, one of the agents from the office drove to my house to find out if I was okay since the telephones were still out. Tornadoes were yet another reason to get out of Louisiana.

FBI New Orleans Division Directory 1998

CHAPTER 18

PENNSYLVANIA

On May 6, 1999, I moved my family once again across the country, this time to a beautiful home on over three acres in Belleville, Pennsylvania, located twenty-five miles south of State College. Belleville was in the middle of Kishacoquillas Valley, a scenic rural area populated with Amish farms, complete with horses and buggies on every road. It was a throwback in time, very quaint, and almost idyllic. Cindy loved the Union Elementary School in Belleville, the teachers, the neighbors, and just about everything about this unique community. Our house was a gigantic 3,700 square foot brick rancher with a two-car garage and a built-in swimming pool, purchased for a mere $185,000. I thought I would spend the rest of my life there.

Work in the SCRA started out very well for me. I was assigned an espionage case immediately that had originally been assigned to another agent. This other agent convinced the SSRA that he had another big case which demanded his full attention and he did not have the time to work on this one. I was happy to work the case. I knew working in the SCRA was not going to be anything like working FCI in Washington, D.C. However, the FBI's FCI mission in State College was essentially the same as anywhere else in the United States. The FBI's strategy, known as the National Security Threat List (NSTL), involved an issues threat list and a country threat list. The issues threat list involved eight issues: terrorism, espionage, proliferation, economic espionage, the targeting of national information infrastructure, the targeting of the United States government, perception management, and foreign intelligence activities. The countries listed on the NSTL were then and are now classified.

My subject was a visiting research scholar on a J-1 visa believed to be trying to steal classified military information. He was reported to have previously worked at an institute in his home country for a known intelligence officer at the institute. My case involved obtaining warrants from the FISA Court to monitor his telephone, e-mail, and facsimile machine. I utilized a military translator who flew in for sixty days. All the monitoring was stored on a hard drive. The translator converted everything into English. After sixty days, however, no shred of evidence regarding espionage was uncovered. The visiting scholar did send a voluminous amount of information back to the intelligence officer at the institute, but all of it was public source material. Nothing was sent that was classified. He had no apparent access to any classified materials. The only valuable information derived from my effort was learning who his contacts were in the United States.

My only option was to interview him and hope to gain his cooperation. Before interviewing any foreign national in the United States who possessed an F-1 student visa or a J-1 visiting research scholar visa, I first had to request approval from FBI Headquarters. The FBI then had to send a request to the USDS for a "No Foreign Policy Objection Statement" (NFPOS) to interview the subject. The USDS had oversight in order to ensure that no international incident might occur as a result of the interview. It generally took about six months to get the NFPOS approved.

Upon approval, I immediately called my subject to come into the FBI office for an interview. These types of interviews were not supposed to be confrontational, per the USDS. The subject admitted working for the reported intelligence officer from the institute in his country, but he had no knowledge of him being affiliated with intelligence. It was clear the subject was not going to cooperate with the FBI fully. He admitted sending public source information back to the institute, but he said it was all part of his studies.

One of his contacts was a fellow countryman who owned a restaurant in State College. I interviewed this restaurant owner who said he met the subject only after he came to the United States. My subject was planning to attend Shippensburg University the next semester. The restaurant owner said the subject had to attach a copy of his bank statement on his application to the college and on his USINS forms to prove he had the financial ability to attend school. The restaurant owner said that he assisted him by writing a $25,000 check for him to deposit into his bank account. The subject paid him back in two weeks, but in the meantime, he made a copy of his bank statement to show he had the financial means to attend school.

Upon learning of this information, I called the university admissions office and the USINS to inform them of the subject's application falsification. Consequently, the college did not accept him and the USINS did not renew his visa. Although I did not prove espionage against him, at least my investigation exposed his dishonesty, resulting in the denial of his visa and his return to his home country.

Department of Justice
Federal Bureau of Investigation

Performance Award

Presented to
William A. Larsh

in recognition and appreciation of exceptional performance of official duties throughout the past year.

March 31, 1999
_____
Date

_____
Federal Bureau of Investigation

Department of Justice
Federal Bureau of Investigation

Performance Award

Presented to

William A. Larsh

in recognition and appreciation of exceptional
performance of official duties throughout the
past year.

March 31, 2000
Date

Federal Bureau of Investigation

I mainly worked FCI cases in the SCRA, but occasionally I was assigned other matters. I worked one bank robbery case during my tenure at the SCRA. The bank robbery occurred in Lewistown, a depressed town about thirty miles southeast of State College. Very few bank robberies occurred during my four and a half years assigned there. This was not the ORA where they had eighty pending bank robbery cases at any one time. This was the only pending bank robbery case in the SCRA at that time. These were relatively easy cases. This particular bank robber was later identified and eventually apprehended. I was also assigned a civil rights investigation involving a mentally ill man who died during an arrest by officers at a local hospital. He had gone to his doctor's office for an early morning appointment to receive his medication. When he discovered he would not be seen by his usual doctor, he became upset, and then violent, assaulting a nurse. He stormed out of the office pushing the lobby door so hard, he left a hole in the wall. A warrant was subsequently issued for his arrest.

When he was confronted by police officers in a hospital parking lot later that morning, the psychotic man, roughly 6 feet 3 inches tall and weighing well over 250 pounds, punched an officer in the face. This very large and angry man put up a tough fight with the police. It took seven officers to wrestle him to the ground and subdue him. At least five or six officers ended up on top of him. He was finally handcuffed, but was unconscious. He was placed into the back of a squad car and taken to the emergency room. He was found to be brain dead. His wife made the decision to pull the plug on his life support system a few days later and he died. The wife was furious at the police and believed he was unnecessarily killed. My investigation determined that all of the police officers and witnesses to the incident were consistent in their version of events.

The coroner ruled his death a homicide by traumatic asphyxia. A homicide in medical terms meant that he died by the hand of another. A homicide did not mean murder in the legal sense. Traumatic asphyxia was the result of the police sitting on his chest and diaphragm which prevented him from breathing. It was an accidental death. The police were justified in their actions in trying to restrain this rather large and belligerent individual who was suffering a psychotic episode after not being prescribed his medication. The wife called me several times demanding justice. I could never tell her the results of my investigation. I was not allowed. At the conclusion of my investigation, I advised her that the results were forwarded to the Civil Rights Division at DOJ. They would decide whether prosecution was warranted. I knew it did not. The Civil Rights Division took nine months to make this determination. After being advised by DOJ, I called the wife to advise her of their opinion. She remained very angry and believed an injustice was perpetrated. She had no interest in hearing that the evidence did not support charges being brought forth against the police.

My FCI cases were somewhat mundane over the next several years. They basically consisted of identifying the foreign nationals who were from the countries on the NSTL, conducting backgrounds on them, and then obtaining the NFPOS in order to interview them. I interviewed hundreds of these individuals and the majority of them said they were in the United States because of better educational opportunities and/or a superior standard of living in the United States. I never gathered a bit of intelligence from any of them. I supposed the only good it may have done was to put them on notice if any of them had actually been in the United States for nefarious purposes.

I soon learned that there was not enough work for the agents in the SCRA. I kept busy, but it was dull and overall was not very fulfilling work. I realized that the agent who had the espionage case transferred to me when I first arrived to the SCRA was either a fraud or a complete nut. His big case that he worked on for over five years and his excuse to work on little else was targeting a woman who had worked as a secretary for a suspected intelligence officer at an institute from her home country. She became a United States citizen after marrying an American-born individual. She had been living in the United States with her husband and child for ten years. The agent collected her trash for five years hoping to gather evidence to prove she was connected to intelligence. The trash often smelled up the office. The SCRA office was too small for all the trash he collected, so he would often take it home to his garage to search through it.

Early on in his investigation he found a flattened "Dots" candy box in her trash. The inside of the candy box had a rudimentary map drawn on it indicating the location of a hostel in central Pennsylvania. The goofy agent extrapolated that this was a "drop site" for an intelligence officer because of an "X" marked on the map indicating the site of the hostel. This agent had apparently read one too many spy novels. His investigation was completely ludicrous. No evidence existed that she ever returned to her home country or maintained any contact with her old boss after coming to the United States. It was even more ridiculous that FBI management allowed him to continue with this farce for five years.

The SSRA of State College had no experience in FCI work and took the agent's word for the importance of the case. The SSRA also might have wanted to keep the case on the books to make the FCI program look good. The management in the Philadelphia Division probably wanted the case kept open for similar reasons.

Annual reports were furnished to FBI Headquarters by field offices regarding not only FCI cases, but all cases. These reports were used as justification to have more agents added to certain programs and to the office overall. A lot of the reporting was only a game to gain resources for the division.

A new ASAC in Philadelphia finally did recognize that this agent's case had gone on long enough. The ASAC ordered the idiot agent to interview the woman. The former secretary admitted to working at the institute for the suspected intelligence officer, but she claimed no knowledge, affiliation, or ties to intelligence. Her last contact with the individual at the institute was when she left her home country almost ten years ago, she claimed. The agent's five-year investigation, based entirely on supposition, was finally closed. Any other normal agent would have interviewed the subject years before to determine what knowledge, if any, she may have had.

On September 11, 2001, I participated in a Career Day at Fulton County High School in McConnellsburg, Pennsylvania. I set up at a table to answer questions about the FBI and to provide informational pamphlets. The Career Day had barely gotten started when people started talking about a plane crashing into the World Trade Center in New York. Then a second plane crashed into the second tower. Everyone was now convinced this was no accident. People began hovering around a television set in a room off the school cafeteria. I remembered one man asking me, "How will they ever find out who did this?" I told him with great confidence that the FBI would be able to identify everyone who was on those planes. The perpetrators would definitely be identified.

Further news reports revealed the complexity of this terror incident as a plane crashed into the Pentagon and another crashed into a field in Somerset County, not more than sixty miles away from McConnellsburg and less than one hundred miles from the SCRA. The man asked me, knowing I was an FBI agent, "Shouldn't you be doing something?" Other individuals began asking me the same thing. I began to feel very self-conscious about being at the Career Day. I did indeed believe that I should be doing something. I had already called the FBI office in State College and spoke to my partner. The FBI did not officially have "partners" like in local police departments, but we investigated everything together and considered ourselves partners in that sense. He said that the SCRA had not heard anything, but that he would call me back the minute he heard something. He called back about twenty minutes later and said he had gotten a call from the ASAC in Philadelphia. The ASAC told him that the SCRA agents should go home, pack, and be on standby. We assumed we would be going to the United Flight 93 crash site in Somerset County.

It took me about two hours to drive from the Fulton County High School to my home in Belleville. I got home at about noon, packed my bag, and ate lunch. I watched the news reports on the television the rest of the afternoon waiting on the call from my partner. I was filled with emotion, as were most Americans that dreadful day. As an FBI agent, I felt a special sense of duty in wanting to do something about it. I was very anxious to assist in Somerset County at the crime scene in whatever manner possible.

At about 4 p.m., my partner finally called to say that the SCRA agents were told to stand down. He said we would not be helping at the crash site in Somerset County. Somerset County was part of the FBI Pittsburgh territory and not FBI Philadelphia's territory. The executive management in Pittsburgh evidently told the ASAC in Philadelphia that the agents from the Johnstown RA, part of the FBI Pittsburgh Division, would handle the crime scene. The agents from the SCRA were not needed or wanted. I could not help but think, knowing the FBI management the way I did, that this was a result of some stupid territorial issue between the two divisions. It did not make sense that they would not welcome assistance from agents so close in proximity to one of the worst crime scenes in our nation's history. This news was a huge letdown to me. The man's comment from the Career Day at the school earlier "Shouldn't you be doing something?" resonated with me forever.

With the exception of the months following September 11, 2001, when everyone in the office was busy working counterterrorism matters, work in the SCRA was slow. Nearly all of the counterterrorism cases in State College investigated following 9/11 turned out to be nothing. Citizens were calling the FBI all over the country accusing every person of Middle-Eastern descent as would-be terrorists. At a library, a Middle-Eastern student was seen throwing away a flight manual. He was an American citizen of Pakistani descent, born in Brooklyn, New York, who had been taking single-engine plane flying lessons for two years. He was not a terrorist. A pizza delivery man called and said he saw Middle-Eastern men watching a terrorist training video in the apartment where he delivered their pizza. Investigation at the apartment determined no Middle-Eastern men living there, but two students from India attending school. They said the terrorist training video was footage being shown on CNN.

Things went from bad to worse for me at the SCRA. I worked as hard as I could, but it was not satisfying work interviewing foreign nationals. I could not stand the idiot agent who worked the trash case either. Despite every meaningless thing he did, he made it appear as if he was actually doing something important. I was sickened by his stupid case with the endless trash collection and the Dots candy box, but the last straw came when he wanted to use my cases as statistics for his source. When I arrived at the SCRA, the only way I was opening cases against foreign nationals was through a list this agent obtained. He never opened a single case from this list because he always claimed he was too busy. He was in fact quite occupied for years collecting and analyzing trash. It did not take me long to realize I could obtain a list myself. I developed my own contact so that I would not have to interact with him or depend on him to open cases. After my second year there, he again requested from me a list of all the cases I opened on foreign nationals so that he could credit his source with the opening of these cases. I explained to him that I had my own source who gave me the list of foreign nationals. He stated that his source was my source's superior and that his source had been credited with these case openings for years.

When I told him I was not going to give him the list, he said he was going to talk to the SSRA. The SSRA had recently been promoted to be in charge of two RAs, including the SCRA. He had been an agent working criminal matters for the past twenty years. He had a questionable reputation, was ignorant of FBI policies and procedures, and had no experience in FCI matters. Normally, supervisors were selected from FBI Headquarters, but because the last supervisor from FBI Headquarters had not worked out and ultimately quit the FBI altogether, the SAC in Philadelphia decided to select someone from within the office. The SAC in Philadelphia happened to be related to my partner by marriage. However, my partner's influence on the SAC was minimal. The SAC told my friend he would not discuss business or personnel matters with him to avoid any appearance of favoritism. My partner tried to tell the SAC that the new SSRA was not supervisory material, but his advice was ignored.

The SSRA's reputation was all about making money for himself and his buddies. I was told that in a white collar crime case some time previously, a golf course had been seized by the FBI and forfeited to the government. The SSRA and his friends were rumored to have been planning to bid on the low-priced golf course until the United States Marshals Service told them they could not, due to an obvious conflict of interest. After becoming SSRA, he became obsessed with power. He disliked two younger agents and did everything he could to make their lives miserable.

The first young new agent was one of the most intelligent and accomplished agents I had ever known. He was a computer genius, a martial arts expert, a firearms instructor, and a smart, aggressive investigator. When he came into the Bureau, he lived out of state with his wife and two children. He previously received permission by the Philadelphia front office to commute back and forth to his home about 100 miles away. When the SSRA became supervisor, he decided that this agent could not commute this far. The young agent did not want to move his family so he rented a room near the office during the week and went home on the weekends. The SSRA never seemed to appreciate the young agent's talents. After about a year of their deteriorating relationship, the SSRA arranged with the front office for a permanent transfer to Philadelphia for the agent. This agent ultimately resigned from the Bureau after a few months in Philadelphia.

Another young agent was also the target of the SSRA's wrath. The young agent was the nicest guy you'd ever want to meet. The SSRA's dislike for him seemed unbelievable. He applied to become an FBI polygrapher and was approved. He attended the FBI's polygraph school, completed the training successfully, and returned to the office ready to administer polygraph examinations as needed by the Bureau. Even though he was a polygraph examiner, he had to continue working his own cases. Polygraphers were requested to assist in criminal investigations, security background investigations, applicant cases, and vetting sources. If requested to conduct a polygraph examination, he could only do so with the approval of the SSRA. Normally, supervisors would grant approval, but not this SSRA.

The SSRA decided that the agent could not conduct polygraph examinations at the expense of his own cases. The agent was unable to utilize his new skill which had been obtained at a considerable cost to the FBI. The agent complained to the front office in Philadelphia and to the Polygraph Unit at FBI Headquarters. The response was always the same. His assistance on polygraph examinations was at the discretion of his supervisor. Years later, I learned through my best friend who was assigned to the Polygraph Unit at FBI Headquarters that this agent was rumored to have sued the FBI and was awarded $200,000 for the grief and ill-treatment he received at the hands of the SSRA and the FBI.

The SSRA also disliked me and my partner intensely. After I refused to hand over my list of new case openings for statistical credit to the other agent, the SSRA targeted me with retaliation. No matter what I worked on or what I accomplished, the SSRA found reason to criticize my performance and/or threaten me with non-existent misconduct issues. My performance appraisals were never better than average. The only reason he could not justify a poor performance rating was because I always had cases and accomplishments, albeit only minor ones. I was working in the SCRA after all. The SSRA would tell me that I did not go to lunch with the other agents in the RA besides my partner. He kept needling me in my file reviews that I should go to lunch with them and be friends with them. Finally, I got fed up and told him that I had been an SSRA once and I didn't have to be friends with anybody, including the supervisor, to do my job. I emphasized that I spoke to my co-workers regarding any pertinent business, as I did with him, but that was all that was required of me. I felt good about speaking my mind, but this behavior only made the SSRA more resolute in his efforts against me.

He repeatedly threatened me with referrals to OPR for misconduct issues. His idea of misconduct, however, was me just doing my job. For example, I had a lead from FBI Headquarters in the FBI's anthrax investigation to determine who at Penn State University handled or had access to anthrax. My partner and I met with a professor who was the contact for compiling the list of students and faculty members. The professor seemed less than enthusiastic in assisting the FBI, despite our informing him of the urgency from FBI Headquarters. He seemed bothered by our request, which was surprising considering the national attention the case had received. After meeting with him initially, he never called me again. I called him for weeks to obtain the list of names. Finally, I told my partner I was calling the Dean to get this guy to cooperate. My partner thought that was a great idea.

After informing the Dean of the situation, the professor called me the next day and said the list was ready. When my partner and I met him at his office to pick up the list, the professor was indignant and angry. He insisted that he had been working on it and that there had been no cause to call the Dean. I told him that he hadn't returned my calls and we couldn't wait any longer. The FBI provided us with a deadline and we were long past it. This professor evidently called my SSRA complaining I was unprofessional by going over his head. The SSRA threatened to refer the matter to OPR until my partner convinced him that I actually had done a good job getting information from a less than cooperative individual. This type of nonsense from the SSRA never stopped.

He retaliated against me in other ways. For example, he continually assigned me the worst vehicle in the SCRA. I was also never assigned any good cases. On one occasion, a big case developed in State College through an informant from Philadelphia. The source knew an anti-government individual living in a trailer in central Pennsylvania who said he was going to blow up the FBI office. The SSRA assigned this high priority domestic terrorism case to an agent with a reputation for doing nothing. He was the type of agent similar to the agent collecting trash. He touted his cases as something far more significant than they really were. An old friend from the ORA worked with this same agent years before. He said that he would disappear from work during the day and go to the movies. A local detective described him as "dumb as a rock."

My partner and I were assigned a lead in this case to interview the suspect's parents at their home. We spoke to the father at his front door. He was polite, but did not appear to want to cooperate. We asked if we could come into the house to look around. The father volunteered that his twenty-seven-year-old son was not currently residing with him, but had lived with him and his wife up until a year ago. The father, however, still refused to allow us to come in. My partner was about ready to leave when I asked the father to come outside on the front porch. I figured I would try to bluff him by explaining to him that if he didn't let us in to look around now, we would be back the next day with a search warrant. In actuality, no probable cause existed to justify a search warrant of the parents' house, but the father did not know that. I told him that it would be a lot easier and less intrusive if he allowed us to look around now. I told him that if we had to get a search warrant, it might get in the newspapers and there would be a lot more commotion at his house tomorrow. He agreed to let us in to search the house and signed a waiver indicating he gave us permission.

This initiative on my part made the entire case. The Philadelphia Division SOG had the suspect under surveillance, but no evidence had been obtained against him. When my partner and I went into the basement of the parents' house, we observed a large caged area filled with canned foods, ammunition, guns, and even grenades. The father said this part of the basement was prepared by his son as part of his Y2K survival contingency. It was now 2002 and nothing obviously went wrong when the year 2000 arrived. Nevertheless, the father said that his son was convinced anarchy would ensue following Y2K. The father said he was aware of all the food storage, but he had no idea his son had horded guns, ammunition, and grenades. We called the office for assistance to seize the evidence. My partner made it plain to the other agents, including the case agent, that through my conversation with the father, I was the one who made it possible to collect this evidence. The other agents could have cared less.

The next day, a search warrant was obtained based on the evidence found at the father's house to search the son's residence. The search of the son's residence resulted in more weapons found, some of which were illegal automatic weapons, more ammunition, homemade bombs, and numerous marijuana plants. This evidence was sufficient to arrest, indict, and convict the subject. The case agent later received a substantial incentive award. I got nothing, as expected.

One day at about 3:30 p.m., my partner and I were returning to the SCRA from Erie, Pennsylvania. We had been to the state prison in Erie interviewing a potential witness in my partner's drug case. We drove by one of the SCRA agents' house, which just happened to be on our route, and saw him on his tractor cutting his grass. When we got to the office, we saw that he had written on the eraser board that he was going to the township police department where he happened to live. We had noticed that he often left the office around 3:30 or 4:00 p.m. and wrote on the board that he was going to the township police department. My partner and I had departed that morning and wrote on the board that we were going to the state prison in Erie. Everyone in the office wrote on the eraser board every day where they were going. This agent was apparently getting so bored in the office, he would write down he was going to the police department when he was in fact going home, as we witnessed that day on our drive back from Erie.

This behavior was typical in the SCRA. There clearly was not enough work for the agents in the office, but going home to cut grass while still on the books was too much. This kind of fraud against the government really galled me; particularly since the agent cutting his grass on Bureau time never did anything by the book anyway. He once was assigned a child pornography case wherein he seized the subject's computer containing the alleged child pornography. The USAO declined to prosecute this particular case. The pictures looked as if they were minor children, but the prosecutor said there was no way to prove their ages. They may have been eighteen years of age and just looked like they were minors, the AUSA reportedly advised. The case was closed and the evidence was supposed to have been destroyed. Instead of carefully removing the hard drive and destroying it, this agent threw the entire CPU in the dumpster in the building where the FBI leased its office. The maintenance man found the computer, took it home, and discovered the child pornography. He provided the computer to my partner the next day reporting the child pornography. My partner recognized the case number on the computer and returned it to the case agent. I presumed the case agent then destroyed the computer and hard drive more appropriately the second time.

This agent later made me so mad that I reported these incidents to OPR. He was a rotten son of a bitch to me and his behavior was so egregious that I felt compelled to put an end to it. He sat only two desks away from me. One bitter cold winter morning at about 7:30 a.m., I arrived at the office. The rotten agent was at his desk. The trash-collecting agent was at the other end of the office at his desk. The other agents had not yet arrived. This agent had the patio door wide open making the room we were in quite cold. I immediately said, "Hey, it's a little cold to have the door open." He said nothing, obviously just ignoring me. I then said, "Come on, can we close the door?" He said in a defiant abrupt tone, "No, I want the door open." I became annoyed and went over to shut the door. As I shut the door I said, "It's too cold in here." He jumped up and pulled the door open. I then went back over and pulled it shut. He jumped up again and opened it. I looked at him and said, "You're a real asshole." He then went bananas and began to call me every name in the book. By this time, I was back sitting at my desk. He continued cursing and was pacing back and forth at his desk in a tizzy. I had really pushed his buttons. I sat at my desk, looked over at him and said, "You're a real class act." He only got angrier. By this time, the other agent came from the other end of the office to see what the commotion was about. He said, "Come on, guys." Then the other agents wandered in seeing that something was wrong, but having no idea what.

Another time, this same agent put the air conditioner on in the middle of winter shortly before I arrived in the morning, just to rile me I assumed. I switched it over to the heat. No incident ensued like it had with the patio door. However, I was fed up with him and decided to write OPR regarding his time and attendance fraud and the manner in which he disposed of evidence in his child pornography case. When I was later assigned to OPR after being promoted to FBI Headquarters, I reviewed the OPR file on this very matter. I read my partner's signed, sworn statement he gave in the case. My partner lied regarding the agent cutting his grass during business hours. He told the investigators I had told him about it and he had not witnessed it. The agent ultimately got a letter of censure for improperly handling evidence when he threw the CPU containing child pornography in the dumpster. The maintenance man was interviewed by the OPR investigators and did not lie. OPR never interviewed me. I can only assume it was because he made counter allegations against me.

He wrote a letter to OPR alleging that I played golf on Bureau time. This was the best he could come up with. He knew I did everything by the book. He took a shot in the dark with the allegation about golf because I frequently took a half a day or left work an hour early to meet my family at the golf course. However, I always took annual leave. OPR investigators actually went to my country club to check my tee times. After comparing them to my annual leave, it was determined that I did in fact always take leave to play golf. My old partner later bragged to me how it was he who saved me from the OPR investigators. I knew that was another lie. I could never view him in the same way again. My partner had been my best friend, but he had lied to protect my worst enemy.

I actually almost died shortly after I arrived in the SCRA, long before my aforementioned problems. It was a rainy evening on September 22, 2000. I left the office in State College to go home at about 5:30 p.m. I was assigned a 1991 Chevrolet Tahoe with 140,000 miles on it. The brakes were not good and the tires were worn. I had been assigned the vehicle only a short time and had not yet gotten a chance to take it in for repairs. I drove over two mountains to get to my home in Belleville. The first mountain was located shortly after leaving State College. The second mountain was past Greenwood Furnace descending into Kishacoquillas Valley where I lived.

As I descended the steep terrain, I came to an S-curve halfway down the mountain. As I applied the brakes, I began hydroplaning. I then made two critical errors. First, I began pumping the brakes. This reaction was almost instinctive as I was taught to pump the brakes at the Perry Hall Driving School where I learned to drive in 1978. The problem with pumping the brakes in the year 2000 was that all cars now had disc brakes, not manual brakes. By pumping the brakes, I negated the computerized disc brake system. I then made another crucial error as I was sliding off the road. I tried to turn the steering wheel in the direction I was sliding to straighten out. The result was catastrophic. As my front tires went off the road in the top part of the curve, I turned the steering wheel too sharply causing the truck to flip and start rolling down the mountain until I was upside down at the bottom of the curve.

Somehow I landed on my feet like a cat, crouching below the steering wheel looking up at the gas and brake pedals. I immediately felt a panic that the truck would collapse, leaving me trapped or just crushing me altogether. I couldn't open the driver's side door so I crawled to the rear of the truck where a window was broken out. I stood up as I exited the vehicle. I took stock of myself, looking down at my cowboy boots I had purchased in Louisiana, then my pants, and finally at my out-stretched arms, first to the left and then to the right. A euphoric feeling came over me. I was standing there in my suit and tie without a scratch or even a scuff on my leather boots. I looked up to the heavens and thanked my mother and father out loud. At that moment, and to this day, I knew they protected me. I hadn't even been wearing my seat belt. I realized that I could have easily been killed. I looked back at the upside down truck. The engine was still running with smoke coming from the engine from leaking oil. I crawled back into the truck and turned the engine off.

CHAPTER 19

OPR AGAIN

After four and a half years in State College working with people who did little work and who did nothing but try to ingratiate themselves to the supervisor to mask their less than stellar output, I decided to leave and put in for OPR again. I had lost all enjoyment and any self-satisfaction in my work. I thought maybe going back to FBI Headquarters would be better than working with agents desperately trying to justify their existence. I knew I could not work the rest of my career in that type of environment.

I was lucky to be selected again to be an OPR investigator. I started work there in February 2004, but this time I did not move my family. They stayed in Belleville for the next two years while I worked in Washington, D.C. Working in OPR was enjoyable. The steady stream of cases rolled across my desk and I was always busy. I worked for the Unit Chief who replaced the guy that didn't give me the QSI. The new Unit Chief had been working there since right before I left in 1997. He liked me and knew I was hardworking and reliable. He gave me an interesting bit of news about my former SAC from New Orleans. He was forced to retire after the DOJ report on the scandal he investigated criticized him for whitewashing the investigation. He went to work in a private sector job that required a security clearance. However, my Unit Chief told me he quickly lost his security clearance and his job after returning from an overseas trip and failing to declare to United States Customs some expensive items he had purchased. The Unit Chief said his bad behavior and lack of morals had finally caught up with him. The

Unit Chief was a great guy and I was deeply disappointed when he decided to retire less than two months after I came back.

His career had come to a screeching halt following his appearance on CBS' *60 Minutes* in the fall of 2002. The DOJ Office of the Inspector General (OIG) later conducted an investigation of allegations that officials in the FBI retaliated against him for comments he made on *60 Minutes* where he suggested that there was a continuing double standard of discipline in the FBI. After the broadcast, FBI executive management turned against him. His career was completely over. He had already been passed over for promotion numerous times after he lead the OPR investigation of the mishandling of the 1992 Ruby Ridge, Idaho, incident. The wife of white supremacist, Randy Weaver, was killed by an FBI sniper as she stood inside her home in Ruby Ridge. Their fourteen-year-old son had been killed days before by United States Marshals Service deputies attempting to serve an arrest warrant on Randy Weaver. The OPR investigation concluded that six senior FBI officials had lied or committed misconduct in their handling of the case at Ruby Ridge. Despite these findings, none of them were disciplined. The only people punished were subordinate FBI employees. The Unit Chief later testified about the Ruby Ridge case in 2002 at a congressional hearing describing the inequities in discipline in the FBI.

The Unit Chief retired in March 2004. He had dared to speak out against the so-called FBI family only to be cut off at the knees for doing so. He was a fine, honest, conscientious man, whose career was halted by the vindictiveness and retaliatory nature of FBI management. DOJ recommended six months after his retirement that OPR be completely reorganized. This occurred as a result of the Unit Chief's assertions in his testimony before Congress, and from subsequent recommendations made in a DOJ study called the Bell-Colwell Commission.

The Bell-Colwell report concluded that there was a perception of disparity between FBI agents and management with regard to OPR punishment for misconduct. The report stated that the incidents at Ruby Ridge and Waco (the FBI assault on the Branch Davidian compound in 1993) created the "well-justified perception that FBI management received favorable consideration in disciplinary matters." The most significant change that occurred following the issue of the Commission's report was bringing in an outside person to be in charge of OPR adjudications. The current OPR had the investigative and adjudicative units all within the Inspection Division and under the supervision of the Assistant Director of the Inspection Division. The reorganization called for the adjudication units to be in a separate division under a different Assistant Director. A DOJ attorney was appointed as the new Assistant Director over adjudication.

When I had first worked in OPR in 1995, the investigative unit was attached to the Director's Office and run by an Inspector-in-Charge. The adjudication unit was called the Personnel Summary Unit and was completely separate on a different floor within the Personnel Division. In 1996, the OPR investigative units were reorganized and became part of the Inspection Division. The Personnel Summary Unit was also moved into the Inspection Division and renamed the Adjudication Unit. In 2004, the reorganization took place based on the recommendations by the Bell-Colwell Commission. The Commission's report indicated that having the investigative and adjudicative units under the same umbrella gave a perception of collusion. The investigative units subsequently remained in the Inspection Division, but the adjudication units were put under a separate division called the OPR Division. It was headed by the DOJ attorney, even though the adjudication units remained in the same hallway next door to the investigative units.

At least the reorganized OPR no longer had an SAC Review Board for Disciplinary Matters. This review board had been the real reason that SACs and executive management were treated differently in OPR matters than the rest of the FBI employees. The old adjudication unit judged every case the same, whether it involved an SAC or a file clerk. Each case was adjudicated based on the evidence and punishment was handed down according to precedent set in previous cases. The problem was that although adjudication was consistent, if the case involved Senior Executive Service (SES) personnel such as an SAC, a Section Chief, a Deputy Assistant Director, or an Assistant Director, the SAC Review Board reviewed the case and invariably reduced the punishment. I was involved in one such case involving an SAC. Allegations surfaced from several women in a different division that this individual had sexually harassed them while he had previously been the ASAC there. Suffice it to say that the evidence from these women revealed that he had been a sexual predator.

Many of his female subordinates felt pressured to go on dates with him, inasmuch as he was the boss and was also widely known to be vindictive. Some of them admitted to having sexual relations with him. One young girl, a secretary in the front office, broke out in hives denying to us that she ever had sexual relations with him. I was never so embarrassed for anyone in my life. She wore a top that showed part of her shoulders and chest. When she was asked whether she had sexual relations with him, she flatly denied it. Her skin was revealing otherwise, as she began to practically turn purple on her neck and chest. I guess she was dying inside. We did not press the issue, as it did not really matter. The bottom line was that all of the women, with the exception of one agent, dated him out of fear. One female agent benefitted greatly by dating him. She received a new car and the cushy position of media spokesman for the office.

I was anxious to interview this SAC and ask him about his dalliances. I pictured this guy as looking like Burt Reynolds in his prime. I was very surprised to find a very odd-looking fellow in his late forties with bugged-out eyes resembling more of the late comic, Marty Feldman, than any handsome movie star. The evidence clearly proved that he sexually harassed several women while working as ASAC. The Adjudication Unit recommended he be dismissed from the FBI. This determination was based solely on precedent OPR cases in the FBI. Previous offenders of this nature had been fired. The SAC Review Board chose not to fire him. They did not reverse the findings of the OPR case, but merely reduced the punishment. The SAC was transferred to a different field division and demoted to a GS-13 street agent to finish out his career. He had only about a year until he reached retirement age. The SAC Review Board once again protected one of their own. Under the new reorganization of OPR in 2004, this would supposedly no longer happen.

My years of experience in the FBI were definitely not appreciated at FBI Headquarters in 2004 with Director Robert Mueller in charge. He was of the belief that "fresh eyes" were needed in the FBI to make it a better law enforcement organization. I was amused at the "reorganization" of OPR and how everyone thought they were creating a new and improved OPR. OPR simply reverted to what it was in 1995. Little was actually changing in OPR except for the elimination of the SAC Review Board and the appointment of the DOJ attorney to head adjudication.

When Director Mueller came on board, he made a lot of changes in the FBI, mostly to placate Congress. As a result of the many changes he made, he was not very popular among the rank and file agents. After 9/11 and the criticism of intelligence failures by the FBI, Mueller began transforming the FBI into more of an intelligence gathering organization by putting less emphasis on what the FBI did best, conducting complex criminal investigations. The first thing he did after 9/11 was to create "Field Intelligence Groups" or FIGs in every field office. He also created the Directorate of Intelligence at FBI Headquarters, an integrated central location for intelligence analysis. Creating a system to better gather intelligence to prevent major terrorist attacks was a seemingly good idea. The terrorist attack on 9/11 was arguably the result of intelligence failures and a lack of coordination between intelligence agencies.

One such intelligence failure occurred in July 2001 after an agent in the FBI Phoenix Division sent an intelligence report to FBI Headquarters indicating that Arabs possibly connected to Al Qaeda were enrolled in flight training. Then, in August 2001, Zacarias Moussaoui was arrested on immigration charges after the FBI learned of his flight lessons at a Minnesota flight school wherein he expressed to the flight instructor no desire in learning to land the plane. In a May 2002 memo to Mueller, a senior female agent in the FBI's Minneapolis office accused FBI Headquarters of having repeatedly refused requests she had made before 9/11 for a warrant to wiretap and to search the computer and belongings of Zacarias Moussaoui, the alleged "twentieth hijacker." A search of his computer after 9/11 reportedly revealed data about the cockpit layouts of commercial aircraft and telephone numbers that possibly could have led authorities to the conspirators.

FBI Headquarters apparently failed to connect the Moussaoui case to the July 2001 report from the FBI Phoenix agent. FBI Headquarters reportedly rejected the FBI Phoenix agent's proposal to investigate other flight schools. Mueller's ideas to improve the FBI's intelligence gathering and coordination were well-intentioned at first. The FIGs and the Directorate of Intelligence were initially an improvement in FBI intelligence. However, Mueller took it to an extreme. Within a short period of time, twenty or more analysts were hired in every field office, many more for larger field divisions, and a thousand more at FBI Headquarters. Director Mueller wanted to model the FBI's intelligence gathering after the CIA, where the analyst was "king."

In the FBI, the agent was king, at least until Director Mueller arrived on the scene. The problem was that the analysts were all new to the FBI. FBI agents possessed the experience, expertise, and practical working knowledge on the streets to obtain intelligence information. Another big problem was that the FIGs in smaller-sized field divisions had little or no terrorism threats. What eventually happened was that the analysts and the FIGs had to broaden their intelligence gathering beyond just terrorism to justify their very existence. It was not long before FBI agents were being required to provide intelligence reports to the FIGs not only on terrorist threats, but on the entire realm of the FBI's jurisdiction, to include drug trafficking, organized crime, violent crime, gang activity, bank robberies, public corruption, health care fraud, bank frauds, wire/mail frauds, foreign counterintelligence, computer crimes and a variety of other criminal violations.

The FIGs were now in a position of having to justify their existence with all kinds of idiotic intelligence reports that derived from the agents' investigative work. The FIG analysts were merely required to take the information, put it in the proper format, and disseminate the intelligence reports. The agents were burdened with quotas of producing intelligence reports for the FIGs from criminal matters. The agents' time and efforts were being diverted from criminal investigations and prosecutions to providing meaningless intelligence reports on such things as health care fraud and other criminal matters where intelligence reports were not necessary. The agents working criminal matters always had their number one priority of putting people in jail, but now their priority had become the dissemination of intelligence reports for the FIG. The purpose of the FIG was no longer simply about preventing terrorism. It morphed into something completely different in its mission.

Agent morale had reached a new low under Director Mueller, in my opinion. Another policy Director Mueller implemented was a seven-year "up and out" term for all field supervisors. In other words, field supervisors could not stay in their position beyond seven years. They had to either take a transfer back to FBI Headquarters or step down from management and revert back to being a street agent. These options were not practical for every supervisor. Many supervisors had no desire to move to Washington, D.C., some because of family issues or other personal reasons, and others for economic reasons. This policy was most detrimental to the FBI because it eliminated experienced and knowledgeable supervisory personnel from field offices.

Director Mueller also reinstituted the rotational transfer policy for new agents. All new agents assigned to small or medium-sized field offices were transferred after three years to a Top-15 office. The Bureau added three more offices to the list since my rotational transfer. The rotational transfer was eliminated in 1993. A good friend who was two weeks behind me at the FBI Academy remained in Orlando for ten years until he opted for an OP transfer to Rapid City, South Dakota. He was an avid outdoorsman who enjoyed fly fishing, hiking, and horseback riding. He found his niche investigating crime on Indian reservations and loved his job. He retired from the FBI in Rapid City in 2010. Sadly, nine months later, he took his own life after a battle with depression.

At a health care fraud conference in Las Vegas in 2007, a Deputy Assistant Director from FBI Headquarters advised the group that even Director Mueller's closest advisors tried to dissuade him from his transfer policies, but he was adamant about keeping them in place. His inner circle was against his transfer policies mainly because of the cost to the Bureau, but also due to draining expertise from the field. He often cited proudly in speeches how he had transferred sixteen times during his career in the military and as a prosecutor. In 2011, his ten-year term as FBI Director ended. Congress and the President made an exception to the ten-year term rule and gave him a two-year extension. This level of hypocrisy did not go unnoticed by FBI agents. Agents were disappointed that Mueller was not "up and out" after his ten-year term expired. His eyes had long since ceased to be fresh. In May 2017, his double standard went further after he accepted the Special Counsel position to lead the investigation of alleged Russian interference during the 2016 Presidential election.

While at OPR for the second time, my goal was to do my time and then try to secure a field desk in Baltimore or Pittsburgh. However, with some exceptions, I had not made the contacts I had made during my first tenure in OPR. With the reorganization of OPR, I traveled very little on my cases. Most cases were now delegated to field office personnel. The OPR SSA mainly provided oversight and direction from FBI Headquarters. I was being passed over for the jobs closest to home. I realized I would need to apply to more field offices in order to be transferred. I could not continue the separation from my family every Monday through Friday working in Washington, D.C., while my family was in Belleville, Pennsylvania.

My son, his friend, my daughter, and me, outside the JEH FBI Building in 2004.

I applied for an SSRA position in Dayton, Ohio, in the FBI Cincinnati Division. I was rated number one for the position by the local Cincinnati career board. The Cincinnati Division requested OPR to investigate the theft of funds from their office break room the year before. Cincinnati had a break room with drinks and snacks to be purchased on the honor system by putting cash in a box. After six months, an inventory and audit of the drinks and snacks revealed a $1,200 shortage. A hidden camera was placed in the break room that showed fourteen employees, three agents and eleven support personnel, making suspicious transactions. The majority of the suspects appeared to be taking candy or soda without paying, but not in every instance. One support person, whose father was in executive management in a different office, appeared to be one of the worst violators. On one occasion, he filled up a cooler with sodas without paying. Another support employee was seen in the video putting his hand in the cashbox and removing a handful of money.

This case could not be delegated to anyone in the Cincinnati office for obvious reasons. The case was assigned to me. I took an agent from OPR, who had become my best friend, to assist me with the investigation. Two employees ended up being fired, the executive manager's son, and the employee seen taking the fistful of cash. Both had no choice but to confess after being advised of their actions in the video. The common defense among the other twelve employees was that when they did not pay one day, they paid what they owed on their next purchase. The evidence on the videotape could neither prove nor disprove their assertions, so they were given the benefit of the doubt when the case was adjudicated.

I first met the OPR agent who had become my best friend on my first day back in OPR in February 2004. He was very friendly, and immediately asked me to assist him on a case in the Baltimore Division. I don't even remember what the case was about. I clearly remembered the other OPR SSAs from our unit confronting me about partnering with him. One agent told me flat out that I would not like working with him. I said, "Why not? He seems like a nice enough fella." The agent quickly responded, "Oh, it's not that. He's a good guy. You'll see what he does at the conclusion of his interviews and you won't want to work with him anymore, I'll just say that. Nobody wants to partner with him because of it." I thought this was the rudest thing I had ever heard. The other three agents in the unit were standing by him, all nodding in agreement. This group mentality against the agent really put me off. I was curious to see what in the world he was going to do, but at the same time I immediately didn't like these four co-workers in the unit.

At the end of our first interview in Baltimore, he asked the witness, "Is there anything else you would like to add to your signed, sworn statement that maybe we did not ask?" I knew this could not possibly be the objectionable question. This follow-up question was completely logical. It was clearly the next question he asked which they found offensive. I personally would not have asked it only because it was not my style. It frankly never even occurred to me to ever ask this type of question. He asked what I would call a "touchy feely" sort of question. He queried, "Do you think you were treated fairly during this interview and do you think we should have done anything differently?" He did nothing wrong in asking this question. I really could not understand why it bothered the other OPR investigators.

In my experience, I routinely warned individuals to be fully candid. I would explain that I had seen individuals fired for a lack of candor in signed, sworn statements for misconduct issues they would never have been fired for had they been honest about it. However, it did not bother me a bit if this agent wanted to soften up the OPR image. I really did not care one way or the other, as it had no bearing on the case. The only thing that mattered was whether or not he conducted straightforward, in-depth interviews, resulting in a thorough investigation. He did just that. I told the critical agent in OPR the very same thing when I returned to the office the following day. I later conveyed to my new friend what his co-workers had said about him and that the entire incident only made me think less of them, not him. He and I became best friends and worked most of our cases together.

My friend had a heart of gold. He was happily married, a father of two, and a devout Catholic. He divulged to me his bout with cancer a few years before and how he had survived. He displayed a courage and spirit I found admirable. The more I got to know him, the more I liked and respected his outlook on life. He made a poignant comment on one occasion I would never forget. It stemmed from his own brush with death. He said, referring to the other OPR supervisors in the unit who seemed obsessed with getting promoted, "They think they've got a bead on everything and have it all figured out...but they have no idea."

We did a lot of traveling together and had fun. He was, and remains to this day, a devoted and loyal friend. I truly enjoyed his company. He only really made me angry one time. We went to Cleveland together on an OPR case, the subject of which I have since forgotten. We stayed downtown at the Ritz-Carlton. I was very impressed and could not believe we had gotten a government rate at such a posh hotel. Upon our arrival, we checked into our respective rooms. He was on the floor above mine and came to my room about ten minutes after checking in to go to dinner. He knocked on my door, came in, and said he needed to use my bathroom before we left. I said fine, and ten minutes later, he opened the bathroom door releasing the foulest odor that permeated my entire room. It was as if open sewage was pouring out of the bathroom. He laughed so hard he was doubled over. I was not amused. I said, "Thanks for ruining my experience in the best hotel I have ever stayed in." We departed quickly to escape the stench and headed for dinner.

THE FBI – THEY EAT THEIR YOUNG

My most satisfying case I worked in OPR was one concerning a support employee assigned to the Training Division. My friend assisted me on the interviews of the subject and his wife. The OPR investigation was initiated upon receipt of information from the Training Division that the employee was the subject of a criminal investigation by the Spotsylvania County Sheriff's Office (SCSO) in Virginia for sexual molestation of his eleven-year-old adopted daughter. The Spotsylvania County District Attorney's Office (SCDAO) initially advised that they intended to present a case before the Grand Jury with the intent of obtaining an indictment against the subject for criminal sexual assault on a minor. However, shortly after the child was removed from the employee's home by Spotsylvania County Social Services on February 24, 2004, the employee and his wife, also employed in the Training Division, both received transfer orders to the FBI Jacksonville Division. On February 26, 2004, his wife provided the SCSO a blanket from the daughter's bedroom that she thought had semen on it.

The SCSO obtained a search warrant to obtain a DNA sample from the employee to compare with the alleged semen on the blanket. The blanket was never tested by the SCSO, inasmuch as the case was dropped after the employees moved out of state. The SCSO continued to advise OPR of their intention to obtain an indictment through the SCDAO. Upon the eventual return of an indictment, the SCSO detective assigned to the case had planned to travel to Jacksonville to arrest the subject and interview his wife to secure her cooperation and testimony. However, in January 2005, the SCSO detective advised that the case had been closed after the SCDAO declined prosecution due to a lack of evidence. The detective provided me a copy of his investigative file in order that I might pursue the OPR case against the employee. My investigation would be administrative, meaning that as FBI employees, they would be compelled to cooperate, but any evidence obtained would not be permissible in criminal proceedings. Ultimately, if the employee was compelled through an OPR interview to incriminate himself criminally, it would violate his Fifth Amendment right against self-incrimination and be disallowed in any criminal proceedings.

A review of the SCSO file revealed that both the SCSO and the SCDAO believed that the victim in the case provided credible and consistent statements concerning her allegations of sexual abuse on the part of the employee. The file further revealed incriminating statements from his wife and from the employee's biological sons. The sons observed their father and the victim in awkward or compromising situations, such as seeing their father in his bedroom with the victim giving him a back or leg rub. The police report indicated that his wife reportedly stated that on one occasion, she walked into the child's bedroom and she thought she saw her husband's pants down with her daughter there.

On February 22, 2005, my partner and I interviewed his wife in the FBI Jacksonville office. She said she had never seen her adopted daughter giving her husband a back rub in their bedroom, but her son told her he had. She said her son told her he saw his father and their daughter lying in bed and she offered to rub his legs. His wife told us she confronted her husband about the incident, but that he said their daughter was watching more television than rubbing him. The most damning information from his wife was that she said she walked into the daughter's room at 1 or 2 a.m. one morning and thought she saw her husband in the motion of pulling up his pants or adjusting his shorts while the daughter was kneeling in front of him. She said she immediately stated to her husband, "Were you pulling your pants up?" He told her "no" and that "she was cold so I was putting her window down." The wife said that on another occasion at bedtime after walking into the daughter's bedroom, she observed her hand ready to go up the back of her husband's boxer shorts to rub his rear end. She immediately asked, "What are you doing?" but got no response since the daughter had not yet touched him.

We then interviewed the father. He categorically denied that he ever sexually assaulted or molested his adopted daughter. He would only admit that she rubbed his knee in bed while he was wearing blue jeans. When confronted about what his wife had said about him pulling up his pants, he denied it saying, "I never had my pants down in front of her. My wife is not correct in thinking I was pulling up my boxer shorts." He recalled the incident saying he had gone into his daughter's room to turn off the fan in her room because she was cold. He said he was in his boxer shorts that he slept in. He said she was not kneeling on the bedroom floor as his wife had stated, but that she was lying on the floor in the middle of the room. The father said, "I don't know why she was lying on the floor. She often behaved strangely." At the conclusion of the interview, he told us he would be willing to take a voluntary polygraph examination.

A few weeks later, his wife resigned from the FBI. I believed she did so to avoid any more compelled interviews regarding the horrid allegations against her husband. I am sure deep down she believed her husband molested their adopted daughter, but she was never going to admit this during our interview, despite what she had seen with her own eyes. She was a woman in denial, not wanting to think her husband was a monster who was destroying her family. She had initially given the police the daughter's blanket which she thought had semen stains on it. The SCSO turned the blanket over to me. I had it checked by the FBI Laboratory Division, but analysis did not reveal the presence of semen. On March 25, 2005, after the Assistant Director of the Inspection Division granted my written request for the approval of a voluntary polygraph examination for the employee, I learned that he was not available. He was called up for active military duty and assigned to the Jacksonville Naval Air Station.

I called him at the base to schedule the polygraph exam, but he began making repeated excuses to avoid the test. On one occasion, he left me a voice message that he could not be released from the Sensitive Compartmented Information (SCI) facility at the base where he worked. On another occasion, he stated that he could not work joint operations with the FBI. It was clear from his absurd excuses that he was hiding behind the military to avoid the polygraph exam. Finally, in September 2005, after getting the runaround, I decided to contact his superior at the base, a Lieutenant Colonel, and advised him of the entire situation. The Lieutenant Colonel released the employee from his duties on September 30, 2005 in order for him to be available for the polygraph examination.

The employee arrived at a Jacksonville hotel at about noon. I escorted him to the room where the polygraph was set up. In the pre-polygraph interview, he gave a signed, sworn statement that his adopted daughter rubbed his groin and performed oral sex on him. There was no need for him to even take the polygraph exam. The case was proven. Upon returning to FBI Headquarters, I prepared my report in order for the employee to be summarily dismissed from the rolls of the FBI. I consulted with the FBI Office of General Counsel (OGC) with regard to advising the military and the SCSO of his admissions. OGC advised that although the employee's admission could not be used against him criminally, inasmuch as it was obtained in an administrative inquiry, his confession could be disseminated.

Consequently, he was discharged from the military and the FBI. The Spotsylvania County District Attorney later charged him for sexual assault against a minor.

On February 22, 2007, he entered an Alford plea in Spotsylvania County Circuit Court to nine counts of felony indecent liberties upon a child. An Alford plea meant that he did not admit guilt, but there was enough evidence for a conviction. Under the plea agreement, he was sentenced to seven years in prison with another fifteen years suspended. He also was ordered to pay $10,000 in restitution to cover the cost of his adopted daughter's mental health counseling. He admitted to the SCDAO that he engaged in a sex act with her nine times, beginning when she was nine years old. According to the plea, he actually said he was a victim in the case saying that the girl initiated the contact. I could only assume that this statement might not have helped him during his sentencing before the judge.

I felt a great sense of accomplishment in this case. Most agents, I believed, would have given up on the employee once he began dodging the polygraph examination. I was very persistent, calling him for months, despite his repeated excuses. The polygraph examination was voluntary, but I kept pursuing him. Calling the Lieutenant Colonel was critical in getting him to take the polygraph exam. Had it not been for my perseverance in this case, this employee, I suspected, would never have been brought to justice, prosecuted, and sent to jail for his heinous crime. Nailing this deviant gave me tremendous satisfaction.

My diligence in this case or any other case at this point in my career rarely brought me any recognition or gratitude from anyone in the FBI. In the child molestation case, it brought the opposite. After I met the employee at the hotel and escorted him to the polygrapher's room, I went back to my room. The polygrapher told me he would handle the polygraph and that I was not needed. After two hours, I called the polygrapher's room to ask him if he was finished yet. It was 12:30 p.m. I explained that my flight was leaving at 3 p.m., but I would stay if he needed me. He told me to catch my flight. He explained that the employee had admitted to the sexual molestation. He said he was getting him to write a written confession and he could handle it himself. I departed the hotel and caught my flight out of Jacksonville to Cincinnati. I then got on a connecting flight to Harrisburg, Pennsylvania, which arrived at 8:30 p.m. I did not arrive home in Belleville until after 10 p.m. that night.

THE FBI – THEY EAT THEIR YOUNG

On Monday morning, I was confronted by my new Unit Chief, who had been recently promoted, and the other OPR Unit Chief from the other unit, who said the Polygraph Unit Chief had called and said I left the polygrapher so I could go play golf Friday afternoon. I explained to both of them the situation and what the polygrapher told me. I had been sitting at my desk preparing my voucher for the trip and had my airline tickets on the desk. I showed them the tickets and the itinerary, which revealed that my flight arrived in Harrisburg at 8:30 p.m. I surmised what had happened. I had told the polygrapher on the night of my arrival that I had played golf that day before getting my flight.

My Unit Chief said that the Polygraph Unit Chief was upset because his policy was to have a witness with the polygrapher for anyone's signed confession. The polygrapher apparently deflected the wrath of his supervisor by blaming me for wanting to leave to play golf, which was not true. He obviously did not want to admit to his boss that he told me to catch my flight. My Unit Chief understood and accepted my explanation, most likely because I had the airline ticket in my hand showing them when my plane arrived in Harrisburg. I told them I was going to call the polygrapher and confront him about this. They asked me not to do that as it might cause tension between our units which had to work together so frequently. I agreed not to call him. However, a few days later, the polygrapher called me to advise that his polygraph report was finished and he would forward it to me. I asked him why he told his Unit Chief I left early to play golf after telling me I was not needed. He flatly denied saying anything to his Unit Chief and said his Unit Chief must have come to that conclusion on his own. I did not argue with him. I just told him he made me look bad to my bosses about something that was not true and hung up.

I was starting to believe that nothing ever went my way in the FBI. Prior to the unpleasant incident involving the allegations from the Polygraph Unit Chief, the Inspection Division handed out numerous cash incentive awards for its employees in the Inspection Division conference room one morning at an all-employee division meeting. The OPR investigators watched as nearly every Inspector received an award from the Assistant Director while they got nothing. The Inspection Division was made up of the two OPR investigative units and the Inspectors. Inspectors were supervisors from the FBI that came to FBI Headquarters on an eighteen-month Temporary Duty Assignment (TDY) to conduct inspections of field offices. The Inspectors received TDY per diem for lodging and meals during their entire time at FBI Headquarters.

Generally speaking, Inspectors at FBI Headquarters raked in the money. On a TDY assignment, an employee received a fixed amount of money each day for food regardless of how much money was spent. For instance, if the per diem rate for food was $50 and the employee only spent $30 per day on food, then he/she could pocket the remaining $20. On a long-term TDY assignment, this could become quite profitable for an employee if he/she was frugal. During an eighteen-month TDY, an Inspector might pocket $5,000 to $10,000 in per diem by making economical expenditures for food. Knowing this and then seeing them awarded thousands of dollars more added insult to injury. When the OPR investigators left the conference without a single award, one of the OPR employees disclosed that no one in our section was even recommended for an award because our Section Chief did not believe in incentive awards.

After this stupid and thoughtless Section Chief was later transferred to head the Anchorage, Alaska Division (probably the only transfer she could get, I imagined) and her replacement arrived, I decided to meet with him. I was already scheduled to transfer in only a matter of weeks to the Oklahoma City Division to be the SSA of the White Collar Crime squad, so I figured I had nothing to lose. I explained to our new Section Chief about his predecessor's policy and how unfair I thought it was that no one in either OPR investigative unit received an incentive award. I told him that my unit had been down two agents for nearly six months and four agents carried the workload for the six-man unit. I advised that I was leaving in a few weeks so I did not expect an incentive award. He was very nice about it and thanked me for letting him know. The following day, my Unit Chief told me that the new Section Chief spoke to him and that the next time incentive awards were given out, the OPR investigators would get incentive awards. He advised that I would receive one, too, even though I would be in Oklahoma City by then. I was very appreciative, but I never received the incentive award, which was really no big surprise to me.

CHAPTER 20

THE MICKEY MOUSE KILLER

The FBI continued to disappoint me. During the summer of 2005, I applied for the SSRA position in Dayton, Ohio, in the FBI Cincinnati Division. I had apparently impressed the front office there with my handling of the OPR investigation of the stolen funds from the break room. The Cincinnati front office ranked me number one for the position. The application package was sent back to FBI Headquarters to the Executive Development Selection Process (EDSP) Unit in the Human Resources Division. An FBI Headquarters career board convened every month to approve the selections by the field offices. The career board consisted of the Unit Chief of the EDSP Unit and several Deputy Assistant Directors and Assistant Directors from the various divisions at FBI Headquarters. Unfortunately for me, an Assistant Director, who had formerly been an SSA in the ORA subsequent to my transfer from there, was on the career board.

I did not know the former SSA personally, but I knew of him. After I transferred from the ORA to WMFO, the ORA was expanded and several squads were added through the years. This particular SSA headed one of the squads there. He had previously worked in OPR. The SSRA and my other old friends from the ORA told me that he immediately clashed with them. The SSRA was in charge of the overall office, but he and this SSA were both currently on the same level of management. They both answered to the ASAC in Tampa. My old SSRA was a laid-back type personality who left the agents alone to work their cases. The ASAC was a micromanager wanting to know every detail of what was going on. Needless to say, the new SSA got along splendidly with the ASAC while the SSRA did not.

Besides clashing with the SSRA, the new SSA objected to ORA employees receiving free tickets to Disney World. He not only believed this was a serious conflict of interest, but that all FBI employees accepting free tickets were misusing their position in violation of FBI policy. His first order of business was reporting this to the ASAC and the front office in Tampa. He reportedly asked the front office, as he had to everybody else in Orlando, "What if we had to conduct an investigation of Walt Disney World?" The front office, at the SSA's insistence, subsequently had every employee in Orlando sign a form stating that they would be under an OPR administrative inquiry should they accept any tickets.

I found out about the new policy years after my transfer to WMFO when I called the SSRA to ask for free tickets for a planned trip to Disney with my family. He told me of the new policy, but defiantly said, "I'll get you tickets anyway." He did it, I think, more for his own satisfaction to put one over on his nemesis. I was extremely grateful and always thought the SSRA was a great guy. I had gone to Disney for free for years, as had every member of my family and my wife's family while I had been assigned there. Years later, I was quite amused when speaking to an SSA at FBI Headquarters and the former ORA SSA's name came up in our conversation. The SSA at FBI Headquarters said, "I know who he is. He's the Mickey Mouse killer."

This was the first and only time I ever heard him referred to as the Mickey Mouse killer. Nearly everybody I knew in the ORA just thought he was a jerk. My Army Ranger friend told me of a bizarre incident involving this guy during an SAC Conference in Orlando. An SAC Conference had been held in Orlando when I had been there. The SSRA had asked me to organize a golf tournament for the SACs since I was the only golfer in the ORA. I organized a four-man scramble and a chip and putt tournament at the Orange Tree Country Club. I played with them and was the only non-senior executive person there. I had a great time. I had only been an FBI agent for two years and admired the SACs. I thought they were pretty cool guys and all very confident, even though some of them were downright cocky. I remembered at the chip and putt tournament after the scramble, several of them were drinking and smoking cigars, declaring "It's good to be an SAC!" It looked good to me, too.

Years later, my Army Ranger friend did not have as good of an experience as I had. My friend was responsible for picking up Director Louis Freeh's family and then taking them to the airport at the end of the conference. Director Freeh had several small children at the time and brought them along so his wife could take them to Walt Disney World. I was fairly certain the Freeh family did not get into the park for free! My friend had two small children of his own, so he put his two child car seats into his FBI vehicle to transport the Director's children safely to the airport. The ORA SSA noticed the car seats in his Bureau vehicle that day. He confronted my friend and asked him what he was doing with car seats in his FBI car. My friend said he accused him of having his children in the car, a misuse of the car and grounds for an OPR inquiry. He responded that he took them out of his personal car that morning to put in his FBI car because he was taking the Director's family to the airport. The SSA said, "We'll see." My friend did not like the accusation, but shrugged it off as he had done nothing wrong. This fact did not deter the SSA who was apparently convinced that having the car seats in his vehicle was misuse, despite being told they were for the Director's children.

On the last day of the conference, the SAC from Tampa came into the ORA office. The SSA called my friend into his office with the SAC and began to explain to the SAC the car seat situation. He was convinced my friend should be put under OPR inquiry. The SAC was dumbfounded and told him, "The car seats were for the Director's children." He responded, "I think we should forward this to OPR." The SAC was not of the same ilk as the Mickey Mouse killer, and said, "I am not sending this to OPR, end of story." The SAC, thankfully, demonstrated some common sense. This was typical of this SSA. He was arrogant and unreasonable. The SSRA told me that the SSA had bragged to him about finishing second in his class in law school. However, this jerk added the caveat that he would have graduated first, but the classmate that was first cheated.

When I applied to field desks from FBI Headquarters years later, the former SSA was in executive management at FBI Headquarters sitting on a career board. He undoubtedly saw my SSRA's name listed on my job application as my former supervisor. The application consisted of all of my greatest accomplishments during my FBI career. Many of them were while working in the ORA. Each accomplishment had to have a supervisor listed to verify them, so my SSRA's name was all over the application. The FBI Headquarters career board was usually a rubber stamp to the field office's local career board selection, however, this was not the case for me, thanks to the Mickey Mouse killer.

The career board was supposed to be held in secret, but observers were allowed in. On the day of the career board for the Dayton SSRA position to which I had applied, a colleague of mine from OPR was observing. She approached me in confidence after seeing what happened with my application. She said she was not supposed to disclose what she had heard, but she believed it was so egregious and unfair that I should be aware of it.

She said that the Mickey Mouse killer completely derailed my application for SSRA Dayton and swayed every member of the career board, all subordinate to him, to vote me down. She said that he told the career board that I should not be rewarded this job since I had dropped out of the management program once. He further reportedly stated that giving me this position was the equivalent of an OP transfer, which I had already received once. She then told me he speculated to the career board that I might try to become an ASAC and leave the Dayton job after only six months. He told the career board that I had been a supervisor for a year and half in the field previously. The requirement for becoming an ASAC was having two years of experience as a field supervisor. Therefore, he concluded, it would be a waste of the Bureau's money to transfer me to Dayton only for me to leave after six months to become an ASAC.

This argument directly contradicted his first argument that I was trying to get another OP, which would indicate I would stay in Dayton for the remainder of my career. It was clear that he said anything to prevent me from being selected. He managed to sway the career board to vote for a supervisor from his own division who FBI Cincinnati had rated number two behind me. I asked my colleague what the Deputy Assistant Director from the Inspection Division said during all of this, considering she was supposed to be representing my interests as an employee from her division. The Deputy Assistant Director apparently said nothing. I subsequently asked my Deputy Assistant Director what happened at the career board. She confirmed what my colleague told me. Her reaction was to advise me that I probably would never leave FBI Headquarters as long as the Mickey Mouse killer was on the career board.

Her response infuriated me. She obviously did not care about the unfairness or the corruption inserted into the process.

She was a typical manager in the FBI. She was not going to put up a fight for me or anyone else. FBI managers like her were commonplace, too afraid to rock the boat for fear it might jeopardize their chance for advancement. I immediately went to see the Section Chief in EDSP with whom I had worked in OPR in 1997. He listened to my story and said it was wrong what had happened. He said I had a very good case to appeal the decision. I asked what would happen if I won the appeal. He told me that I would not get the Dayton SSRA position since the individual selected had already received his transfer orders.

He explained that if I won the appeal, I would be placed in the next supervisory position available in the region. He said it might not be in Cincinnati, but possibly in Indianapolis, Cleveland, Louisville or Chicago. I told him, "No thank you, I have already worked in a field division where I was not wanted. I am not putting myself in that position again." I was, of course, referring to my assignment in Shreveport where the SAC for whom I ended up working for had not selected me. I told him, "I'll wait and take my chances that I am ranked number one again." I further advised that his Unit Chief was at the career board meeting, but reportedly said nothing during this entire incident. The Unit Chief allowed this corrupt individual (the Mickey Mouse killer) to circumvent the entire selection system. The Section Chief had no response and did not seem to care other than to say that it was wrong what happened to me and to explain the aforementioned options for me.

I was ranked number one a couple of months later for the WCC SSA in Oklahoma City. I knew the ASAC in Oklahoma, as well as an SSA there, both of whom had worked in Louisiana when I was the Shreveport SSRA. I thought I would finally work in a place where I had friends. Luckily, the female Deputy Assistant Director in the Inspection Division who did not go to bat for me at the last career board had transferred by this time. I explained to her replacement what happened to me at the last career board. The new Deputy Assistant Director representing the Inspection Division said to me, "Don't worry, that won't happen under my watch." He was true to his word. I got the job in Oklahoma City. I felt fortunate to be getting out of FBI Headquarters. I had been commuting to Washington, D.C. from Belleville, Pennsylvania, staying in Baltimore during the week for the previous year and a half. I was becoming depressed being separated from my family. I was feeling like a bad husband and father. I thought that now I could move Cindy and the children to Oklahoma City and get back to a normal family life.

I was very happy to have learned a few years later that Director Robert Mueller forced the Mickey Mouse killer into retirement. Prior to coming to FBI Headquarters, the Mickey Mouse killer had been an SAC. Two highly publicized whistleblowers were in his division when he was in charge. Following 9/11, two female agents made accusations against the FBI which made national headlines. One female agent saw a Tiffany crystal globe on a secretary's desk that had come from "ground zero" at the World Trade Center. An agent allegedly kept it as a souvenir while collecting evidence at ground zero and subsequently gave it to a secretary in the field office.

Taking a souvenir from this site was not only unethical and possibly criminal, but also downright disgusting. The whistleblower apparently had already been retaliated against by the FBI for an Equal Employment Opportunity (EEO) sexual discrimination complaint she filed in 1998. Throughout the 1990s, this agent reportedly received superior and exceptional performance ratings for her work against child sex-abuse offenders and murderers on Indian Reservations. After her discrimination complaint was filed, she received poor performance appraisals. Then, the SAC transferred her from her RA to the field division headquarters city, a move that she alleged was part of the retaliation against her.

The other whistleblower criticized FBI Headquarters after 9/11 for failing to investigate Zacarias Moussaoui prior to 9/11, despite intelligence information indicating he was a prime suspect. She later testified before the United States Senate regarding this perceived failure. Both of these female agents claimed retaliation by the FBI and sued. The FBI management in their division continued to give them poor performance appraisals and treated them as if they were traitors to the FBI.

The FBI retaliation and reprisal eventually forced one of the agents to retire from the FBI in 2003 after twenty-five years of service. In January 2007, a federal jury awarded her hundreds of thousands of dollars for lost wages and emotional stress. In January 2008, the government was ordered to pay an additional $1 million in legal fees to her lawyer. The jury found merit in her allegations that FBI supervisors falsified negative performance reviews in retaliation against her.

I was advised by an individual working at FBI Headquarters that the Department of Justice subsequently advised Director Mueller of the outcome of the lawsuit. Mueller had evidently not been aware that the SAC, now working in a high-ranking position at FBI Headquarters, was in charge during the retaliation. Upon learning of his involvement, Mueller reportedly told him he would have to retire. He could not remain as one of Mueller's senior executive managers following a federal jury finding that he was responsible for the retaliation. If this story was true, then the Mickey Mouse killer finally got his comeuppance and justice was served.

CHAPTER 21

OKLAHOMA

I began the last phase of my career in Oklahoma City as the WCC SSA. I invited my former colleagues, the ASAC and the SSA, and their wives to my house for dinner when I first arrived. We shot pool and talked about working in Louisiana. I thought I was finally in a job with good people and in a place where things would go my way. I could not have been more wrong.

A few months later, prior to issuing annual performance appraisals for the members of my squad, a support supervisor in the office approached me. She had prepared an appraisal of "Minimally Acceptable" for one of my support employees on my squad, which I was supposed to sign. An odd performance appraisal system was in place for support employees, wherein support supervisors prepared performance appraisals for individuals not working directly for them. I was not allowed to prepare the performance appraisal for my own employee, but I was supposed to sign it. I told this support supervisor that I did not think her rating was appropriate. Although the support employee had only worked for me less than three months, I noted nothing to indicate she was only performing at a minimum level. In fact, I told the support supervisor that I was very happy with the performance of her duties. She had a great attitude, filed everything immediately, answered the telephone professionally, kept my calendar for me, and handled herself professionally at all times.

My employee had a sick husband, grown children, and several grandchildren. She had done nothing in three months for me to have any cause for concern in the manner in which she carried out her responsibilities. The support supervisor was adamant, telling me how she never volunteered for other duties and did nothing extra in her job. I asked her what she was supposed to volunteer for. She said that the communication center in the office was manned twenty-four hours a day and was often in need of personnel to fill in for the employees assigned there when they went on leave or were sick. She said she had never volunteered to fill in. I said, "So what, that's not in her job requirement." She claimed that all of the other support employees pitched in and volunteered.

I was getting annoyed at this point. I told her I was not comfortable signing off on a poor performance appraisal and I would not do it. That same day, the ASAC called me into his office. He told me I yelled at the support supervisor and made her cry while refusing to sign the performance appraisal. I had not yelled at her and she was not crying. She was fine. I told him I had a very professional conversation providing reasons why I could not sign the appraisal. To my surprise, the ASAC said to me, "Why don't you just sign it?" I said back, "I cannot sign that performance appraisal in good conscience. I think she is doing a fine job for me and I have no complaints." He said, "What if I told you she was the worst employee in this office in the last five years?" I responded, "I don't know what she did in the office the last five years, but in the last three months working for me, she surely has not performed minimally. I am not saying she has done anything spectacular, but she has certainly done her job for me." The ASAC was visibly annoyed with me. He said, "Okay, that will be all." He never said another word about it, but the next week she received her performance appraisal with the minimally successful rating. Another support supervisor signed it in my place.

The ASAC turned out to be no friend. He was vindictive and he intensely disliked being challenged by me or anyone else. He was another little Napoleon who enjoyed his power. I also discovered he was the biggest liar I had ever met. He was never on my side on any issue for the remainder of my time in Oklahoma City. He criticized the performance appraisal ratings for my agents saying they were too high and he never gave me more than just a satisfactory rating, despite my squad's high quality cases in all areas of WCC, including public corruption, health care fraud, government fraud, and bank frauds. The only compliment I ever received from him was for my writing skills. My written reports to the front office and to FBI Headquarters were always of the highest quality, so he could not fault me for that.

After fourteen months as the WCC SSA, I was very comfortable and enjoyed working with the agents on my squad. The SAC who selected me was promoted to FBI Headquarters. The Section Chief from EDSP, who I had complained to about my Dayton SSRA job, was selected as our new SAC. An SSRA in Oklahoma City stepped down to take an OP transfer at about the same time.

A female supervisor at FBI Headquarters was selected as the new SSRA. An agent from my squad happened to be on TDY in her unit when she was selected. He told me that the designated female supervisor was the new SAC's girlfriend. She reportedly had even helped him move on his transfer to Oklahoma City. The agent on TDY told me that she was very nervous about being SSRA, inasmuch as her only experience in the FBI was in white collar crime. She was apparently very uncomfortable being in charge of an RA, which required knowledge of all FBI programs and violations. She was clearly selected for the job because of her status as the SAC's girlfriend.

Two days later, the ASAC informed me that the new female supervisor would be taking my position as the SSA of the WCC squad. I would be transferred to an off-site location in charge of the covert surveillance groups, SOG and SSG. In my experience with the FBI, being sent to SOG was usually a form of punishment. Generally, agents who were no longer producing results were sent to SOG.

As described previously, SSG came into existence in the early 1980s when the FBI figured out that agents did not have to be used on surveillance in FCI cases. Since FCI activities were not criminal in nature and presented no violent situations, armed agents were not required. Support personnel were hired and trained in surveillance techniques to alleviate agent resources. Normally, SSG personnel did not testify in court and they did not have weapons. The SSG program had grown in the FBI over the last thirty years, wherein nearly every office had an SSG team. The cities with foreign diplomatic missions had numerous SSG teams.

In Oklahoma City, however, there were no diplomatic missions. SSG followed around suspected foreign students and/or visitors from NSLT countries believed to be involved in foreign counterintelligence activities. Following 9/11, SSG began to be utilized in some instances to follow suspected terrorists, albeit those believed not to be dangerous. However, suspected terrorists were by definition inherently dangerous, so SOG was primarily used for these surveillances.

The ASAC tried to con me that I was needed for my experience and professionalism on SOG because of personnel problems that developed there. The ASAC said that the SSA of SOG/SSG was taking over the RAs, and the new supervisor (the SAC's girlfriend) would take over my squad. The ASAC was a natural born liar. The truth was that the SAC's girlfriend did not want the RA job. She was more comfortable with white collar crime and obviously told the SAC. In most circles, sleeping with the boss, the FBI being no exception, usually got you what you wanted.

The ASAC, the SSA who formerly worked in Louisiana, and the new SSRA, were good friends. The three of them were inseparable. They went to lunch every day together, chatting it up like three gossipy old women. The ASAC depended on them to tell him every piece of hearsay that went on in the office. The ASAC and the SSRA were both pilots as well. The SSRA would lend the ASAC his personal plane and they flew together frequently, another cozy superior/subordinate relationship. The entire episode was yet another unpleasant experience for me in the FBI. I viewed it as another example of FBI management making decisions not for the good of the FBI, but for their own selfish interests, and nothing more.

Ironically, as it turned out, I began to very much enjoy working at the covert off-site supervising SOG and SSG. It was an easy job too. The FBI Oklahoma City squads would request SOG or SSG assistance on their cases and I would accommodate them. I got the best Bureau vehicle I had been assigned since the 1986 Mercedes-Benz 450SL convertible I had at WMFO. I assigned myself a brand new Ford Mustang 5-Speed V-8 GT Deluxe, easily the coolest FBI vehicle in the division. I didn't feel bad about taking it because the Bureau accidently ordered it with a manual transmission. Surveillance agents could not easily drive a stick shift while simultaneously operating the Bureau radio.

My Ford Mustang 5-Speed V-8 GT Deluxe and me.

I did not have to deal with the front office very often, but the down side was that I still had to work for the annoying, spiteful ASAC. He never liked me after the situation with my subordinate's performance appraisal and he continued to be a major asshole to me. Unfortunately, he knew every detail of everything that happened on my squad. The former SOG SSA had a good friend on SOG who was like a spy in the midst. He informed his friend of every move I made. The SSA, in turn, filled in the ASAC on everything that went on at the off-site. The former SSA was also interested in what I was doing because he strangely wanted everything to run the same way as he had run things. Shortly after I took charge, the former SSA confronted my secretary in the mailroom, questioning her about how I assigned vehicles.

The issue was a trivial one, but one that the former SOG SSA apparently did not agree with. An agent from SOG had transferred out of the division. He was a smoker, unbeknownst to me. I subsequently assigned his car to a non-smoker. The SOG agent relayed this information to his friend, who in turn, relayed it to the ASAC. The ASAC then telephoned me telling me not to transfer the car from a smoker to a non-smoker. I immediately asked him how he would know about this inconsequential matter, knowing full well what had transpired. He lied, as always, making up some ludicrous story how he had a meeting regarding the division fleet management and heard about it. As usual, his lies made no sense.

I went into the office the next day and told the former SOG/SSG SSA that if he was so concerned about how I ran his old squad, then we should go talk to the SAC immediately. I told him that he could tell the SAC he wanted to return to his old position and I would have no objection. The man was like a deer caught in the headlights. He denied any knowledge of the matter. He continued to deny it even after I said to him, "My secretary told me you confronted her in the mail room about car assignments." I determined then and there that this guy was a complete squirrel. He was not even man enough to admit what he said.

I was sure word had gotten back to the ASAC about my confrontation with his buddy. I also made the mistake of saying how much I enjoyed my new Mustang in front of the SOG agents. The day after I confronted my predecessor, the ASAC telephoned me and insisted that I participate on surveillances. I told him that the FBI manual specifically stated that the SOG SSA should not participate in surveillances with the team. The SSA's job was an administrative one. For the same reason, I told him, an SSA of a WCC squad or any other squad did not go out on the streets to conduct interviews or collect evidence. This was the job of the street agent and the SSA's job was to manage. I further informed the ASAC that the SSA might be put in a position to testify in court on a case, thereby preventing him or her from performing supervisory duties.

The ASAC knew I was right but said, "We're going to be innovative, go out on the street once a week." I stopped arguing since I was not going to win. The little Napoleon was going to have his way. I wanted to tell him that the reason my predecessor had problems with his SOG personnel was because he insisted on participating on every surveillance after he was promoted to SSA, but I refrained.

My personal philosophy as a supervisor was that individuals performed better when given independence. For the most part, FBI agents were self-starters and highly motivated individuals. It was true that many SOG agents were older guys and maybe not as aggressive as they once had been, but they still did not need a supervisor holding their hand to perform their job. These were seasoned and experienced agents. In addition, SOG performed as a team at all times. No one wanted to let the team down by being responsible for losing the subject or getting burned on the surveillance.

My next run-in with the ASAC came when the Oklahoma City Division hosted an SAC Conference. The last time I had taken part in an SAC Conference was when I was a new agent in Orlando. I had nothing but good memories of that experience. However, this one would be quite different. At the Oklahoma City supervisor's conference, the ASAC gave instructions for the upcoming SAC Conference to the SSAs to pick up FBI executive management personnel from the airport. My assignment was to pick up the Chief of the Technology and Management Division at FBI Headquarters. We were further instructed to pick them up the second day of the conference and drive them to a special luncheon downtown. The ASAC stated that all supervisors were to be present at the conference each day dressed in suits.

At the conclusion of the supervisor's meeting as we got up to leave, I made a comment to the Acting WCC SSA, who had previously worked for me, that "I guess we're going to be a bunch of chauffeurs for these guys." He responded to me by shaking his head, acknowledging my sentiment. Unfortunately, I was overheard by one of the ASAC's spies. I saw his head turn sharply toward me when I made this comment. I knew immediately that this would be a topic of conversation with his two buddies at lunch that day. I didn't care though. I thought it was ridiculous that all the supervisors had to treat the executive management as though they were royalty. The only reason we had to do this was because our SAC wanted to impress them so he could get promoted.

On the Friday before the start of the SAC Conference the following week, I passed the SAC in the hall as I was walking out of the building. He told me that plans had changed for the SAC Conference. The supervisors were no longer required to stay each day at the conference. They only needed to pick up their assigned people from the airport and to take them to the luncheon on Tuesday. I told him, "Great, I really didn't want to be standing around all week at the conference."

On Sunday evening, I picked up the Chief of the Office of Technology and Management Division. He was about fifty years old and had just recently been appointed to his position by Director Mueller. He had not been a career FBI employee. He did not say what career he had previously been in. When he learned I was the supervisor of the surveillance teams, he asked a lot of questions about the equipment we used. I think he was surprised at the lack of technical equipment we employed for surveillance. I did not explain it to him in any great detail, but I basically told him we just followed around our subjects and took pictures. We seldom had subjects with trackers on their cars or anything like that. Tracking devices were reserved for the bigger cases. Generally, our cases in Oklahoma City were not life or death situations. If surveillance teams lost the subject, it really did not matter and surveillance would continue the next day. Most of the SOG/SSG cases were to gather intelligence on suspected terrorists or FCI subjects. The teams would sometimes be called out on TDY to other offices to assist on major cases. The FBI Oklahoma City never had a major case requiring outside assistance during my tenure as SOG/SSG supervisor.

I was assigned to pick up the Chief on Tuesday for the luncheon, wait in the car while he ate lunch, and then return him to the conference. I spoke to the ASAC's two spies outside the building at the conference while waiting for the Chief to take him to the restaurant. I was surprised to learn from them that they were attending the conference every day. I told them what the SAC had told me.

Later that day, I got a call from the ASAC who was very irritated that I was not in a suit when picking up the Chief and that I was not attending the conference. I told him that the SAC told me I did not have to attend and that I had come from the SOG off-site where I never wore a suit. He told me I should have had a suit on and hung up on me. Two days later, an agent from the office told me how angry the ASAC was with me. This agent had heard him talking about me in the gym and how I was not at the conference. He was furious that when I did show up at the conference, I was dressed casually. I immediately sent an e-mail to the SAC advising him of the situation. I asked him to let the ASAC know that he (the SAC) had told me I did not have to attend, because there evidently seemed to be a misunderstanding. The next day, the ASAC called me and told me to be in the SAC's office on Friday afternoon.

I showed up at the SAC's office on time and dressed casually, as I had come from the off-site. The ASAC was sitting in a chair to the right of the SAC's desk. I apologized for the misunderstanding and told the SAC I hoped he could tell the ASAC of our conversation the previous week. I further said to the SAC, "If you don't remember our conversation, then I guess I don't have a leg to stand on." The SAC responded back immediately in a very abrupt tone and said, "You should have known better and stepped up like all the other supervisors and attended the conference." My heart sunk at that point. I knew I was toast. He didn't care what he had said to me about not being required to attend. He was taking the ASAC's side, which was about to get even worse. The SAC asked me what I was wearing when I picked up the Chief of Technology at the airport. I told him I was dressed casually. He then asked what I was dressed in when picking him up for the luncheon. I said, "Pretty much like what I am wearing now, a golf shirt, nice slacks, and this spring jacket."

The ASAC jumped into the conversation and said that the Chief was embarrassed that I was not in attendance at the conference and that I was the only supervisor not in a suit when picking him up. I knew this was another one of the ASAC's ridiculous lies, but I did not argue. Then the SAC asked me if I spoke to the Chief at any time. I said somewhat indignantly, "Of course I did. He asked me all about what technical equipment we used on SOG. We had a very nice conversation in the car from the airport to his hotel."

The SAC then said something very troubling and threatening. He said, "If you cannot step up as a supervisor, we have other people that will." I was shocked at the level he was taking this incident, particularly since it was he who told me not to attend the conference. It became abundantly clear on his next line of questioning that the ASAC was behind all of this. The SAC next accused me of not putting enough time in as a supervisor. The SAC said that last year after the ASAC had advised me that my overtime was short of the required two hours per day, my response was that I was not worried about it. The SAC went on to reprimand me that as a supervisor I was required to set an example and he expected me to be the last person gone at night from my squad. At that moment, I knew the ASAC had dredged up everything he could think of to put me in a bad light.

All agents were required to work an average of two hours per day overtime, called Availability Pay, or AVP. It was previously referred to as AUO, or Administrative Uncontrollable Overtime, when I first became an agent. As explained before, AVP was a part of an agent's salary automatically. The AVP alleviated the FBI of dealing with overtime pay. All agents received this AVP as part of their pay, which amounted to twenty-five percent more in salary. The result of this was that FBI agents were on call 24/7 and had the responsibility to respond to any situation or incident without worrying about how much overtime they would get. Every quarter, the FBI distributed a list of agents who were short the required two hours. Their supervisor was to inform them so they could increase their AVP average and not lose their AVP, or twenty-five percent of their pay.

I explained to the SAC that my AVP had gone below two hours in the fall of the previous year. I told him that because I had been under transfer back at FBI Headquarters, my AVP average had dropped. I told him that when I arrived in Oklahoma City, I stayed more than two hours every night in an effort to get the AVP back to averaging two hours. I assured him that I was always the last one to leave my squad. It took about six months to finally get my AVP average over two hours again. I said that, "This is out of context. I did tell the ASAC that I was not worried about it because I knew I was working extra hours every day to rectify it." This was the only issue in which the SAC seemed to understand my point of view. However, the SAC never did acknowledge our conversation from the previous week and reiterated that I had to work harder.

This was a case of the ASAC's vindictiveness working in full force. The SAC was taking the side of his immediate subordinate and I had no chance to win. They both humiliated me purposely to keep me in my place. I wanted to tell them both to go to hell, but I was thinking of my paycheck. If they had wanted to, they could have fixed it to have given me terrible performance ratings and demoted me. This was another example of the FBI family eating its young, but I did not want to be its prey. I was not anxious at that late stage in my career to take a drop in pay from a GS-14 to a GS-13 street agent's pay, which would have been a substantial pay cut. I swallowed my pride which stuck in my throat for a very long time.

This ASAC's spiteful nature was well known. An agent in the field office once parked his Bureau vehicle in a no parking zone of the FBI building for a few minutes while he stopped into his office. The ASAC punished the agent by sending him on a fourteen-week assignment to the FBI Academy in Quantico, Virginia, twelve hundred miles away. This type of TDY as a field counselor was normally filled on a voluntary basis. The agent was the husband of a female agent in the office and the father of three young children. The TDY was a huge inconvenience and an unwanted sacrifice for him and his family. Yet, he was ordered to leave home by his FBI family for three and a half months for a minor parking infraction. This nasty ASAC was quite proud of his actions and bragged about it for years.

The ASAC never stopped with his vindictive ways. In another incident, he directed my Pilot-in-Command on SOG to draft an Electronic Communication (EC) to FBI Headquarters to approve him and his buddy, my predecessor on SOG, as co-pilots in the Oklahoma City Division. I knew this was wrong. The FBI manual clearly stated that the only management personnel allowed in the FBI's aviation program was the supervisor of SOG. My predecessor had been a pilot as supervisor of SOG, but he was now the supervisor of the RAs. The two of them wanted to be in the aviation program mainly for the free flying time and the free pilot license renewals. I reluctantly signed off on the EC and forwarded it to the front office. The ASAC signed off on it, but the SAC recognized that they could not be pilots for SOG. The SAC sent it back to me with a note on it indicating this fact.

A couple of weeks went by and the ASAC asked for the EC back. He said he wanted to discuss it with the SAC. I then received the same EC again wherein the SAC's initials were on it, thereby approving the document. I emailed the ASAC indicating that I was confused about the EC. I had the note from the SAC stating that this could not be approved. The ASAC said he initialed the EC in the SAC's absence. The SAC had gone back to FBI Headquarters on an extended TDY. The ASAC said he was the Acting SAC. We exchanged several emails whereby I informed him of the SAC's note and the FBI policy regarding pilots. I quoted the FBI manual and also advised him that I had discussed the matter with the Aviation Unit at FBI Headquarters who said they would not approve it. The ASAC's tone in his last e-mail was clearly filled with irritation. His final words on the matter in his e-mail to me were, "Fine, bag it."

The next week, I was on annual leave in Flagstaff, Arizona, where my sixteen-year-old daughter was playing in a

PGA Junior Series golf tournament. My daughter, Mary, my wife, Cindy, and I were all having a great time as Mary had her best performance in a national junior girls golf tournament, finishing second with scores of 76, 73, and 75. We were scheduled to leave Flagstaff on Saturday morning on our ten-hour drive back to Oklahoma. However, on Thursday evening, my secretary called to advise that the Acting SAC called her at the off-site asking her exactly where I was. When he found out I was on vacation in Flagstaff, he told her, "Good, then he can go to Phoenix on TDY on Monday for an FBI Headquarters Inspection for two weeks since he's already in Arizona." I then received a call from the other ASAC in the Oklahoma City Division. This ASAC said that I had to report to Phoenix on Monday morning for an inspection.

I was an Inspector-in-Place, however, I had no desire at this point in my career to become an ASAC, the next step on the FBI management ladder. I hated nearly every ASAC I ever knew, particularly the two current ASACs in Oklahoma City. I had completed three inspections in the past, one in the Buffalo Division, one at CJIS in Clarksburg, West Virginia, and an emergency inspection in Houston a few months previously. In order to become an ASAC, supervisors had to complete six inspections. I actually had four inspections to my credit since an OPR investigation counted as one. In prior years, inspections were done at every field division every three or four years. The FBI offices were usually turned upside down during inspections while inspectors reviewed virtually every file, program, and administrative piece of paper, and interviewed every supervisor, agent and support person in the office.

While at OPR, I volunteered for the Buffalo Inspection. I also volunteered for the Baltimore Inspection, but was turned down. It was very political in getting assigned to an inspection. Other supervisors in OPR would befriend and schmooze the management personnel in the Inspection Division in order to get picked for inspections. The entire process turned me off. I had no desire in becoming an ASAC anyway. I had already capped out in my salary, making the same amount of money as an ASAC. Unless a government employee was in the SES, a cap was placed on one's salary. I reached Grade 14, step 9 on the pay scale, which was a higher salary on paper than I was actually paid. An ASAC was a Grade 15 position, not an SES position, so a promotion to ASAC would have been in name only with no monetary gain.

After arriving in Oklahoma City, I volunteered for the CJIS inspection, largely because my old friend from my 1990s OPR days was going to be on it. Director Mueller later changed the inspection process and decided to do inspections based on problems arising in offices. For example, the Houston Division inspection came about because a DOJ OIG report presented before Congress indicated a problem with the volume of National Security Letters (NSL) being issued by the FBI. I did not volunteer for this particular inspection. Two other Oklahoma City supervisors and I were asked to go to Houston on a day's notice to review that division's files concerning NSLs.

In the Phoenix inspection, I was the only supervisor from Oklahoma City being sent. This inspection was also the result of a DOJ OIG report presented before Congress involving NSLs, but this time it was specifically regarding the misuse of NSLs by the FBI in obtaining telephone records. It turned out that NSLs were not being misused, but that the telephone companies were sending too many records to the FBI. The FBI was justified in using the NSLs as an investigative tool to request toll records of suspected terrorists or individuals suspected of being affiliated with foreign counterintelligence. The problem was that the telephone companies were sending records beyond the dates asked in the NSLs. This was more of an administrative error rather than any kind of misuse of the NSL. For example, the FBI might ask for telephone toll records in an NSL, dated 3/1/2007, for the period of 1/1/2002 to the present. The telephone company would then gather the records maybe a month or two later and include toll records beyond the date of the letter.

I tried to explain to the ASAC that I had to drive ten hours with my wife and daughter on Friday back to Oklahoma City, a day earlier than planned, and could not even arrange my flight or hotel. I also asked why some other supervisor could not go since this was an inconvenience for me. I told him I had annual leave scheduled in two weeks to take my daughter to Hartford, Connecticut, to play in the USGA Girls Junior Golf Championship. I had three plane tickets and a hotel stay that were already paid for. He could not have been less understanding. He obviously did not care and abruptly told me to get on the phone with my secretary to make flight and hotel arrangements.

He said I was the only supervisor in the Oklahoma City Division available to go. I clearly was not available. I told him that these were usually voluntary to which he replied this was not. He said that inspections usually end the second week on a Thursday night and that I should be able to fly back to Oklahoma City and then be able to catch my flight on Friday for Hartford. I was being ordered to go and there was no recourse for me. I knew it was the Acting SAC getting even with me for not sending in his request to FBI Headquarters to be part of the aviation program. This was more vindictive behavior by him, pure and simple. Every time I disagreed with him about anything, I had to pay the consequences.

When I arrived at the Phoenix inspection, the first thing we were told was that no one was allowed to leave early. Everyone would have to stay through Friday of the second week. I couldn't believe it. I thought I would just have to tell them I was leaving a day early and damn the consequences. I had planned to wait a few days to advise the individuals in charge. In the meantime, I was working with a team of agents and explained my situation to them. One agent said he knew our superior on the inspection quite well and he would explain the situation to him. The agents on my team could not believe the circumstances in which I was sent on this inspection. They thought it was awful. The next day, the agent on my team told me he spoke with his friend and it was not a problem for me to leave a day early. I was relieved and thankful to my colleague on the inspection.

The SAC in Oklahoma City went back to FBI Headquarters, having been promoted to a Deputy Assistant Director. I laid low after that and tried not to say much to anybody in the main office, particularly to the ASAC's spies. When the new SAC arrived, a rumor circulated that the new SAC had not gotten along with Director Mueller. He had reportedly disagreed with Mueller too often and put in for a lateral transfer as an SAC.

His reported disagreement with Mueller was deemed as a badge of honor, insofar as Mueller was unpopular among most of the field agents I knew. Mueller was widely viewed as arrogant, egotistical, and unbending on his policies, even those that clearly did not work. As described previously, he instituted the seven-year up and out policy for supervisors and the three-year rotational transfer policy for all new agents. Even after his inner circle at FBI Headquarters advised him that these policies were unpopular among the field personnel, as well as not being cost-effective, Mueller still refused to change them. The rotational transfer policy had been in effect when I was a new agent, but was discontinued in 1993 after it was concluded that it was too costly to the FBI's budget. Mueller reinstituted it after his appointment in 2001.

A visit by Director Mueller to the Oklahoma City Division. I am second from the right. Director Mueller is second to the left of the television screen.

The ASAC continued to be a thorn in my side, but I grew to intensely dislike the other ASAC as well, particularly after my conversation with him regarding going on the Phoenix inspection. The two ASACs were not much different. They were both pricks. They were also both "yes men" through and through, always towing the company line and playing the game so they could stay in good standing for promotion. Ironically, neither was ever promoted. The second ASAC was not unlike his slimy colleague, especially with regard to his treatment of subordinates. He expected his subordinates never to disagree with him. Prior to the previous SAC's transfer to FBI Headquarters, he reorganized the ASAC's responsibilities in the division. I ended up working for the second ASAC, who I thought could not be worse than the first ASAC, but he was at least his equal.

My first experience with him had been at a meeting a couple of years before involving grade promotions for analysts on the FIG. I was the supervisor on the WCC squad at the time. The supervisor on the FIG recommended several analysts for grade raises. One analyst had assisted two of my senior agents on a public corruption case. Both agents raved about him, his work ethic, and his immeasurable help to them on their case. At the meeting with the ASAC, the FIG supervisor presented this analyst's application packet for consideration for the grade promotion. Five analysts submitted write-ups justifying their grade raises. The FIG supervisor had signed and approved all five analysts' requests for promotion. The write-ups were to be voted upon by the Oklahoma City local career board. The applications were then to be forwarded to FBI Headquarters for approval.

The local career board was usually a fairly routine matter. However, when the one analyst's submission came up for consideration, the ASAC began criticizing his writing ability. He said that he often had to send his intelligence reports back to him for re-writes and corrections. The ASAC did not think he deserved a grade promotion. I spoke up and described his excellent working relationship with my two agents and his invaluable assistance to them. I also argued that although some agents investigated major cases, they were not great writers and needed help writing Title III affidavits or undercover proposals. They were, nonetheless, excellent agents deserving of promotions. The FIG supervisor said absolutely nothing, even though he was the analyst's immediate supervisor. He had signed and approved the request for the grade promotion and was making the recommendation to the board, yet he wouldn't argue for the promotion due to the fact that the ASAC was against it.

When it came time for the vote, the ASAC, the FIG supervisor, and the other supervisors present voted against the analyst's submission. I was the lone vote for it. I thought the ASAC was rotten not to have sent it to FBI Headquarters. The other four analysts' applications were approved and forwarded to FBI Headquarters. They subsequently got their raises and their colleague did not. The FIG supervisor revealed himself as a hypocrite with no backbone or conviction. He was the worst yes man in the division. I never heard him disagree with the ASAC ever. The analyst later resigned from the FBI after being hired at a national counterterrorism center in North Carolina.

After this ASAC became my immediate supervisor, I realized how stupid he really was. One of my support employees volunteered to assist the FBI contingent in Iraq for a three-month TDY as a supply technician. While this employee had loyally served her country in the military reserves for over twenty years, she had never been in combat or involved in any real wartime activities. She felt it was her chance to serve her country in a war zone. Many agents and support personnel had been volunteering to go to Iraq and Afghanistan. The FBI had been involved in both operations from the start in an effort to interrogate prisoners from the battlefield and gather immediate intelligence information regarding terrorism. Many viewed this as an opportunity to do something really special and different in their careers. Others merely wanted to collect the combat pay, which usually amounted to about a $20,000 bonus for agents after three months. In Iraq, the FBI occupied a building in the green zone in Baghdad. I fully supported my employee's request to serve there.

After a time, she called me from Baghdad. She was getting very little sleep, but she was enjoying the opportunity to serve her country in wartime. She told me of a mortar that had landed in the nearby vicinity of her building. She said she was especially excited to be carrying an automatic weapon. I was stunned and asked why in the world she would be carrying a weapon. She said that she often had to walk to the front gate escorting visitors. She carried the weapon for security. I told her she should not be doing that for a number of reasons. First, she was not trained on that weapon or any other. I was deeply concerned she might hurt herself or others if she ever used the weapon. Secondly, she was making herself a target by carrying the weapon. Lastly, I did not believe FBI Headquarters policy sanctioned an FBI support employee to carry automatic weapons.

She argued with me vehemently that I did not understand that she was in a war zone. She told me that her FBI supervisor there had authorized her to carry the weapon. I told her that he was clearly wrong. I ordered her not to carry the weapon, not just because I was certain it was against FBI policy, but because as a friend, I was very concerned for her safety. She continued to argue that it was quite necessary and that I could not understand because I had never been in a war zone. I continued to implore her not to carry a weapon by telling her that I was sure her husband, her children, and her grandchildren would be worried sick if they knew about this. I ordered her not to continue this activity and that I was calling FBI Headquarters to make sure she stopped.

I immediately called the unit at FBI Headquarters responsible for deploying FBI personnel to Iraq. The individual with whom I spoke advised that he was a contract employee with the FBI. He said, however, that FBI support personnel should not be carrying weapons, only agent personnel were authorized to do so. He advised that he would make it known to the FBI management and to the FBI supervisor in Baghdad.

A half an hour later, the ASAC called me to advise that my employee had just spoken with him on the telephone from Baghdad. She was very upset that I had told her not to carry a weapon. The ASAC said that another support employee from Oklahoma City had been on TDY to Baghdad the previous summer. He had been allowed to carry a pistol. The ASAC told me that it was all right for her to carry a weapon and that I should "just let it go." He further told me I had supported her TDY to Iraq so I should accept this. I was very happy to have been able to tell this idiot, "Sorry, too late, I have already called FBI Headquarters concerning the matter. They told me it was against Bureau policy and they would inform the appropriate personnel that she was not allowed to carry a weapon." I further told him that I personally felt that she might harm herself or others if she was in a situation wherein she believed she might have to use the weapon, having never been trained with it. He had no response and no further say in the matter anyway. I was glad that for once common sense won out. I felt such gratification at not having to listen and follow another stupid order from FBI management, especially from this fool.

Later on, I would be assigned the additional responsibility over the Language Services Unit in the Oklahoma City Division. This move was one of the dumber management decisions I had ever seen. I was in charge of a covert off-site. I supervised fifteen covert employees. In order to maintain my covert status, one would logically think I should not be supervising another dozen people in another building ten miles away in an overt FBI office. As usual, it made no sense. The Language Services in Oklahoma City was comprised of mainly part-time contract FBI employees who were fluent in various different languages, as well as one full-time FBI linguist, and the Language Services supervisor.

Shortly after I took over Language Services, a linguist requested I meet with her privately. She was the daughter of my predecessor on SOG. She was in the process of becoming a permanent full-time FBI employee. She told me that the Language Service supervisor was very unpopular among the contract employees. He was perceived as condescending, abrupt, rude, and offensive. Before providing any details, she made it clear that she did not want to go to the front office with these complaints. Her father advised her that it was not a good idea to become the center of controversy, particularly at a time when she was trying to become a permanent employee. I assured her that I would not take her complaints to the front office, but that I would handle it.

She said that she did not personally like the supervisor because of the rude and condescending manner in which he would speak to her. She said he was abrupt with the other translators too. The major problem with him, she said, was his inappropriate remarks. She said that the Arabic translator heard him refer to Arabs as "sand people," a highly offensive and racist remark. I told her I would speak to him, but would not let him know who complained.

I spoke to him the very next day. He had previously been a Language Specialist at FBI Headquarters prior to his promotion in Oklahoma City six months previously. I told him there was talk in the office of him being a bit heavy handed with his employees. I told him to be careful not to get too power hungry as a supervisor, as I had seen many people change after getting promoted. He seemed to take my advice without any indignation. When I told him he had been overheard in the office using the term "sand people" in reference to Arabs, he laughed a little and said he was referring to the sand people in the movie, *Star Wars*. He said he never made any racist remarks against Arabs. I told him to be very careful what he said in the office. I explained that the Oklahoma City office was relatively small and people loved to gossip.

I ran into his subordinate in the hallway about a week later. I asked her if everything was going well, to which she replied yes. I told her I had spoken to her supervisor about her complaints without revealing her identity. She said that he had been very nice the past week. She thanked me for handling the problem and was extremely grateful for keeping her name out of it. I told her to call me if she had any more problems with him. I never heard from her again.

Six months later, however, the SAC called me about the Language Services supervisor. He said that the Arabic translator in Language Services wrote a letter to him and to FBI Headquarters alleging that the supervisor was a racist, referring to her as sand people and criticizing Muslims, among many other issues. The SAC asked me if I knew anything about this. I immediately realized that my predecessor told the ASAC about his daughter's complaints. I told the SAC that I had spoken to the language supervisor six months ago regarding the sand people issue and for him to be extremely careful what he said in the office. I told the SAC that he said he was referring to the movie, *Star Wars*, and he said he was misinterpreted. The SAC asked me why I had not brought it to the attention of the front office. He was very annoyed. I explained why, but he said I should have brought it to his attention anyway. The SAC said that another Arabic FBI employee from another office had recently testified before Congress regarding alleged racism toward Muslims in the FBI. He said that he did not want this to end up before Congress.

The SAC decided that he did not want this individual supervising Language Services. He referred the letter to OPR for misconduct and contacted FBI Headquarters to have him removed as supervisor. OPR referred the case to the Equal Employment Opportunity (EEO) for investigation. FBI Headquarters said they could not remove him as supervisor until the EEO investigation was concluded. EEO determined that the alleged comment had occurred six months to a year ago. Complaints to EEO had to be reported within forty-five days of the incident, so EEO did not investigate. The SAC was completely frustrated. He told me that I would have to give him an unacceptable performance rating so he could get rid of him. The problem was that his performance as Language Services supervisor met all of the minimum efficiency requirements, at least quantitatively.

The SAC really wanted to fire this guy. However, the SAC did not have that authority. Since FBI Headquarters did not do anything, the SAC decided to conduct his own investigation. All of the translators were interviewed. The language supervisor was then interviewed having to answer all of the allegations. He admitted to making many inappropriate remarks with regard to his opinions on religion, specifically Muslims; and race, but not specifically pertaining to Arabs, but with regard to his wife's sister's black husband; and abortion. His admissions, coupled with most of his subordinates' repulsion to his comments, provided sufficient justification in his performance appraisal report to justify that he caused a hostile working environment.

In the meantime, the SAC did not want him supervising Language Services or being near any of the translators. The SAC made the terrible decision, probably to punish me as well, of sending him to my covert off-site while the case was being made to fire him. Everybody on SOG and SSG thought this was a horrible idea due to the fact that it was a covert off-site and might be compromised. He was an overt FBI employee who obviously possessed terrible judgment. Furthermore, he probably resented being removed as supervisor, ostracized from the main office, and possibly anticipated being fired. The SAC's decision to send this person to a secret off-site was nothing short of completely stupid.

Only a year before, the owner of the previous SOG/SSG off-site building we were leasing compromised our location. Fortunately, the owner of any FBI covert off-site had to sign a confidentiality agreement with the FBI as part of the lease, promising not to disclose the identity of the FBI. With over a year left on the lease, the previous owners were attempting to sell the building. Selling the building would have been acceptable as a new lease could have easily been drawn up with new owners. However, the owners were using the fact that the FBI was leasing the building as a selling point to potential buyers.

One of the SOG agents overheard the owner's realtor telling the potential buyers that they would have a built-in lease with the FBI. These people did not end up purchasing the building, but the off-site was definitely compromised. The realtor had not been cleared or signed a confidentiality agreement, nor had the potential buyers. There was no way of knowing how many people the realtor told, the potential buyers might have told, or how many other potential buyers knew the building was leased by the FBI. I spent months after that incident looking for a new building, and then another six months with FBI Headquarters finalizing a new lease. The leased building required moderations in its construction for security purposes, to include soundproofing the walls, installing a vault, building a secure entrance, alarming the building, and providing security cameras inside and outside the building. This was accomplished at considerable time and expense to the FBI. Now the SAC was placing an overt FBI employee he was trying to fire in our new off-site. Fortunately, the Language Services supervisor was transferred to Language Services at FBI Headquarters after several months and the new off-site was not compromised.

FBI management not only made these types of stupid, illogical decisions, but they made others out of spite and pure meanness. One female agent who had previously worked for me on the white collar crime squad was one of the most hardworking agents on the squad. On top of that, she was a genuinely sweet person with no pretensions. She was also a diligent, thorough investigator who produced quality prosecutable white collar crime cases in the areas of health care fraud and fraud against the government. After I left the squad, she put in a request to transfer to the Norman RA near her home.

She had two severely autistic boys, ages four and five, at the time. The boys had to adhere to very strict routines. If deviations occurred from their routines, the boys would react in a visceral way. At a squad party at an agent's home on one occasion, I observed one of the boys scream and squeal because his water was not coming out of his baby sippy cup properly. Virtually any minor problem encountered would result in the boys becoming hysterical. If this female agent did not come home every night from work at exactly 6 p.m., her stay-at-home husband would have to console two frantic young children. As a result of her unique personal situation, the previous SAC had given her permission not to have to work late. She was assigned to white collar crime, since most of these investigations, with exception, such as my telemarketing case in ORA, did not usually require odd hours.

The University of Oklahoma in Norman had a special educational program targeted precisely for severely autistic children. The FBI management transferred her to the Norman RA so that she could be in close proximity to the school. The FBI at times did have a heart, but justification to FBI Headquarters was required for this type of transfer, more commonly known as a hardship transfer. Generally, if an FBI employee had an immediate family member requiring long-term specialized medical care which was not available in their present assignment locale, the FBI could approve a hardship transfer for the employee to transfer them where the medical attention was available. Her transfer was much easier than most since she did not have to transfer out of the division or purchase a new home. This type of transfer was referred to as a no-cost transfer. All she had to do was commute to the Norman RA, a couple miles from her home, instead of thirty miles north to the Oklahoma City office.

This good will by the FBI was spoiled by her SSA, my predecessor on SOG, who was supervising the Norman RA. After she was there about a year, the SSA decided that she needed to attend an SSA Conference for two weeks. She was a relief supervisor on the squad at the time. However, several SSAs, including her SSA, had already declined to go to this conference with no repercussions. When she declined, she was threatened with losing her AVP. The previous SAC had exempted her from training at Quantico due to her children's condition, just as he had exempted her from working late. Her new SSA was having none of this. He told her it was not fair that she never had to go to training at Quantico.

All the other agents from the RA attended some type of training periodically at Quantico and she could not be an exception, he said. She was getting nowhere trying to explain to him that her children would not be able to cope with her long absence. She then went to his boss (his best friend), the ASAC, to plead her case. She was not surprised that her SSA's flying buddy stood behind his decision. She then went to see the new SAC, telling him the previous SACs had exempted her from traveling. The SAC told her flat out he was supporting the ASAC and her SSA. When she told the SAC about the threat of taking away her AVP, the SAC later told her that her SSA denied ever saying that.

She then called me on the telephone to tell me of this horrible situation. She was crying and did not know what to do. She and I had become good friends when she worked for me. She knew that she could trust me. She had called me for advice in other matters through the years. She also knew my background in OPR at FBI Headquarters. I was also very knowledgeable regarding the Bureau's policies. She said she was a member of the FBI Agent's Association so I advised her to call them for an attorney. She did so and the SAC changed his tune the second he received a very long e-mail from her attorney, which ultimately threatened litigation against the SAC, the ASAC, her SSA, and the FBI under the Americans with Disabilities Act of 1990. Suffice it to say, she was not required to go to Quantico at that time or any other. However, the entire unseemly episode caused her to drop out of the relief supervisory program.

Unfortunately for me personally, I rarely won any battles with FBI management. About six or eight months before my retirement, I received yet another ridiculous telephone call from FBI management, this time from my original ASAC, and an acting ASAC, a fellow who was an SSA and now my supervisor. The SSA temporarily replaced the other idiot ASAC who retired.

This SSA was another spineless wonder who never, ever, disagreed with the front office. The front office loved this SSA. He had an agent working for him who stole informant payments for five years totaling $50,000 to cover his gambling debts. An informant clerk finally noticed that the signatures on the receipts did not match the informant's. The agent was apparently forging the informant's signature, as well as the required witnessing agent's signature. The Oklahoma City agent was subsequently arrested, indicted, and convicted. The SSA missed this for five years. He was never even criticized for this outrageous supervisory oversight. Instead, the Oklahoma City management made him the Acting ASAC. I shudder to think what would have happened to me had this agent been on my squad. I would have been disemboweled like William Wallace before the citizens of London.

The two had me on a conference call and asked me where a certain SOG agent was, who I'll just refer to as Joe. Joe was a seasoned agent and a former SSA, but was now an SOG agent who had recently received an OP transfer to Oklahoma City. Joe told me he had hated the ASAC in his former office for the same reasons I hated our ASACs. He thought they were idiots who never supported any of his decisions. He stepped down as an SSA and took his OP to Oklahoma City. Joe was a man of many talents. He was a West Point graduate, confident, intelligent, competent, as well as conscientious. In addition, he was very likeable and an individual who I would describe as "a class act."

Joe also happened to be a firearms instructor and the best pistol shooter in the division. For this reason, the SAC wanted him to participate with the FBI team in a local law enforcement pistol competition the following day. The problem was that Joe was at the Wiley Post Airport leaving on an SOG TDY to support a national priority FBI terrorism case. Joe was a Bureau co-pilot working toward becoming a licensed pilot. He and the division's pilot were preparing to fly across country when the two morons from the front office called on behalf of the SAC. I advised them that the SOG team was leaving on TDY. The ASAC then ordered me to find out if they had gone yet.

It was a Thursday morning at about 9:30 a.m. When I called, they were about to take off in the plane. The pilot said that if I had called just thirty seconds later, he would have already turned his cell phone off in preparation for takeoff. When I told the pilot that the SAC wanted Joe to participate in a pistol shooting competition, he said that he needed Joe as the co-pilot to help him through some overcast and rainy weather. The pilot further advised that he was presently on the radio talking to the airport tower. My gut instinct was to tell them to just go and I would tell the ASAC they had already taken off. However, I was not a liar, so I told them both to stand by.

I called back the ASAC who had me on speakerphone with the Acting ASAC. I told them that the pilot and Joe were preparing for takeoff and that the pilot needed Joe as co-pilot. The ASAC told me to get Joe off the plane; the SAC wanted him to compete in the firearms competition. This was another prime example of complete lunacy in the FBI. I said to them, "This is ridiculous. They are seconds from taking off on a TDY on a national priority terrorism case and the pilot does not want to fly across country alone through bad weather." The ASAC immediately shot back, "Then you fly with him. Just get Joe off the plane." I responded, "I am not a pilot or a co-pilot. I would be of no help." The ASAC became completely agitated with me. He ordered me to get Joe off the plane so he could shoot in the competition. I said, "Okay, but this is crazy." I called them and told Joe he would have to make arrangements to fly commercially following the firearms competition. The pilot was furious at having to fly alone. He said, "The ASAC should know better, he's a pilot!"

This episode was yet another example of arguing with FBI management to no avail over idiotic and nonsensical decisions. Nobody was going to challenge the SAC, least of all the ASAC. The ASAC was following orders from the SAC, carrying them out unapologetically like a Nazi subordinate. His mission was to please the SAC, plain and simple. He continued to be a little Napoleon and never liked being challenged, particularly by me. The Acting ASAC, being true to form, never said a word during the entire conference call. I was too low on the totem pole to win at challenging stupid management decisions. This decision was particularly annoying because it was all about the SAC wanting the FBI to win the local pistol competition. The FBI did in fact win the competition the following day with Joe on the team. The SAC's pride and ego were saved at the expense of the FBI's time, money and resources in fighting terrorism, as well as at the risk to the pilot's safety.

The following week I attended firearms training. A new ASAC (a third one for the division and not needed) and one of his supervisors remarked with great amusement at how Joe was pulled off a plane to win the pistol competition for the FBI. I immediately called them out telling them it wasn't funny. Joe was not only called away from a national priority terrorism investigation, but his absence from the airplane put the pilot at personal risk flying across country in bad weather. The new ASAC and supervisor wiped the smiles off their faces immediately following my admonishment, hopefully realizing that it was neither funny nor a prudent move on the part of management. Both of these individuals later rose to Senior Executive Service positions in the FBI after my retirement.

One of my big pet peeves working for the FBI was the amount of money that was continually wasted. As the supervisor at the off-site, I was in charge of an approximately $200,000 annual budget, a relative pittance compared to the FBI's total budget of $5 billion, and the total federal government budget that was in the trillions. I was annoyed, however, at the end of every fiscal year when I had money left over in my budget. FBI Headquarters supervisors explained to me that if I did not spend every last dime of my budget, then my budget next year would be less. This fact applied to all government budgets everywhere, no matter how big or small. If the money allotted was not spent during one fiscal year, then it was only reasonable to assume that you could get by on fewer funds the following fiscal year. The problem was that no government entity ever wanted to give up funds.

My father told me that when he worked as an engineer as a civilian for the Department of the Army back in the 1960s, the same rules applied. This was how the federal government worked. Nobody cared because it was not their money. This was why the national debt grew leaps and bounds each year and continued to do so with no end in sight. This drove me crazy. From 2007 to 2012, the national debt had risen from around $9 trillion to $16 trillion. In 2017, the national debt had grown to almost $20 trillion. After my third year of frittering away money at the end of each year, I had over $20,000 near the end of fiscal year 2009. The government fiscal year began on October 1st and ended September 30th the following year. Every August, FBI Headquarters personnel would telephone me to remind me that I needed to spend any excess money from my budget.

In August 2009, I had over $20,000 to spend from my budget. When FBI Headquarters called, I told them I did not know what to spend all of this money on. I believed I had everything I needed for my surveillance squads to operate sufficiently. The previous years I had purchased cameras and camcorders for the surveillance agents, special aviation binoculars for the plane, Garmin GPS units, and a number of other items for the off-site, including furniture, desks, and chairs. I honestly did not know what else I could buy. I suggested buying new computers since my personnel had to share computers. To my astonishment, I was not allowed to purchase any computer equipment. FBI regulations dictated that only the FBI's Operations and Technology Division was authorized to purchase computer equipment. Any request for new computers would have to go through them and could not be from my budget.

The supervisor from FBI Headquarters made numerous purchase suggestions, such as a new Xerox machine, a new refrigerator, or new tires for vehicles. I told him that we already had these items in working order, and they were not that old. Besides, these items would not cost $20,000 combined. I was getting frustrated and finally e-mailed, "I have an idea. Give the money to another office that really needs it, or better yet, why don't you apply it to the national debt?" The supervisor at FBI Headquarters was not amused, even though I was really not joking. He called me, clearly annoyed, and said, "I have never spoken to any FBI supervisor before who did not want to spend money!" I took that as a great compliment, although he was trying to insult and shame me.

The next day I received a call from his Unit Chief. The Unit Chief told me in no uncertain terms that I had to spend the money. He said, "You don't understand. If you don't spend this money this year, you'll lose the money from your budget next year." I completely understood. I didn't say so, but this thinking was what was entirely wrong with the federal government and why it would never get out of debt. I didn't bore him, however, with my philosophy of the way things ought to be. I was already bringing more wrath upon myself than I needed.

I asked him if he had any ideas how to spend this large sum of money. I had previously explained to his subordinate that I believed my off-site and my surveillance group had everything it needed. He suggested buying new Nikon cameras with telescopic lenses, which cost $5,000 - $7000 each, depending on the size of the lens. I already had numerous Nikon cameras for all the surveillance personnel, however, these would at least be the latest and best cameras available. The down side was that the cameras on hand, which were not that old and in perfect working order, would now go to waste. I was really in no position to refuse. I certainly would have been referred to OPR for insubordination and would have lost my supervisory position had I not depleted my budget. I purchased three new cameras and later gathered many of our old cameras and provided them to the Oklahoma City Division photographer. The photographer said that she would keep them for agents in the division to check out if they needed them. She said that she would send the older ones back to FBI Headquarters as surplus.

I was always appalled at the money wasted by the FBI. The ASAC told me that the Oklahoma City Division building was leased, even though the building was exclusively for the FBI. In 1999, the Government Services Administration (GSA) contracted out for the FBI building to be constructed at a cost of $3 million. The ASAC told me that the FBI paid rent on the building to the owners at a cost of $150,000 per month. The owners, therefore, made back their construction costs after only twenty months. In ten years, they accumulated a $15 million profit. They continued to make $1.8 million annually off the federal government. It made no sense for the government to have leased this building when they could have built it for $3 million and then owned it.

Another waste of government money involved hundreds of Tommy guns from the 1930s in the FBI's possession. A supervisor in Oklahoma City who previously worked in the Firearms Unit at Quantico told me that Congress had passed legislation directing the FBI to destroy all its outdated firearms, to include these valuable Tommy Guns. These antique Tommy guns were selling on the Internet for $25,000 to $30,000 each. This supervisor said the firearms instructors at Quantico were sickened at having to destroy these valuable weapons. When I retired, I had to turn in my Bureau-issued weapon, a Sig Sauer P226 9mm automatic pistol. I had carried it for over twenty years and would have loved to have been able to keep it. I would gladly have purchased it. Instead, the FBI destroyed it. The same thing happened years before with my Smith & Wesson, Model 13, .357 caliber magnum revolver, issued to me as a new agent at the FBI Academy. The FBI collected all revolvers and destroyed them. Both guns had sentimental value for me. I had wished I could have paid to have kept them.

CHAPTER 22

USA TODAY

By October 2010, I was beyond caring about the FBI management. I had only a year and a half left in the FBI until retirement. I was fed up with the power plays, the pettiness, the vindictiveness, and the bad decisions made by small-minded people with either inflated or fragile egos. I was never in any kind of trouble in the FBI other than telling a supervisor exactly what I thought. However, in late October 2010, I wrote a letter to the editor of the *USA Today* newspaper regarding Director Mueller's responsibility for a failed FBI computer system. An article appeared in the *USA Today* describing the failed computer system in the FBI and the hundreds of millions of dollars spent on it. I wrote the following letter that was published on October 29, 2010:

"In response to *USA Today*'s article **'FBI two years behind on computer system, Justice Department finds project is $100M over budget and only half-finished,**' I find it interesting that nothing is mentioned about Director Robert Mueller being responsible for this debacle (News, Oct 21). Mueller has been Director of the FBI since 2001. If Mueller was in the private sector, he certainly would have been fired back in 2005 for spending $170 million on a system that did not work. Now, five years later, with an incomplete system, one would think his job would have been on the line.

Having worked in the FBI for more than 26 years witnessing the waste of taxpayers' money, and seeing how deep in debt this country has become, I can only hope that taxpayers and our elected officials in Washington have become as exasperated as I have, and demand drastic changes in spending, budgeting and accountability not only in the FBI, but throughout every government agency. Bill Larsh, Edmond, Oklahoma"

Note my Horoscope for the day, "You express yourself without seeking the agreement of others. You actually don't even care what they think."

I immediately became the subject of scorn by the FBI Oklahoma City management. The ASAC instantly began questioning the SOG and SSG personnel regarding how this had affected my ability to manage them, even though it had not. This was another case of going against the FBI family, thereby becoming a target by FBI management. The retaliation and vindictiveness toward me was in full force for the remainder of my career. My performance ratings were lowered due solely because of my letter to the editor. In fact, the ASAC had already prepared my performance appraisal for the year prior to my letter to the editor. It was not a great performance appraisal, but it was better than my usual average rating. Unfortunately, it had not been signed by everyone, including the SAC, so the ASAC asked for it back. He made several revisions, referring to my poor judgment for sending the letter to the editor, as well as the so-called negative effect it had on my supervisory abilities. The rating was lowered, but he put it at "Fully Acceptable." The narrative written was negative and insulting, but he could not justify my performance as being anything lower.

He knew that I had been solely responsible for finding a new covert off-site location, coordinating with FBI Headquarters for the five-year lease, and working with FBI Headquarters and the appropriate Oklahoma City personnel to ensure the security of the new off-site. The surveillance program in the Oklahoma City Division had received the highest ratings from FBI Headquarters across the board. I was the only supervisor in Oklahoma City whose program had all top ratings from FBI Headquarters for their program. The other supervisors in the division in charge of the other programs, such as white collar crime, violent crime, drugs, counterterrorism, and foreign counterintelligence, did not receive anywhere near the high ratings I had gotten for my program.

I was also in charge of the FBI's Undercover Program in the division for which, prior to my letter to the editor, I had received a $1,000 incentive award annually for my work. I went above and beyond in the program, encouraging several qualified newer agents to apply to be undercover agents. The supervisors preceding me on SOG, who were also in charge of the undercover program, never had any agents from the division apply. My secretary told me that her previous supervisors paid no attention to the undercover program. For the first time in years, the Oklahoma City Division sent agents to attend and get certified at the FBI's Undercover School, probably the most difficult and stress-filled training in the FBI. I never even got a simple "thanks" from any management personnel in Oklahoma City. The only people who appreciated how diligently I worked were those I was helping, i.e., the undercover applicants themselves, and the FBI Headquarters personnel running these programs. In Oklahoma City, I was just a bum to the front office.

I was blamed for every subordinate's shortcoming or performance issue following the publication of my letter. Even if I advised the front office of a problem with a subordinate, it would always be turned around on me. The SAC and ASACs would either say I did not bring it to their attention soon enough, or the employee's behavior or problem was the result of my lack of supervision. My only consolation was that I would be retiring in less than a year and a half.

Numerous agents in the office told me they loved my letter and it was entirely true. A supervisor at FBI Headquarters even told me he had a copy of it hanging in his cubicle. None of these people, however, could help me with the retaliation I endured.

I joined the Federal Law Enforcement Officers Association (FLEOA) immediately after the backlash from the FBI management following my letter to the editor. My old ORA colleague would have been proud. FLEOA enabled me to retain counsel from them for free, which I knew I would soon need. An OPR investigation was initiated against me. I never thought I would ever need an attorney in my career until this incident. It was clear that the FBI Oklahoma City management wanted me tarred and feathered. When I called the FLEOA attorney, he seemed to believe that my letter was a matter of free speech. However, after being interviewed by OPR, I eventually received a one-week suspension as punishment.

The FLEOA attorney appealed the OPR decision in January 2012 on the basis of my freedom of speech to write such a letter. The Assistant Director deciding the appeal had close ties to the Oklahoma City Division. He had been my predecessor on the WCC squad. He had also been the EDSP Unit Chief on the career board who said nothing when the Mickey Mouse killer derailed my selection as SSRA Dayton. The timing of my punishment was also suspect. I submitted my retirement papers in mid-February 2012 with a retirement date for April 29, 2012. Within two weeks, I received the letter from OPR suspending me. I am certain the adjudication of my case was expedited in order to suspend me before I retired. When an agent under OPR inquiry retired, their case was terminated. The Assistant Director disagreed with FLEOA's appeal and ruled that I violated the FBI media's policy by not gaining approval for the submission of my letter to the editor. The one-week suspension was not in line with punishment for other more serious misconduct issues in the FBI. For example, an employee found guilty of sexting on a Bureau telephone received only a three-day suspension.

In an OPR case years before, my ASAC (the little Napoleon) was suspended for only one week after being discovered during an FBI Headquarters office inspection of having downloaded more than 800 pornographic images on his Bureau computer. I seriously did not think that writing an honest letter about government waste was on the same level as looking at pornography on a Bureau computer or worse than sexting on an FBI cell phone. I did feel some consolation knowing that as part of his punishment, the rotten son of a bitch ASAC had been precluded from ever being promoted to an SES position. Unfortunately, this punishment caused him to remain in Oklahoma City for years on end, making my life miserable. My father had always amused me when he was extremely irritated with someone. He would hold his left hand out and press the middle of his palm with his right index finger, while stating, "I wish I had an exterminator button in the palm of my hand." If I had possessed that button, the dirty rotten ASAC would have been gone.

CONCLUSION

I retired from the FBI on April 29, 2012, with little fanfare. I probably should not have written that letter to the editor. It made the remainder of my career unpleasant, specifically with regard to every interaction I had with the FBI Oklahoma City front office. The majority of street agents seemed to have enjoyed my letter to the editor, particularly due to the fact that the majority of them disliked Director Mueller. However, the management hated me for going against the FBI family. As I said before, I made some life-long friends in the FBI, but I would hardly ever refer to the FBI in any way, shape or form as "my family."

Through my experience working at the FBI, I firmly believed that the FBI did in fact "eat its young." I was one of its victims. I supposed, however, I would rather have been eaten up than to lose my self-respect. I did have the satisfaction of knowing I was never a yes man. I nearly always spoke my mind regarding what I thought was right or wrong, even to the detriment of my career or personal circumstances. I was never happier in my life than to leave the organization. I would never again have to be in a subservient role taking orders from mindless managers and sycophants.

My wife and I attended an FBI Retirement Conference in Sacramento, California, in June 2010. It provided the basic information regarding pensions, health care, and other benefits, as well as what to expect in retirement. Most of it I already knew, but the conference confirmed a few things. For instance, the amount of one's pension was explained. It was calculated based upon one's salary and years served in the FBI. The FBI figured the average of an employee's highest three annual salaries and an equation was computed for this average high-three salary with the number of years served. My pension ended up being about forty-one percent of my salary. Since I didn't get another job after retirement, I was also paid Supplemental Security Income (SSI) by the federal government. I had also been contributing to the Thrift Savings Plan (TSP), the federal government's equivalent to a 401K plan, for twenty-five years. I was able to take a small percentage monthly from the TSP without penalty before turning fifty-nine and a half years of age, at which time more could be designated for withdrawal. Financially, I would be very comfortable without taking another job.

The speaker at the FBI Retirement Conference was a retired FBI agent. He told the audience that he had an agent friend who told him he planned to do nothing but play golf when he retired. The speaker said that after six months, his friend told him he got tired of playing golf and wanted to find a job. The speaker said to the audience, "So don't think that you are going to be able to retire and just play golf every day, you're going to have to do something else." My wife, Cindy, laughed and said to the people seated near us who we knew from the FBI Oklahoma City office, "He doesn't know my husband very well!" Since retiring, I proved the speaker at the conference to be wrong and Cindy to be correct. I have played golf practically every day, weather permitting. Since I became an agent at the age of twenty-five, my goal was always to retire at the age of fifty and do nothing but play golf. The only time I ever played golf every day was when I was seventeen years old during the summer between my junior and senior years of high school. Until now, that was the happiest I had ever been in my life.

I was not exactly unhappy in my career, but I clearly did not like management. I had an epiphany of sorts concerning FBI executive management about halfway through my career. I was able to sum up my moment of clarity in two simple sentences. In fact, my best friend related to it quite well and told me he repeated my philosophical quote often to others regarding FBI management. I had told him, "If they like you, it doesn't matter what you do. If they don't like you, it doesn't matter what you do."

William A. Larsh
Supervisory
Special Agent
Oklahoma City
27 Years

Career Highlights: I have worked for the FBI since age 22. I spent three years at FBIHQ as a narcotics analyst, then the next 24½ years as an agent. My first office was the Orlando RA. I always said it was downhill after that because my experience there was fantastic, personally and professionally. I recovered a kidnapped baby, arrested maybe 100 to 200 fugitives, helped convict several drug traffickers, and was successful in two telemarketing fraud trials that yielded numerous convictions and the forfeiture of more than $3 million in cash and other assets—more money than I made my entire career. My next assignment at Washington Field Office resulted in my greatest accomplishment outside the criminal realm: two recruitments-in-place at a hostile foreign embassy who provided top secret intelligence on two occasions to the Secretary of State. I was a supervisor twice at FBIHQ; a Supervisory Senior Resident Agent in Shreveport, Louisiana; worked for five years in State College, Pennsylvania; and spent the last 6½ years as a supervisor in Oklahoma City.

Looking Back and Forward: I am not looking back, but looking forward to life as a free man.

MAY/JUNE 2012

Retirement Credentials presented by my good friend and co-worker.

Perry Hall High School Hall of Fame Induction, 11/2/2012.

GLOSSARY OF TERMS

Administrative Uncontrollable Overtime (AUO)
Overtime pay built into an FBI agent's salary, later called
Availability Pay (AVP).

Advanced Interactive Communications, Inc. (AICI)
An illegal telemarketing firm investigated by the FBI.

Assistant Special Agent in Charge (ASAC)
The ASAC is usually the second tier management who works
directly for the Special Agent in Charge (SAC) in an FBI field
division.

Assistant United States Attorney (AUSA)
A federal prosecutor working on behalf of the USA.

Availability Pay (AVP)
Overtime pay built into an FBI agent's salary, formerly called
Administrative Uncontrollable Overtime (AUO).

**Bureau of Alcohol, Tobacco, Firearms and Explosives
(BATF or ATF)**
A federal law enforcement agency within DOJ responsible for the
investigation of firearms and explosives violations, arsons,
bombings, and the illegal sale of alcohol and tobacco.

Central Intelligence Agency (CIA)
The nation's foreign intelligence service responsible for protecting
national security. The CIA has no law enforcement function and
is tasked mainly with collecting intelligence overseas.

Criminal Investigative Division (CID)
A division at FBI Headquarters overseeing all FBI criminal investigations in the field.

Criminal Justice Information System (CJIS)
A division of FBI Headquarters formerly known as the Identification Division, the repository for arrest fingerprint cards from police departments. CJIS has expanded its services to law enforcement and is now located in a large complex outside Clarksburg, West Virginia.

Department of Justice (DOJ)
A department of the executive branch responsible for prosecuting violations of federal law. It is headed by the chief law enforcement officer of the nation, the Attorney General.

Deputy Director
The second in command in the FBI behind the Director. This position is held by a career FBI agent promoted through the rank and file. The Director is appointed by the President from outside the FBI for a ten-year term.

Drug Enforcement Administration (DEA)
A federal law enforcement agency within DOJ responsible for enforcing federal drug laws.

FBI Academy
Training site on the United States Marine Corps base in Quantico, Virginia, for FBI new agents, DEA new agents, and continued training for on-board FBI personnel.

FBI Agents Association (FBIAA)
An FBI lobbying group protecting the interests of both active and retired FBI agents.

FBI Director
The head of the FBI appointed by the President to serve a ten-year term.

FBI Headquarters (FBIHQ)
FBI Headquarters is located in Washington, D.C. providing oversight and guidance to FBI divisions and agents in the field.

FBI National Academy (FBINA)
Training site on the United States Marine Corps base in Quantico, Virginia, for United States and international law enforcement officers.

Federal Bureau of Investigation (FBI)
The nation's prime federal law enforcement and intelligence agency responsible for investigating violations of more than 300 federal statutes, protecting citizens and upholding the Constitution of the United States, combatting public corruption, white collar crime, organized crime, civil rights violations and violent crime, as well as protecting the United States from terrorist attacks, foreign counterintelligence, espionage, and cyber attacks.

Federal Grand Jury (FGJ)
A legal body consisting of 16 to 23 jurors meeting in secret wherein a federal prosecutor conducts official proceedings to investigate potential criminal conduct, determining whether criminal charges should be brought in the form of an indictment.

Federal Law Enforcement Officers Association (FLEOA)
A federal law enforcement lobbying group protecting the interests of both active and retired federal agents.

Foreign Counterintelligence (FCI)
The FBI's effort to protect national security from foreign intelligence networks.

Foreign Intelligence Surveillance Act (FISA) Court
A United States federal court within the Department of Justice created under the Foreign Intelligence Surveillance Act of 1978, a statute allowing authorization of electronic surveillance for the purposes of intelligence gathering to protect national security against agents of foreign powers within the United States. The statute has been amended and expanded to allow the FISA Court to authorize secret physical searches.

Frontier Financial Services (FFS)
An illegal telemarketing firm investigated by the FBI.

Intelligence Research Specialist (IRS)
An FBI analyst at FBI Headquarters in the 1980s and 1990s.

Internal Revenue Service Agent (IRS Agent)
A federal agent working in the Criminal Investigative Division of the Internal Revenue Service within the Department of the Treasury.

Investigative Analyst (IA)
An FBI support employee who assists FBI agents in their investigations.

Narcotics and Dangerous Drugs Information System (NADDIS)
An index maintained by the Drug Enforcement Administration (DEA) listing known and suspected drug traffickers and associates.

National Security Letter (NSL)
The equivalent of an administrative subpoena in foreign counterintelligence cases and counterterrorism matters to obtain telephone toll records and financial information concerning targets of those types of investigations.

National Security Threat List (NSTL)
The FBI's foreign counterintelligence mission setting out a strategy for national security concerns.

New Agent Class (NAC)
A training class of new FBI agents at the FBI Academy in Quantico, Virginia.

Northern Virginia Resident Agency (NVRA)
The Northern Virginia RA is a satellite office of the FBI Washington Field Office (WFO), formerly known as the Washington Metropolitan Field Office (WMFO).

Office of Inspector General (OIG)
Investigates DOJ employees and programs.

Office of Preference (OP) Transfer
An FBI transfer for a non-management Special Agent based on seniority and the needs of the Bureau. The FBI now refers to OP Transfers as Personnel Resource List (PRL) Transfers.

Office of Professional Responsibility (OPR)
The internal affairs branch of the FBI.

Orange County Sheriff's Office (OCSO)
A local sheriff's office in Orlando, Florida.

Organized Crime Information Systems Analyst (OCIS Analyst)
An FBI analyst at FBI Headquarters in the 1980s and 1990s.

Orlando Resident Agency (ORA)
The Orlando RA is a satellite office of the FBI Tampa Division.

Quality Step increase (QSI)
An FBI incentive award increasing the salary of an employee through a step increase within their grade.

Resident Agency (RA)
A satellite office to an FBI field division. The FBI currently has 56 field divisions with approximately 375 resident agencies.

Sensitive Compartmentalized Information (SCI)
United States classified information derived from sensitive sources.

Shreveport Resident Agency (SRA)
The Shreveport RA is a satellite office of the FBI New Orleans Division.

Special Agent in Charge (SAC)
The SAC generally is in charge of the FBI field division except in larger divisions such as New York and Los Angeles, where an Assistant Director in Charge (ADIC) is in charge, delegating authority to his SACs.

Special Agent
An FBI field agent or street agent.

Special Operations Group (SOG)
A permanent surveillance squad in an FBI field division consisting of FBI agents.

State College Resident Agency (SCRA)
The State College RA is a satellite office of the FBI Philadelphia Division.

Supervisory Senior Agent (SSA)
A supervisor in charge of a squad of agents in a field division or a supervisor assigned to FBI Headquarters in Washington, D.C.

Supervisory Senior Resident Agent (SSRA)
A supervisor in charge of an FBI Resident Agency.

Special Surveillance Group (SSG)
A permanent surveillance squad in an FBI field division consisting of unarmed FBI support personnel.

Temporary Duty Assignment (TDY)
Temporary duty or travel by a federal government employee to a location more than 50 miles from the employee's permanent duty station subject to voucher reimbursement to the employee for food, lodging, travel, and other incidental costs connected with the authorized travel/assignment.

United States Attorney (USA)
The lead federal prosecutor appointed by the President with jurisdiction in the judicial district. There are 94 judicial districts in the United States with at least one judicial district in each state.

United States Attorney's Office (USAO)
The federal prosecutor's office in the judicial district headed by the United States Attorney (USA).

United States Department of State (USDS)
The lead foreign affairs agency headed by the Secretary of State.

United States Immigration & Naturalization Service (USINS)
Formerly, the name of the federal agency with responsibility for administering immigration services and enforcing immigration laws, under the Department of Justice (DOJ). USINS is now called the United States Immigration and Customs Enforcement (USICE) within the Department of Homeland Security (DHS).

United States Marshals Service (USMS)
A federal law enforcement agency responsible for protecting federal courts and its officers, prisoner transport, and fugitive investigations.

Unlawful Flight to Avoid Confinement Warrant (UFAC Warrant)
A federal arrest warrant pursuant to federal statute Title 18, United States Code, Section 1783, used to assist state and local law enforcement in the apprehension of escaped prisoners.

Unlawful Flight to Avoid Prosecution Warrant (UFAP Warrant)
A federal arrest warrant pursuant to federal statute Title 18, United States Code, Section 1073, used to assist state and local law enforcement in the apprehension of fugitives.

Washington Metropolitan Field Office (WMFO)
The former name of the FBI field division in Washington, D.C., now called the Washington Field Office (WFO).

White Collar Crime (WCC)
An area of non-violent crime motivated by financial gain wherein the perpetrators of the alleged crimes are usually known to law enforcement, but the acts being committed must be proven to be criminal.

ABOUT THE AUTHOR

I was born in Baltimore, Maryland. I worked my entire career for the FBI from the age of twenty-two until my retirement at the age of fifty in 2012. I currently live in Hanover, Pennsylvania, where I enjoy golfing, writing, playing the trombone, shooting pool, riding my bicycle, watching old movies, following sports, working out, and listening to my favorite music. I enjoy spending time with my wife, Cindy, and our two grown children, Ethan and Mary. We also enjoy visiting our extended families who live mainly in Maryland and Pennsylvania. My preferred travel destination is the Highlands of Scotland, the ancestral home of my paternal grandmother. I love golfing on Scottish links courses, hiking mountains, visiting my Chisholm cousins, and taking in the beautiful scenery of the Highlands. This is my second book. I published a novel in December 2016 entitled, *L'Archevêque,* based on the true story of a French fur trader in the 1700s, my direct ancestor, Paul L'Archevêque, also known as Paul Larsh.

Standing on the summit of Ben Wevis in the Highlands of Scotland, 2015.

CPSIA information can be obtained
at www.ICGtesting.com
Printed in the USA
LVHW082132050219
606534LV00020B/829/P

9 781544 029269